SGML and HTML Explained

SGML and HTML Explained

Second Edition

Martin Bryan

Addison Wesley Longman

Harlow, England • Reading, Massachusetts
Menlo Park, California • New York • Don Mills,
Ontario • Amsterdam • Bonn • Sydney
Singapore • Tokyo • Madrid • San Juan • Milan
Mexico City • Seoul • Taipei

Addison Wesley Longman Limited
Edinburgh Gate
Harlow
Essex CM20 2JE
England

Published in the United States of America by Addison Wesley Longman Inc., New York.

Cover designed by Designers & Partners Ltd, Oxford
Illustrations by Margaret Macknelly Design, Tadley
Typeset in 10/12pt Times by Dobbie Typesetting Ltd, Tavistock, Devon
Printed and bound in Great Britain by Henry Ling Ltd,
at the Dorset Press, Dorchester, Dorset

First edition published 1988
Second edition published 1997

ISBN 0-201-40394-3

British Library Cataloguing-in-Publication Data
A catalogue record for this book is available from the British Libary

Library of Congress Cataloging-in-Publication Data is available

This book is dedicated to Yuri Rubinsky, who did so much to make SGML and HTML widely accepted before his untimely death.

Foreword

International Standards come in two flavors. One variety is a useful codification of current practice, providing, for example, an unambiguous definition of a character set for information interchange, as ISO 8859-1 does for the Latin-1 character set. The other category has been aptly described as 'standards imposed by an international body of do-gooders' which, largely as a result of the gestation time of such standards, are found to be largely irrelevant by the time they appear. The Office Document Architecture (ODA) standard is a case in point. The Standard Generalized Markup Language (SGML, ISO 8879) is an honorable exception to this rule: in the ten years since it was first published it has revolutionized the handling of information in industry, commerce and government circles. Large quantities of the world's information are now organized with the help of SGML, and the World Wide Web community is at last beginning to realize that treating HTML in its true guise as an SGML application opens up a future of Web publishing divorced from the power games of Microsoft and Netscape.

For a long time the practice of SGML was a black art, known only to a select few. Foremost amongst these gurus is Martin Bryan, whose book *SGML: an Author's Guide* did much to help the spread of SGML in its early days. This present volume stands as a worthy successor, marking SGML's coming of age and its recognition as a major force both in technical documentation and in the wider world of Web publishing. Attempting to extract the message from the text of an International Standard is masochism of the highest order, and readers who need to understand the precise meaning and significance of ISO 8879 or the HTML 3.2 definition will have cause to be eternally grateful to Martin Bryan for his guidance.

Professor David Barron
University of Southampton
December 1996

Preface

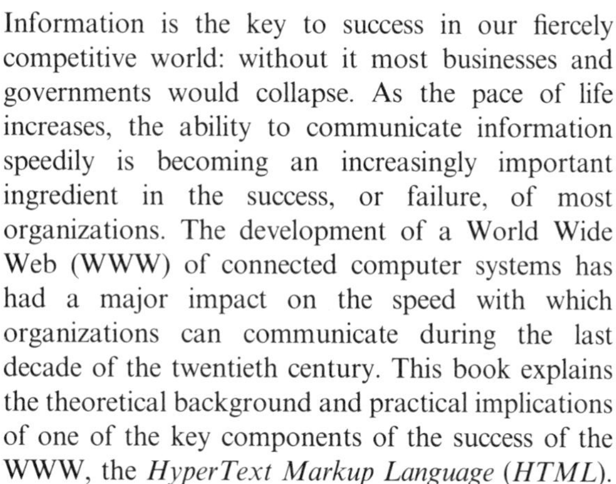

Information is the key to success in our fiercely competitive world: without it most businesses and governments would collapse. As the pace of life increases, the ability to communicate information speedily is becoming an increasingly important ingredient in the success, or failure, of most organizations. The development of a World Wide Web (WWW) of connected computer systems has had a major impact on the speed with which organizations can communicate during the last decade of the twentieth century. This book explains the theoretical background and practical implications of one of the key components of the success of the WWW, the *HyperText Markup Language* (*HTML*).

HTML has been formalized according to the rules defined in International Standard 8879, which defines a *Standard Generalized Markup Language* (*SGML*). This book explains the role of SGML and the concepts for controlling computerized document markup that it has introduced; it then explains how these concepts have been utilized in formalizing HTML.

Rather than concentrating on the 'how to' aspects of producing HTML documents, this book concentrates on 'why it was done this way.' By providing a different perspective on the development of HTML, it is hoped that this book will increase awareness of the benefits that SGML brings to computerized information management.

While this book is specifically designed to appeal to those who want to gain a more in-depth understanding of what makes HTML tick, it also serves a more general purpose in teaching the theory behind SGML. As such, it will be a useful reference book for those being introduced to this important information processing language.

One of the best ways to learn any computing language is by example. One of my principal aims, therefore, has been to try to provide a practical example of the use of every concept in SGML, and every markup tag provided in HTML. To avoid making the book too unwieldy, I have deliberately simplified many of the examples.

To provide a more in-depth understanding of the use of HTML the book is supplied on CD-ROM in the form of a set of HTML-encoded files, which contain navigable hypertext links within and between chapters. Most WWW document browsers provide facilities for viewing the coding of the source document. By using these facilities to view the way in which the files that make up this book have been encoded, you can get some idea of the way in which HTML documents are typically marked up and learn the advantages of electronic cross-referencing, which is extensive in the electronic version of the book.

Until recently, document creation using word processors was seen as a separate activity from other computing activities of a company. Today, companies are beginning to realize that document production of all types needs to be tightly coupled with other forms of information capture and management. SGML provides a generalized mechanism for the identification of manageable units of information and the documents that can be produced from them. Many of today's largest document management projects already use SGML to control information flow. This book explains how document components can be identified and stored as a reusable resource by marking up their information elements in SGML.

The WWW has led to an increasing awareness of the benefits of building compound documents by pointing to many different information sources, rather than copying data directly into new files. Trying to maintain multiple copies of a piece of data is impossible over any length of time. Only by keeping one master copy of each file, and making a reference to this copy at appropriate points from other documents, can document sets be realistically managed over the lifespan of projects, such as that required to build an airliner. Typically, such large capital investment projects involve life cycles measured in terms of decades. To maintain data over such periods using technology that has a lifespan that can be measured in months, rather than years, naturally leads to difficulties. One of the big advantages of SGML is that it encodes documents in a way that can be understood by virtually all computers. This is why HTML-encoded documents can be moved between computer systems without difficulty. This ability to create a document on one platform and then view or edit it on a completely different platform is one of the key aspects to the success of the WWW.

The twenty-first century could be the first for many centuries for which written records are not available. Unless we can learn to archive our electronic mail, our Internet newsgroup discussions, our videoconferences and our telephone messages in a way that will preserve the data over time, future historians will find it difficult to find out about our activities. It is now, at the start of this age of electronic information dissemination, that we need to take a serious look at how we can preserve our electronic data in an easily understood format. As bodies such as the Association for Computing in the Humanities' Text Encoding Initiative (TEI) have already recognized, SGML and HTML will help to provide an electronic record of the twenty-first century.

Acknowledgments

This book would not have been possible without the help and encouragement of my family and friends, or the excellent team of reviewers and copy-editors that my editor, Nicky McGirr, found for me. I would particularly like to stress the contributions made by David Penfold, who had the hard work of copy-editing my bad grammar, and Peter Flynn (Silmaril Consultants, UK), David Barron (University of Southampton, UK), Gary F. Hasman (Graceland College, USA), Jacques Deseyne (SEMA Group, Belgium) and Neil Bradley (Pindar plc, UK) for reviewing the draft text and making substantial improvements to it. David Barron has added to his long list of favors to me by supplying the Foreword.

The CD accompanying this book has been significantly enhanced by James Clark, who has allowed the beta-version of his new JADE DSSSL Engine (© James Clark 1996) to be distributed with the HTML files that were used to create the book. The SGML world is becoming increasingly indebted to James for his excellent freeware. His SP parser is now an industry standard, and many of the new ideas being introduced into SGML and DSSSL are finding their first implementation in his tools. His excellent work on developing DSSSL on behalf of ISO has been widely acknowledged, but I feel I must add my personal thanks for his support for my role as Panel Chairman at the British Standards Institution responsible for SGML and related standards. It is unlikely that UK involvement in the development of SGML would still be possible without James's support.

Using the CD

The files used to create this book have been supplied in electronic form for two reasons:

(1) To allow you to see how much can be gained by reading the text in an interactive environment, where terms are linked to their definitions, and, where possible, references to documents are linked to electronic sources of the referenced text.

(2) To allow you to experiment with some of the latest software for processing SGML and HTML files, using James Clark's DSSSL Engine (JADE).

You will find the chapters on SGML stored in the files called SGML-1.HTM through to SGML-11.HTM; the accompanying figures are stored in the GIF files. Chapters 12–15, which cover HTML, and the future developments of both SGML and HTML, are stored in the files labeled HTML-1.HTM to HTML-4.HTM. You will also find a file called HOME.HTM, which contains the preliminary pages of the book plus an electronic version of the table of contents, from which you can select every section of the book using your mouse.

When you view the files for Chapters 13 and 14 using your favourite Web browser you will be able to see how your browser displays each of the HTML constructs, rather than the way they have been illustrated in the book, where examples have been based on the behavior of the most popular Web browser, Netscape Navigator.

To help you find what you want in the hyperdocument more easily we have modified the first paragraph(s) of the electronic version of the files to provide each chapter with its own mini table of contents. In addition, references to other parts of the book have been highlighted so that you can simply click on the highlighted words to move to information about that subject. In most cases, terms are highlighted in bold the first time they are used, and then marked as references to the bold text for the next two or three references. Once a term has been used more than three or four times it is presumed that you will already know what it means.

Where information sources outside of the book are mentioned you can click on the reference in the body of the text to move to the full citation given in the reference section that has been appended to each chapter. Where the referenced documents are available over the Internet, clicking on the highlighted text in the reference section should cause the relevant document to be called by your browser.

Note: *The references were correct as of December 1996, but you should always remember that electronic files can be moved without warning. If you cannot find the referenced documents call the following file for the most up-to-date set of pointers:* `http://www.sgml.u-net.com/book/refers.htm`

To allow you to see the effect of Java applets we have added a Java program to the CD, courtesy of Sun Microsystems. You will find this program in the Java directory, while the images it needs to call are stored in the flags directory. Whilst your Web browser will allow you to print out the files, it may not allow you to edit their contents or fully control the formatting. The files in the Jade directory will allow you to convert your HTML files into the Rich Text Format (RTF) used to interconnect word processors.

Those of you who are technically minded will find an explanation of what the beta-version of James's DSSSL Engine for Windows 95 can do in the file called JADE.HTM in the Jade directory. This file includes links to the source programs, and to the DSSSL home page James Clark maintains to assist those trying to develop software based on this advanced engine.

Note: *As JADE is a multi-threaded program it cannot be run under Windows 3.1. The CD contains Windows 95 only versions of the JADE files and PC versions of the other files. Users of other systems wishing to experiment with JADE should contact James Clark's site at* `http://www.jclark.com` *to obtain the latest version for their platform, when these become available. (At the time of going to press only the Windows 95 beta-version of JADE had been released.)*

Those of you who are not technically minded, but are users of Windows 95 based systems, can see the effect of this advanced program by first reading and then carrying out the following set of instructions:

(1) Select the `Run...` option from the Windows 95 Start menu.

(2) Enter a command of the form `x:\PRINTOUT x: filename directory` where

- `x:` is the sequence that identifies the CD drive on your system (for example, `D:` if it is the D: drive)

Note: *It is important that the colon follows immediately after the drive letter in each of the two positions it is entered.*

- `PRINTOUT` is the command required to create a version of the chapter that your word processor can print on A4 paper (if you normally use paper of the US Letter size change `PRINTOUT` to `PRINT-US`)
- `filename` is the name of the file containing the chapter you want to load into a word processor (for example, `SGML-1` to create a printout of the first chapter on SGML, SGML-1.HTM)
- `directory` is the full name (including a drive identifier) of a path that identifies the writable directory in which the RTF file is to be placed (for example, `C:\TEMP`)

Note: *Typically, following this instruction will result in a command of the form* `D:\PRINTOUT D: SGML-1 C:\TEMP`

(3) When the Jade MS-DOS window heading changes to `Finished-printout`, click on the Windows 95 Close button (that is, the X in the top right-hand corner of the window) to close the window opened by Jade.

(4) To ensure that any illustrations used in the chapter are available to your word processor, the files on the CD whose extension is GIF should be copied to the directory used to store the RTF files generated by Jade.

For example, to copy illustrations stored on a CD loaded into the `D:` drive to `C:\TEMP` you could use the Windows 95 `Run...` option from the `Start` menu to run the command `XCOPY D:\*.gif C:\TEMP`

Note: *You only need to follow this instruction once for each output directory you use as it copies the illustrations for all chapters you may subsequently choose to print out.*

(5) Start your favorite word processor and open the file identified by the sequence `directory\filename.rtf` (for example, `C:\TEMP\SGML-1.RTF`).

It should be noted that if you attempt to use this procedure with the two files that contain details of how HTML works, `HTML-2.HTM` and `HTML-3.HTM`, you will not get a full copy of the file as the screen displays in the HTML files are intended solely for display on a Web browser, and cannot be duplicated using a word processor.

Martin Bryan
January 1997

Contents

Foreword vii
Preface ix

1 Background to SGML and HTML 1
1.1 What is the Internet? 1
1.2 Interconnecting word processors 2
1.3 The role of markup 3
1.4 Types of markup 3
1.4.1 Specific markup 4
1.4.2 Generalized markup 6
1.5 The role of SGML 7
1.6 The role of HTML 9

2 Document analysis and information modeling 11
2.1 Identifying document types 12
2.2 The structure of documents 12
2.2.1 The structure of a memo 13
2.2.2 The structure of a letter 14
2.2.3 The structure of a report 17
2.2.4 The structure of scientific papers 20
2.2.5 The structure of books 22
2.3 Formatting structured documents 24
2.4 The difference between formatting and structure 25
2.5 Information management 26

3 The components of an SGML system 28
3.1 System components 28
3.2 Selecting an SGML document editor 29

3.3 The role of document analysis/design tools 31
3.4 The role of document conversion tools 31
3.5 The role of an SGML parser 32
3.6 Document databases and repositories 33
3.7 Printing SGML documents 34
3.8 Electronic delivery 36
3.9 The component parts of an SGML document 36

4 The SGML declaration 38

4.1 The role of the SGML declaration 38
4.2 The syntax clause 40
4.2.1 The reference concrete syntax 40
4.3 Other clauses in the SGML declaration 50
4.3.1 The character set description 50
4.3.2 The capacity set 52
4.3.3 The scope clause 52
4.3.4 The features clause 52
4.3.5 Application-specific information 53
4.4 Alternative concrete syntaxes 53
4.4.1 The HTML SGML declaration 54

5 Elements and attributes 59

5.1 Element roles 59
5.2 Element declarations 60
5.2.1 Model groups 61
5.2.2 Text elements 63
5.2.3 Exceptions 65
5.2.4 Comments within element declarations 66
5.2.5 Ambiguous content models 66
5.2.6 Analysing content models 66
5.3 Using elements 69
5.4 Attributes 70
5.5 Declaring attributes 71
5.6 Using attributes 74
5.6.1 Simple attributes 74
5.6.2 Using tokens 75
5.7 Specialized attributes 77
5.7.1 Entity attributes 77
5.7.2 Unique identifiers 78
5.7.3 References to unique identifiers 79
5.8 Controlling attribute values 80

6 Entity declaration and use 82

6.1 Types of entity 82
6.2 Entity references 83
6.2.1 General entity references 84
6.2.2 Parameter entity references 84
6.3 Entity declarations 85
6.3.1 Declaring parameter entities 86
6.3.2 Comments 86
6.3.3 Special forms of general entity declaration 87
6.4 External entities 89
6.4.1 System-specific external entities 90
6.4.2 Alternative markup notations 90
6.4.3 Notation declarations 91
6.4.4 Publicly declared external entities 93
6.5 Character references 100
6.6 Entity sets 101
6.6.1 Publicly declared entity sets 102
6.6.2 Private entity sets 103

7 Short references 104

7.1 Introduction to short references 104
7.2 Short reference mapping declarations 105
7.3 Short reference use declarations 106
7.4 Using short references 107

8 Marked sections and processing instructions 110

8.1 The role of marked sections 110
8.2 Marked section declarations 111
8.3 Using marked sections 112
8.3.1 Ignored sections 113
8.3.2 Temporary sections 114
8.3.3 Combining keywords 115
8.3.4 Storing marked sections as entities 115
8.3.5 Nested marked sections 116
8.4 Processing instructions 116
8.5 Using processing instructions in marked sections 117

9 Tag minimization 118

9.1 Types of minimization 118
9.2 Tag omission 118
9.2.1 Start-tag omission 119

9.2.2 End-tag omission 120
9.2.3 Omitting tags 120
9.3 Short tags 121
9.3.1 Empty tags 122
9.3.2 Unclosed tags 123
9.3.3 Null end-tags 124
9.3.4 Omitting attribute names 125
9.4 Tag grouping (rank) 126
9.5 Automatic tag recognition (data tags) 126

10 Multiple document structures (SUBDOC, CONCUR and LINK) 130

10.1 Types of multiple document structures 130
10.2 SGML subdocuments 131
10.3 Concurrent document structures 133
10.4 Linking document structures 136
10.4.1 Simple links 138
10.4.2 Implicit links 139
10.4.3 ID-specific links 141
10.4.4 Explicit links 142
10.4.5 Using alternative link sets 145
10.4.6 Short cuts 150
10.4.7 Overriding link declarations 151
10.4.8 Using publicly declared link type declaration subsets 152

11 Building a document type definition 153

11.1 The document type declaration 153
11.2 Using publicly declared document type declarations 154
11.3 Element sets 155
11.3.1 The role of comment declarations 156
11.3.2 Modifying existing element and entity sets 157
11.3.3 Creating new element sets 157
11.3.4 Structured element sets 158
11.4 The effect of record boundaries 158

12 Interpreting the HTML DTD 161

12.1 DTD history 161
12.2 DTD identification 162
12.3 Deprecated features 163
12.4 Imported Internet specifications 163
12.5 Shared parameters 164
12.6 Character mnemonics 164

12.7 Text markup 166
12.8 Shared content models 167
12.9 Body components 167
12.10 Anchors and links 168
12.11 Images and maps 169
12.12 Applets 170
12.13 Paragraphs and headings 171
12.14 Preformatted text 172
12.15 Lists 173
12.16 Forms 175
12.17 Tables 176
12.18 HTML document headers 177
12.19 HTML document structure 179

13 The HyperText Markup Language (HTML) 180

13.1 The HTML Header 180
13.2 Text blocks in the HTML body 184
13.2.1 Space-delimited text blocks 185
13.2.2 Lists 186
13.2.3 Preformatted and quoted text 189
13.2.4 The <DIV>ision element 190
13.2.5 Other elements defined as blocks 192
13.3 Embedded text 193
13.4 The role of HTML anchors 196
13.4.1 Link relationships 199
13.4.2 Link management in an HTML environment 200
13.5 Images and maps 201
13.6 Tables 204
13.7 Applets 206

14 Creating HTML forms 209

14.1 Basic principles 209
14.2 The <FORM> element 210
14.3 The <INPUT> element 211
14.3.1 Text input 212
14.3.2 Password input 212
14.3.3 Checkboxes 212
14.3.4 Radio buttons 213
14.3.5 Submit button 214
14.3.6 Reset button 214
14.3.7 Hidden input 214
14.3.8 File selection 215
14.3.9 Image spot selection 215

14.4 The <SELECT> element 216
14.5 The <TEXTAREA> element 217
14.6 The <ISINDEX> element 218
14.7 Form submission 218
14.8 Form processing 220

15 The future for SGML and HTML 221

15.1 What DSSSL brought to SGML 221
15.1.1 SGML groves 221
15.1.2 The SGML Document Query Language 222
15.2 The HyTime SGML General Facilities annex 223
15.2.1 Architectural form definition requirements 223
15.2.2 Formal system identifiers 223
15.2.3 Property set definition requirements 224
15.3 Possible extensions to SGML 224
15.4 Possible extensions to HTML 226

References 227

Index 230

Trademark notice

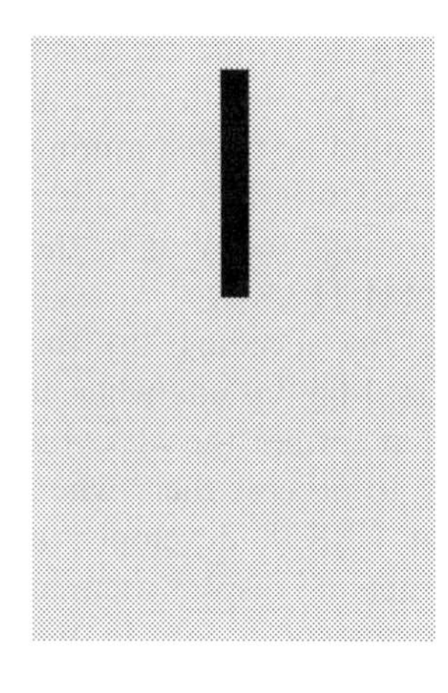

1 Background to SGML and HTML

What is the Internet? • Interconnecting word processors • The role of markup • Types of markup • The role of SGML • The role of HTML

The phenomenal growth of the Internet during the first half of the 1990s has led to an ever-increasing awareness of the benefits of generic markup in the interchange of documents. In particular, the success of the HyperText Markup Language (HTML) has improved awareness of the relevance of the Standard Generalized Markup Language (SGML) developed by the International Organization for Standardization (ISO) as a method for describing documents in a way that makes it easy to move them from one platform to another.

At present there is a large gap between the levels of knowledge of those who work only with HTML and those who have been using the full power of SGML to manage their documents. One of the purposes of this book is, therefore, to try to increase the awareness among those using HTML of the role SGML plays in ensuring that their documents can be easily exchanged between systems. This chapter provides some background material on the history of the development of both HTML and SGML.

1.1 What is the Internet?

The Internet is a set of interconnected computer networks that has been developed over the last three decades of the twentieth century. The US Defense Advanced Research Projects Agency Network (DARPANET) was one of the first networks to interconnect government, academic and private research organizations with one of the early European connections established with the Conseil européen pour la recherche nucléaire (CERN) in Geneva. Today the Internet network of interconnected computer networks developed from this early beginning has been extended to cover many millions of computers located in all the continents of this planet, including Antarctica!

Initially the Internet was used primarily for sending electronic messages and transferring files, but it was not long before groups of people interested in the same subjects set up news groups so that messages could be shared among the relevant user community. To allow people to request files from another system without having to send an email message requesting a copy of it, the Internet community developed a File Transfer Protocol (FTP).

While these early techniques were very helpful in speeding up the interchange of information between researchers, they had limitations when it came to document handling; you could not be sure what format the files you requested would be in, nor whether you would be able to process them when you received them. Tim Berners-Lee, a researcher at CERN, developed a document browser that could request files over the Internet and display them in a predefined format. To do this he introduced two new protocols to the Internet, the HyperText Transfer Protocol (HTTP) and the HyperText Markup Language (HTML). The CERN browser led to the development of the NCSA Mosaic browser at the National Center for Supercomputing Applications in the USA, which soon became the standard tool through which researchers requested documents ('surfed') over the Internet.

As HTML document browsers became readily available, more and more people started referencing existing documents over the Internet. A standard method of identifying files using Uniform Resource Locators (URLs) was developed so that browsers could share files more easily. Files that were interconnected in this manner were seen to form a World Wide Web (WWW) of data. This name is, nowadays, synonymous with the use of the HTTP and HTML protocols to interchange electronic documents.

1.2 Interconnecting word processors

The spread of the Internet has led to an increased awareness of the advantages of transferring documents from one word processor to another in electronic form. Many of the currently available techniques do not, however, allow information to be transferred with the text about how a document is to be presented to the user. Sometimes presentation details cannot be transferred because they are coded in a machine-specific manner that may not be understood at the receiving end; sometimes they are coded using characters that are outside the range allowed by the electronic delivery subsystem. The absence of formatting clues to the 'structure' of a received document can lead to a degeneration of the transmitted message. SGML, however, allows information about a document's structure to be preserved as it is transferred from one computer system to another.

Documents that are to be freely interchanged over the WWW are typically coded using the HyperText Markup Language (HTML), which is a simple application of SGML. For more complex documents users can define the *structure* of their information set using an SGML *document type definition*. This structure can be used directly by a plug-in to a standard HTML document browser that understands SGML to present the stored information in a suitable manner, or can be converted to HTML for display using a basic WWW browser.

The structure of a document can be used to help users identify and move to relevant parts of an electronic document. Electronic documents do not need to rely on the tables of contents, indexes and cross-references used in printed documents to help users find information. By making text *active*, users can move directly to different sections of text without having to scroll through intervening pages.

Electronic books are typically displayed as a continuous set of paragraphs rather than being split up into arbitrary pages. Cross-references to a particular page number are not, therefore, appropriate in an electronic environment. Instead electronic cross-references are presented as an active area that the user can click on to move directly to the relevant point in the text. Indexing is often replaced in electronic documents by features that allow the user to search for particular words or phrases within the document.

1.3 The role of markup

Markup is the term used to describe codes added to electronically prepared text to define the structure of the text. (Markup is spelt as one word when applied to electronic files to distinguish it from the form of mark up traditionally used by graphic designers, which was normally hand-written onto printed copy.)

Any device that stores formatted text for later recall uses some form of markup, though this may not be apparent. Sometimes the points at which markup has been added to a document can only be identified on a display screen by a change of typeface or by the addition of a special marker. Wherever a change of features is found in an electronic document, it can be presumed that some form of electronic markup has been recorded. In many cases some form of *delimiter* will be used to identify the start and, optionally, end of this markup.

Each word-processing program has its own set of markup instructions, though it will often be able to import files coded by other programs. Moving from one word processor to another involves authors in the costly and time-consuming exercise of learning a new set of markup instructions. The changeover may also require the conversion of existing text before it can be used with the new software.

1.4 Types of markup

There are three types of electronic markup in common use today:

- specific markup
- generalized markup
- generic markup.

Specific markup describes the format of a document by use of instructions that are specific to the program used to generate or output the text. Such instructions normally have immediate effect on the appearance of the text. They can affect either the appearance of the characters (for example, by selecting bold or italic text) or the position of characters or lines (for example, by adjusting indent, margin or spacing values). Generalized markup normally identifies a style sheet to be associated with the text that follows it. The name of the style sheet can indicate the basic structure of the document, but in general a different style sheet name is required for each variant. For example, if paragraphs in an appendix are to be set in a smaller size than those in the body of a document, they must be marked up using a different name.

Generic markup concentrates on the role of the associated data, leaving differences in the way the data is to be presented in different contexts to a later stage in the process. Typically, generic markup instructions identify elements such as headings, paragraphs, highlighted words and quoted text. The presentation format of the elements of a generically marked-up document is context specific. For example, a paragraph in an appendix can have the same name as one in the body of the text, but will be presented in a different format.

1.4.1 Specific markup

Specific markup instructions can take many forms. One of the most commonly used forms is the Rich Text Format (RTF) used to interchange documents between different environments using the Microsoft Word program. This format is often used as a common denominator when interchanging documents between different word processors as most programs can import and export files in RTF format. RTF commands begin with a backslash (\) and this is followed by one or more letters identifying the function to be used (for example, `\b` for Bold).

There are three basic types of RTF commands:

- instructions that define or affect only the next character (for example, `\_`=nonbreaking hyphen);
- instructions that affect all subsequent characters until turned off (for example, `\ul`=underline);
- instructions that affect the layout of the page (for example, `\page`= required page break).

Although these three basic types of markup instruction occur in most markup languages, the way in which they are used can differ from program to program. For example:

- Instructions affecting only one character that appear before the character in an RTF file may occur after the character in the markup scheme used by another word processor.

- Instructions that affect all subsequent characters may stay in force until the same instruction is entered a second time, or may, like RTF, be cancelled by entry of a different instruction (for example, `\b0` to switch off bold).
- Instructions that affect the layout of the page may have immediate effect or may only be actioned when the next line or page is started.

Some markup instructions need to be qualified by the addition of one or more numbers or other parameters. As such instructions can be of variable length two basic techniques are used to identify them:

- placing them on a separate line;
- enclosing them within special *delimiter* characters.

Wordstar Dot Commands are an example of text formatting instructions that are placed on separate lines. A Wordstar Dot Command consists of a dot (full stop) followed by two letters identifying the command required and any relevant parameter(s). (The initial dot always appears in the first column of a line.) Parameters may be variable length numbers or one of a predefined set of control words (for example, `ON` or `OFF`).

A typical Wordstar document might start:

```
.PL 66
.MT 6
.MB 9
.UJ ON
^A^BChapter 1
INTRODUCTION^B

The spread of word processors . . .
```

These instructions tell the program that the page length is 11 inches (`.PL 66` = 66 lines of the standard 1/6th of an inch spacing), with a top margin of 1 inch (`.MT 6` = 6 lines) and a bottom margin of 1.5 inches (`.MB 9` = 9 lines). After switching on justification (`.UJ ON`) the first print control command requests that the character pitch be changed to 12 characters per inch (`^A` = Elite) while the second (`^B`) requests the bold version of the typeface. This bolder face remains in force until the end of the heading, where it is switched off by a second `^B` sequence.

RTF uses delimiters to identify the scope of its formatting instructions. For example, to set the above heading without associating a style sheet with it, the following RTF command sequence could be used:

```
\pard\plain\qc
{\b\f4\fs36 Chapter 1
\par INTRODUCTION
\par }
```

The first line defines the style of following paragraphs (`\pard`), identifying it as being based on the default style (`\plain`) but quad centered (`\qc`) rather than left aligned. The text between the curly braces is to be set using the bold (`\b`) variant of the font identified by the number 4 (`\f4`) using an 18 point font size (`\fs36`). The end of paragraph (`\par`) command shows where the quadding rules defined in the paragraph definition are to be applied.

It will be seen from the above examples that interrelating the instructions used by different word-processing programs is not straightforward. To convert a file created using one package to a form that can be understood by another may require the entries to be redefined using different mnemonics in a different sequence.

1.4.2 Generalized markup

To avoid having to respecify markup instructions whenever a change of format, or output device, is required, the concept of a generalized markup language was postulated by Goldfarb *et al.* as part of an IBM research project. The idea was based on two premises:

- Markup should describe a document's structure rather than its physical characteristics.
- Markup should be rigorous so that it can be understood unambiguously by a program or a human interpreter.

These techniques formed the basis of IBM's Document Composition Facility Generalized Markup Language (DCF GML). A typical chapter in a GML coded document might start:

```
:book.
:body.
:h1.INTRODUCTION
:p.The spread of word processors . . .
```

It can be seen that this generalized markup differs from the earlier, specifically coded, examples in a number of important respects. It starts with two instructions identifying the type of document being prepared (a book) and the section of the document in which the text is to be placed (the main body of the book). These instructions clearly show the structure of the document and define the role of the following text.

The next point to notice is the absence of the line containing `Chapter 1`. With generic coding, the format and numbering of chapters (identified by the `:h1.` instruction) can be taken care of automatically by the text formatting program. This has the advantage that the sequence in which chapters are output can be changed without the author having to renumber each one. In addition, decisions as to whether or not the word 'Chapter' is to appear and whether numbers are to be printed using arabic or roman numerals, or simply as words, can be controlled by the person who prints the document rather than its author.

The final point to notice about the GML-coded version of the chapter opening is that it has not been necessary to indicate that the heading is to be set in bold or in a larger point size. The text formatting program knows that, when it reaches the instruction to start a paragraph of text (`:p.`), it should return to the standard form of text, after applying any necessary paragraph indents.

1.5 The role of SGML

Dr Goldfarb used the concepts of generalized markup developed for the DCF GML project as the basis for developing a *generic markup* scheme for the American National Standards Institute (ANSI). This scheme was then internationalized to become ISO's Standard Generalized Markup Language (SGML). Generic markup schemes differ from other generalized ones in that it is no longer necessary to have a one-to-one correspondence between style-sheet names and the names of markup tags. With generic coding the markup tag only identifies the role of the data element. The way this element will be presented to users depends on the context in which it is used. For example, a paragraph may be formatted differently if it appears immediately after a heading, or in a foreword or appendix, without having to be coded differently from other paragraphs.

SGML operates at a number of levels, depending on the features required by the application. The standard provides facilities for defining:

- the structure of permitted classes of documents;
- the characters used for markup, and within the text of a document;
- shared text that is to be used more than once in the document;
- externally stored information that is to be incorporated into the completed document;
- special techniques used in marking up the text, such as tag minimization or identification of different versions of a document;
- the way in which text is to be processed.

The structure of an SGML-coded document, and details of optional SGML features used in its preparation, are formally defined in a set of **markup declarations** that form a **document type definition** (**DTD**). These markup declarations describe a set of markup instructions, known as **tags**, that can be used to identify the start or end of the *logical* **elements** of the text. The start of each element is marked by a **start-tag**; an **end-tag** is normally used to indicate where the element ends.

While separate sets of markup tags can be used for different applications, the same basic elements occur in most documents. For instance, a paragraph of text forms a logical element of a letter, report, paper or book, and can be allocated the same markup tag in each type of document (for example, <p>). In SGML, our example chapter heading would be coded as:

```
<chapter>
<title>INTRODUCTION</title>
<p>The spread of word processors...
```

Where necessary SGML markup tags can be qualified by **attributes**. Attributes are used within SGML to:

- identify specific tags uniquely;
- cross-refer to elements identified by unique identifiers;
- recall externally stored data;
- indicate the role of an associated element.

Attributes can also allow users to control the way in which text is presented to readers.

The amount of keying required to capture a document can be reduced by assigning names to data storage **entities** that contain text that will be used in more than one place. For example, a **general entity reference** called `&SGML;` could be used to enter the phrase `Standard Generalized Markup Language` at relevant points. The replacement text for each entity can either be declared within the document type definition currently being used (local entities) or can be stored in an external file that is recalled as the document is processed (external entities).

Where complex structures are required for specific parts of a document, SGML allows externally stored **subdocuments**, based on an alternative document type definition, to be merged with the main document.

Numeric or named **character references** can be used within SGML documents to request characters that are not included in the word processor's character set. This technique allows characters outside the basic character set of a word processor to be incorporated into a transmitted file in a way that makes them interpretable when received by a different program or operating system.

SGML also provides ways of declaring short cuts to document markup. The amount of markup that needs to be entered or transmitted can be reduced by:

- omitting markup tags that can be implied by the use of other tags;
- using special short forms of tags;
- using shorthand references to identify entities that contain markup tags.

These techniques make it possible to reduce to a minimum the amount of markup required in an SGML-coded file.

Users of SGML systems may hardly notice the difference between their existing word processors and SGML-based programs. Both may use the same sequences of key or button depressions to enter and format the text. The main difference will be that the set of tags/buttons that are permitted/active at a particular point in an SGML document will be restricted to the set that is defined for the containing element in the document type definition. This will mean, for example, that it will no longer be possible to place a third-level heading directly under a first-level heading if the document type definition requires there to be an intervening second-level heading.

Word processors will only be able to import and format SGML-coded documents if they have a program that is capable of converting SGML markup into a form that can be understood by the formatting program used by the word processor. For generalized SGML documents this can be a difficult process. There is, however, one particular application of SGML that is specifically designed to make it as easy as possible to convert word-processed text into and out of SGML – the HyperText Markup Language (HTML) used on the World Wide Web.

1.6 The role of HTML

When Tim Berners-Lee created the first HTML browser at CERN, he was not designing an SGML system. Initially he just wanted a mechanism that would describe the processes going on within his browser in a form that could be safely transmitted over the Internet. As the SGML developers had found, the safest code set for the transmission of information between computer systems is that defined in ISO 646, which formally defines an International Reference Version (IRV) of the code set originally created by the American National Standards Institute (ANSI) as the American Standard Code for Information Interchange (ASCII). To delimit his markup instructions from the text Tim Berners-Lee chose the same delimiters as SGML, the < and > characters. His initial markup instruction set included things like end of paragraph `<P>`, italic `<I>` and bold `<B>`. To end italic and bold text strings Tim Berners-Lee chose to use end delimiters of the same form as SGML, `</I>` and `</B>`.

While at first glance this initial coding scheme looked like SGML, it was apparent to those who knew SGML that there were fundamental differences between the concepts behind HTML and those behind SGML. In particular, the role of the `<P>` tag was fundamentally different. In HTML this tag initially only indicated the point at which a paragraph end was required. In SGML this tag indicates the start of a paragraph, with a matching `</P>` tag identifying the end of the paragraph, where the actual paragraph break occurs.

Another fundamental difference was that HTML originally had no control on when you should switch bold and italic on and off. As with many word processors, there was nothing to stop users from switching on bold in the middle of one paragraph and then switching on italic at the start of the next. In such cases the first part of the second paragraph would be set in bold italic. If bold was then switched off the text would continue to be presented in italic until a command to switch off italic was received.

The problem with this approach is that you could not be sure that all HTML document browsers would work in exactly the same way. Some might choose to automatically switch bold and italic off when they started a new paragraph. This led to the same document providing different results in different browsers.

The philosophical differences between HTML and SGML were resolved with Version 2.0 of HTML (Internet RFC 1866), when it was decided to use an SGML document type declaration to formalize HTML so that restrictions could be placed on where each of the HTML elements could be started and ended. The formal definition made it clear that it was no longer permissible to extend formatting instructions over paragraph boundaries. It also introduced logical equivalents for formatting-related instructions. For example, emphasis (`<EM>`) was introduced to replace italic (`<I>`) and `<STRONG>` was introduced to replace bold (`<B>`).

HTML is not as well controlled structurally as most SGML document type definitions. It is still more presentation-oriented than structurally ordered. Version 3.2 of the standard, which was formally agreed in January 1997, introduced some additional structural elements, including one that can be used to arbitrarily group sets of elements. It is likely that the trend of introducing a greater range of logical elements will develop over time.

HTML is very easy to map to and from word-processing software. At its simplest level it can be looked at as an SGML representation of RTF. HTML is an ideal way of getting users of existing word processors to start to use generic markup tags, because it can be introduced into existing word processors with very few changes to existing document creation processes. This book will use HTML to explain many of the features of SGML that it utilizes, but will also explain why some of the techniques used in HTML still represent poor practice for SGML document creation.

Document analysis and information modeling

Identifying document types • The structure of documents • Formatting structured documents • The difference between formatting and structure • Information management

An SGML document forms a self-contained unit that can be delivered either electronically or in printed form. There are no size constraints on SGML documents – they can range in size from a one-line memo or letter to a multi-volume set such as the *Encyclopaedia Britannica*.

SGML documents consist of a number of interrelated **elements**. Each element contains data which serves a specific purpose. A particular word can be a subcomponent of more than one element. For instance, a word can be part of a highlighted phrase within a paragraph, which forms part of a section in a chapter, and so on.

Each SGML document is associated with a **document type definition** (**DTD**) which defines the structure of the document in terms of the elements it can contain and the order in which these elements can occur. Within the DTD each element in the document is given a name (**generic identifier**) by which its role can be recognized. When placed within **markup delimiters**, these generic identifiers form the tags used to identify the start and end of each element.

To allow large documents to be generated efficiently, SGML documents can be developed as a sequence of subdocuments, each subdocument forming a document in its own right. Authors can opt to process each subdocument separately or can create a master document that links the various subdocuments together in the required order.

To use SGML effectively authors should be able to recognize:

- what constitutes an SGML document;
- the structure of a document;
- how the physical appearance (format) of a document relates to its contents.

Each of these concepts will be explained in this chapter.

2.1 Identifying document types

From the author's point of view the most important thing about a document is that it is a unit that can be passed to another user. How big this unit is will depend on circumstances. For example, if an author has contracted to supply certain chapters of a book to his publisher on specific dates, he will probably find it easiest to treat each chapter as an individual document, whereas, if the contract calls for the delivery of the completed manuscript at one time, the whole book can be considered as the document, individual parts or chapters forming subelements of the main document.

Another consideration in determining what constitutes a document may be the form in which the data is delivered. For example, documents designed to be delivered over the WWW are typically written in smaller units to reduce transmission delays. By linking together a set of related small files, it is possible to create what is referred to as a **hyperdocument**. In this case the contents of each file may be thought of as forming a subcomponent of a chapter, which itself is a subelement of a master document that combines the chapters into a coherent set.

Parts of documents that need separate processing should be treated as separate **entities**. For example, complex tables that require special document type definitions, or features not used elsewhere in the document, can be treated as subdocuments and stored in a separate file. If complex tables are processed separately, the complexity of the DTD used for the main document can be reduced. Where pre-processed graphics are incorporated into an SGML document by reference to external files, however, it is not necessary to create a separate subdocument for the processed data, as an SGML **external entity reference** can both identify the location of non-SGML information and control its processing.

In many applications creating a document can be thought of as completing a preprinted form. For example, a memo will normally be output on a sheet of paper that has been preprinted with the name of the company and special fields for the entry of the names of the sender and recipient, as well possibly as the subject and date of the memo. These preprinted fields do not, as such, constitute part of the document. *For preprinted forms the SGML document just contains the text to be added to the preprinted sheet.*

It is important, when analyzing documents, to separate the role of a piece of data from its format. It is the role of a piece of information that determines how it should be processed. Part of the processing of the element is its formatting but, as you will see, this may be only a small part of the processing required to manage properly the elements that make up a document set.

2.2 The structure of documents

While the structure of a document can vary in complexity from the simple format of a memo or letter to the complex format of a technical manual or a textbook, the concepts used to identify the structure of each document remain

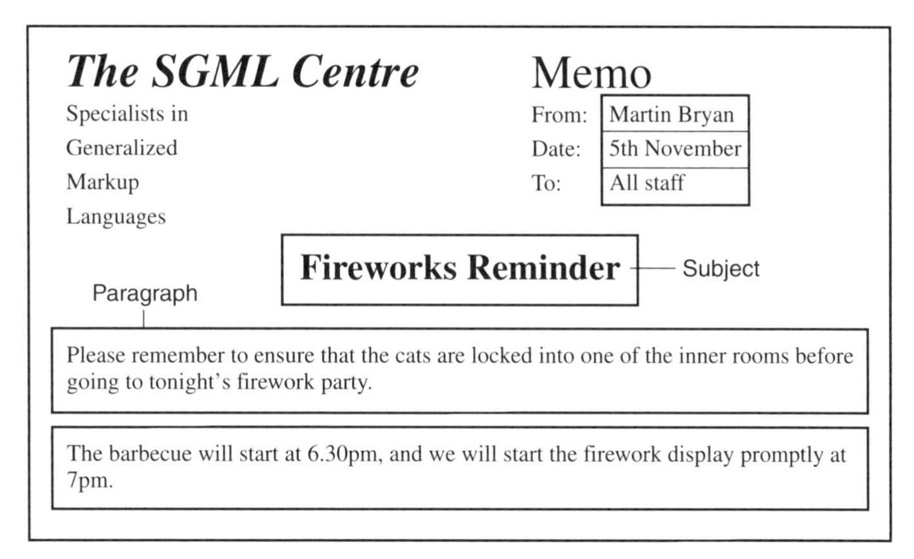

Figure 2.1 The structure of a memo

the same. One advantage of this is that the elements used to generate a simple memo or letter can also be used within a more complex document such as a textbook.

2.2.1 The structure of a memo

Figure 2.1 shows the structure of a simple memo. Each element of the structure has been surrounded with a box and allocated an identifier. In the cases of the first three elements the identifier is the preprinted name of the field (`<FROM>`, `<DATE>` and `<TO>`). The `<SUBJECT>` element can be considered as an optional heading to the memo. The text of the memo, in this case, consists of two paragraphs of text, which have been assigned the generic identifier `PARA` in the marked-up document.

In SGML this memo could be marked up as:

```
<!DOCTYPE memo PUBLIC "-//The SGML Centre//DTD Memo//EN">
<MEMO>
<FROM>Martin Bryan
<TO>All staff
<DATE>5th November
<SUBJECT>Fireworks Reminder
<PARA>Please remember to ensure that the cats are locked into one of
      the inner rooms before going to tonight's firework party.
<PARA>The barbecue will start at 6.30pm, and we will start the
      firework display promptly at 7pm.
</MEMO>
```

The first line of the coded text contains a **document type declaration** identifying the document type definition (DTD) required for the document. In this example the definition required is one declared previously for the production of English (EN) language memos for The SGML Centre. (A document type declaration is required at the start of each document. In many cases, however, this declaration will be generated automatically as part of the file conversion/transmission process to avoid the need for manual entry.)

The document type declaration is immediately followed by an SGML start-tag whose name (generic identifier) is identical to the one used for the document type declaration (for example, <MEMO>). This **base document element** is the markup instruction that is used to check that the correct DTD has been associated with the document.

The elements following the <MEMO> base document element are fairly self-explanatory. The start of each element is identified by a start-tag consisting of the element's name entered between a pair of delimiters (in this case angle brackets).

Notice how the <DATE> element has not been entered in the sequence that might be expected from its position on the printed memo. This illustrates one of the powers of SGML – it is based on the logical structure of the contents rather than their position or appearance. In many cases this will allow entries to be made in a more convenient sequence, the formatting program determining exactly where each element should be placed on the printed page or display screen.

The end of the coded memo is identified by an end-tag indicating that the memo has been completed. The tag consists of the name of the base document element between a pair of special end-tag delimiters (</ and >). In many simple documents this final end-tag will be the only one identifying the end of an element, all other end-tags being omitted to reduce the amount of embedded coding required. (In general, end-tags may be omitted whenever no ambiguity would occur from their omission.)

2.2.2 The structure of a letter

Figure 2.2 shows the structure of a typical letter. This letter could be coded as:

```
<!DOCTYPE letter PUBLIC "-//The SGML Centre//DTD Letter//EN">
<LETTER>
<REF>MTB/290296-4
<DATE>29th February 1996
<ADDRESS>Hugh Tucker
Documenta ApS
Marievej 7
DK-2900 Hellerup
Denmark
<DEAR>Hugh
<P>
```

```
Many thanks for placing the latest version of the editor on your FTP
server. I had no trouble downloading the program and loading it onto
my system.
<P>
I particularly liked the new feature to prompt users for missing
elements if they try to save incomplete files. It certainly helps to
bring home the fact that partial documents are just that - something
that needs completing as soon as possible.
<SIGNED type=grateful>
<NAME>Martin Bryan
</LETTER>
```

As is to be expected, a letter requires more elements to define its structure than a memo, but perhaps surprisingly it does not contain many more markup instructions within the text, despite its greater length. This is made possible by the use of 'implied' tags and short references, as will be explained shortly.

The start of the coded letter is similar to that of the memo, with a document type declaration requesting a previously declared set of element and entity definitions being immediately followed by the base document element, in

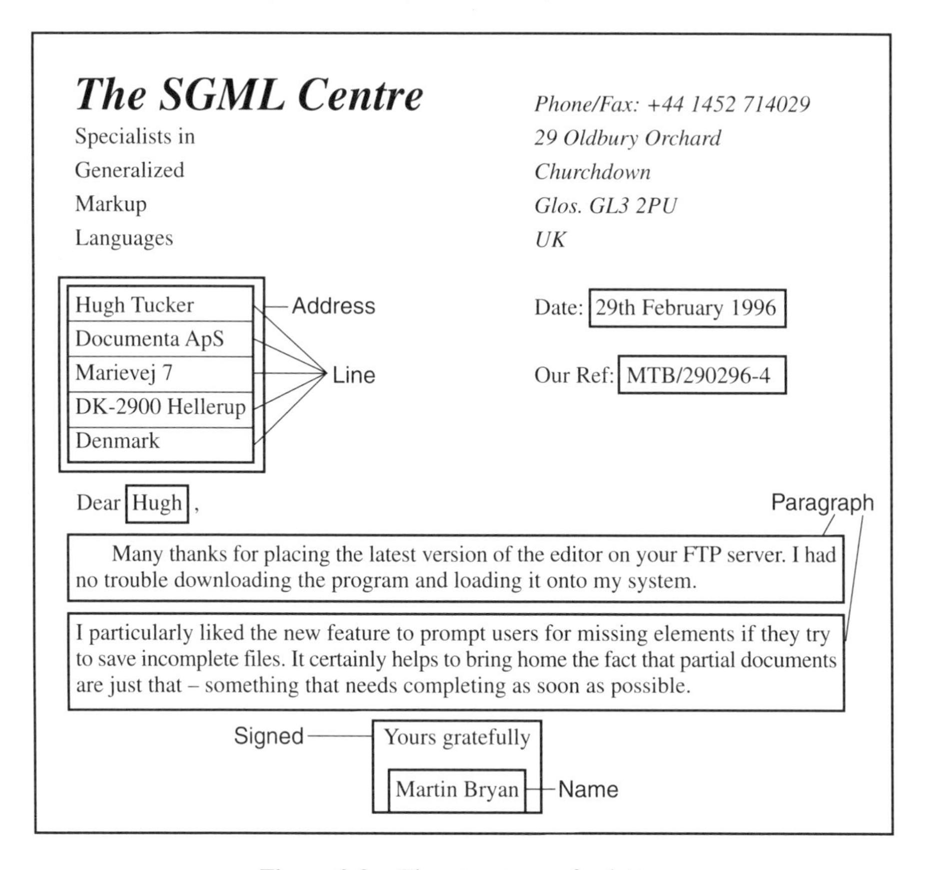

The SGML Centre

Specialists in
Generalized
Markup
Languages

Phone/Fax: +44 1452 714029
29 Oldbury Orchard
Churchdown
Glos. GL3 2PU
UK

Hugh Tucker
Documenta ApS
Marievej 7
DK-2900 Hellerup
Denmark

Date: 29th February 1996

Our Ref: MTB/290296-4

Dear Hugh,

Many thanks for placing the latest version of the editor on your FTP server. I had no trouble downloading the program and loading it onto my system.

I particularly liked the new feature to prompt users for missing elements if they try to save incomplete files. It certainly helps to bring home the fact that partial documents are just that – something that needs completing as soon as possible.

Yours gratefully

Martin Bryan

Figure 2.2 The structure of a letter

this case <LETTER>, that activates the declared set. (Once again this element is the only one with an explicit end-tag.) The next two elements contain the document's unique reference number and its date. Note that these precede the address in the markup, though they appear to be printed after specific lines of the address.

Each address consists of a number of lines, each of which can have a specific purpose. It is here that some care needs to be taken in identifying clearly the true structure of the document, rather than its apparent one. The apparent structure of an address is that it starts with the recipient's name, possibly followed by a company name. This is then followed by one or more lines of address information, which may contain a postcode. But beware: if the markup is simply being entered to produce a printed letter there is nothing to be gained, and much to be lost, by treating the name, company and postcode as separate elements of the document when this information is not used elsewhere in the document.

In the coded example above the various components of the address have not been identified individually. To reduce the amount of markup needed, the document designer has asked the program to recognize the end of each line of the address as the end of a nested <LINE> element, but this fact is not visible to the typist. By using the power of SGML short references the amount of markup required to code the address has been reduced to a single start-tag preceding the first line.

The rest of the SGML-coded letter is fairly straightforward, with <DEAR> being used as the tag for the form of the recipient's name to be placed after the word 'Dear' at the top of the letter and, in this case, <P> being used to identify the start of each paragraph of the text.

As is shown in Figure 2.2, the formatting program may treat two paragraph tags differently, depending on where they occur in the document. Often the first paragraph of a letter will be indented while other paragraphs will be set full out, with a blank line of space identifying the paragraph break. Whereas most current word processing programs would expect the typist to remember to indent the first paragraph manually, such features can be taken care of automatically by SGML's text-formatting procedures. All the operator needs to do is to identify the start of the logical element called a paragraph so that the program can apply the relevant house rules to produce the final letter.

The <SIGNED type=grateful> tag in the coded letter illustrates another SGML feature – the use of **attributes** to qualify a tag. In this case, selection of the appropriate type of signature is all that is needed to tell the formatting program:

- the form of address to be used ('Yours gratefully');
- the space to be left for the signature (which could be added automatically by a laser printer).

For this example the name of the sender has been entered as a separate <NAME> element, embedded within the <SIGNED> element.

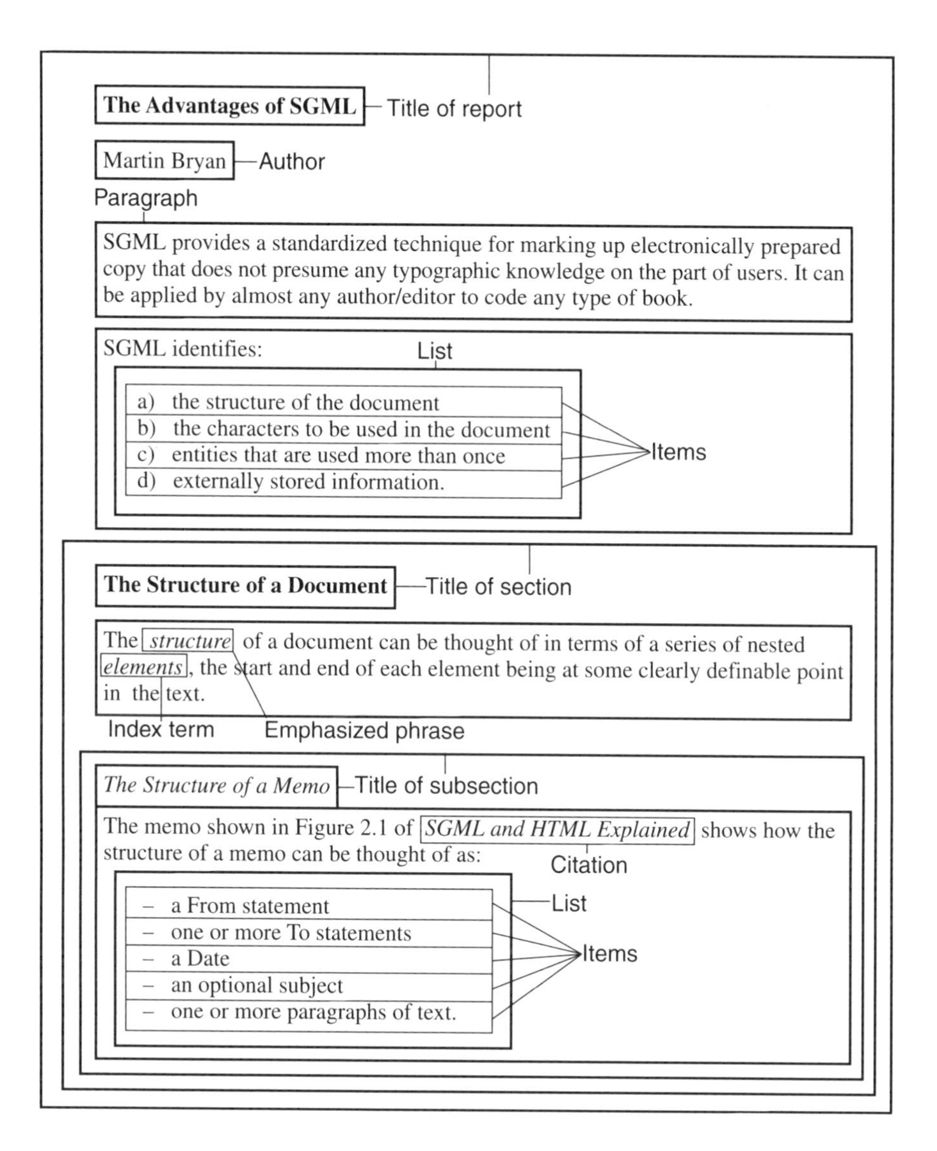

Figure 2.3 The structure of a report

2.2.3 The structure of a report

Figure 2.3 shows the start of a typical report, each element of the structure once again being boxed for clarity.

The report could be marked up, in SGML form, as:

```
<!DOCTYPE report PUBLIC "-//The SGML Centre/DTD Report//EN">
<REPORT>
<TITLE>The Advantages of SGML
<AUTHOR>Martin Bryan
<P>SGML provides a standardized technique for marking up
electronically prepared copy that does not presume any typographic
knowledge on the part of users. It can be applied by almost
any author/editor to code any type of book.
<P>SGML identifies<LIST number=alpha>
<ITEM>the structure of the document
<ITEM>the characters to be used in the document
<ITEM>entities that are used more than once
<ITEM>externally stored information.</LIST>
<SECTION>
<TITLE>The Structure of a Document
<P>The <EMPHASIS>structure</EMPHASIS> of a document can be thought of in
terms of a series of nested <INDEX>elements</INDEX>, the start and end
of each element being at some clearly definable point in the text.
<SUBSECTION>
<TITLE>The Structure of a Memo
<P>The memo shown in Figure 2.1 of <CITATION>SGML and HTML Explained
</CITATION> shows how the structure of a memo can be thought of as<LIST>
<ITEM>a From statement
<ITEM>one or more To statements
<ITEM>a Date
<ITEM>an optional subject
<ITEM>one or more paragraphs of text.</LIST>
...
```

The first two elements of the report (`<TITLE>` and `<AUTHOR>`) have been given fairly self-explanatory identifiers. Note that the `<TITLE>` start-tag has been used in three places. In each place the immediately preceding tag indicates which element the title identifies.

As in the previous example, the start of each paragraph of text is identified by `<P>`. This time, though, the format of the first paragraph of text is the same as that of subsequent paragraphs. Within reports a paragraph can contain a number of embedded elements (such as identifying lists, highlighted phrases and index entries), making the overall structure of the document slightly more complex than was the case for the earlier memo and letter examples.

A level of structure that occurs within a report, but which does not normally occur in a memo or letter, is that of sections (divisions) of text. Such sections are normally readily identifiable because they have headings explaining their purpose. More than one level of such heading may apply, as illustrated in Figure 2.3. The number of different types of headings, and the use to which they are put, varies according to the purpose of the report.

Another point to note about the SGML coding used for the text in Figure 2.3 is the fact that the four elements of the document that are printed in italics have each been coded differently. The advantages of separate coding for the heading, which could end up being set in a different typeface or size, are fairly clear, but the reason for coding the other three italicized phrases differently may not be immediately obvious.

If you look at the wording of text you can see that the roles of these italicized words differ. The first italicized word is simply an *emphasized phrase*, which in this case happens to have been printed in italic. (The graphic designer could equally well have asked for such words to appear in small caps, or another face.) The second italicized word appears at first sight to have exactly the same function as its predecessor, but there is one important difference – this word also has to be included in the index. To indicate this, the word has been flagged by tags identifying the start and end of an *index term* (<INDEX> and </INDEX>) rather than those identifying a particular style of emphasized phrase (<EMPHASIS> and </EMPHASIS>).

The last item of embedded italicized text identifies a book that has been cited in the text. As the publisher may request that such *citations* be expanded to form a bibliography (which may result in their being replaced by cross-references to the bibliography) yet another pair of tags has been used to identify the italicized phrase as a citation (<CITATION> and </CITATION>).

It should be noticed that end-tags have been entered for each of the embedded elements. End-tags are compulsory wherever the end of an element occurs at a point which is not immediately followed by the start-tag of another element or the end-tag of the parent element.

Another form of embedded element shown in Figure 2.3 is a *list*. The start of the list is identified by the <LIST> start-tag, which also marks the point where the program is to output the colon required by the publisher's house style to indicate the start of a list. As with the other embedded items, an end-tag is used to identify the end of a list. Actually, in this example the </LIST> end-tag is not really necessary because end-tags are only compulsory for lists that occur in the middle of other elements, that is, where the list is immediately followed by more of the current paragraph's text, or where one list is embedded within another.

Each list is made up of a number of *list items*, in this case identified by the tag <ITEM>. Each item can, if required, be numbered or otherwise identified on output. In Figure 2.3 the items in the first list have been identified by individual letters, while those in the second list are simply preceded by dashes. This is achieved by the addition of a `number=alpha` attribute to the first <LIST> tag to specify that items in the list are to be 'numbered' alphabetically, whereas the second <LIST> tag contains no attributes, invoking the default style for the item identifier at the start of its embedded items. (The styles applied depend on how the text-formatting program has been set up. There are no pre-defined styles associated with SGML.)

If you look carefully at the coded text, you will notice that the letters used to identify each item have not been specified by the author – they have been added by the program as the text has been formatted for output. Besides reducing the amount of keying required, this also means that a new item can be added to the list without having to renumber all the entries.

Where items in a list are referred to elsewhere in the document, renumbering of individual items can prove to be a trap for the unwary. Fortunately, SGML has provided a neat solution to this problem. Any element can be assigned an attribute that provides a **unique identifier** to specific occurrences of that element. If a list item is given such an attribute, reference can be made to the item by entry of a tag containing a special cross-reference attribute at the appropriate point in the text. For example, if the tag for the fourth item in the first list shown in Figure 2.3 is entered as `<ITEM id="external">` it could be cross-referred to within the coded text as:

```
... as shown in <ITEM-REF refid="external">, the ...
```

An advanced text-formatting program could check the page and number of the item being referred to, which it could then output in the form:

```
... as shown in item d) on page 24, the ...
```

Whenever the list is extended, or positioned on another page, the program will automatically adjust the reference when it reaches the cross-reference point.

2.2.4 The structure of scientific papers

Figure 2.4 illustrates the structure of a simple scientific paper.

As with our report, the basic text consists of a title element, author details, two introductory paragraphs of text and two levels of heading, each with associated text paragraphs. The fact that the title and author elements extend

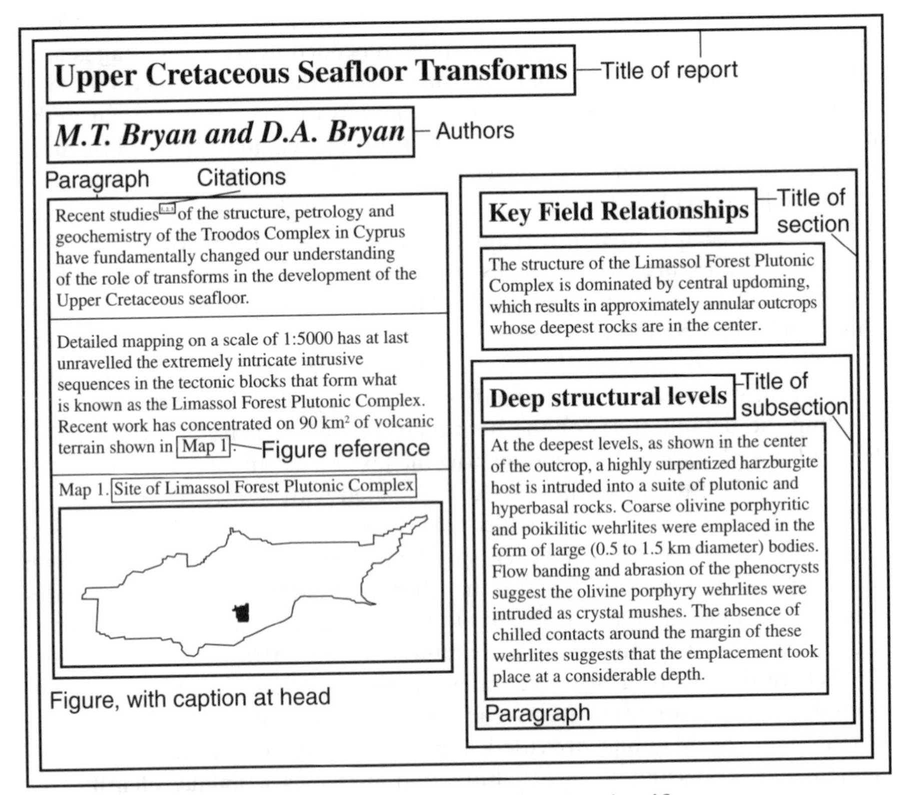

Figure 2.4 The structure of a simple scientific paper

across both columns of the formatted page does not affect the way in which the text is marked up in SGML. As far as the author is concerned, the main structure of this text is exactly the same as for the report example.

Of course, a few additional elements are required for scientific papers, such as those used to reserve space for figures and their captions. Because the position of elements such as figures, tables and footnotes can vary according to the page layout, and to the position at which they are referenced within the text, such elements are sometimes referred to as *floating elements*. To simplify the entry of floating elements, SGML allows them to be defined at the point at which they are initially referenced, their final position being determined by the formatting process on output.

One major difference between this scientific paper and the previous report is in the treatment of citations. Though three different citations are made in the first paragraph, none of the details are shown there because, in common with most scientific papers, the citations have been moved to a separate reference bibliography at the end of the paper, where they have been numbered in the sequence in which they have been referred to in the paper. Within the SGML coded text, however, the citation details can still be entered at the point of reference, even though they are formatted in a different way from the citations in the report shown in Figure 2.3. Typically the citations for Figure 2.4 would be entered as:

```
Recent studies<CITATION>Simonian, KO
<TITLE>Open University Thesis</TITLE> (unpub. 1975).</CITATION>
<CITATION>Bear, LM <TITLE>Geol. Survey Dept. Cyprus Mem. 3</TITLE>,
180pp (1960).</CITATION><CITATION>Panayiotou, A <TITLE>Geol. Survey Dept.
Cyprus Thesis</TITLE> (unpublished thesis, 1977)</CITATION> of the ...
```

Notice that the entered citations have not been given numbers and no commas or spaces have been entered between them; this is all handled by the text formatter, as is the positioning of the references at the end of the main text.

Another feature of scientific papers that is illustrated by Figure 2.4 is the use of mathematical signs such as the superior 2 used to produce the $90km^2$ sequence at the end of the second paragraph. As far as physical appearance is concerned there is no difference between this and the 2 used in the citation at the start of the previous paragraph, but both a reader and an SGML program recognize this symbol as a character with special significance. Such special characters will be entered either by using special entity references of the form `²` or by using a special element to identify the text to be treated in a different way, say `<SUP>2</SUP>`.

At the end of the second paragraph there is a reference to the identifier assigned to the map through its associated caption. Note that this illustration has not been given a figure number; it has been assigned a map number instead. In most SGML-based systems figure numbering is handled automatically by the program. To be able to assign a map number rather than a figure number, the system must be able to identify which figures contain maps. Typically this would be done using markup of the following form:

```
...shown in <FIG-REF idref=cyprus>.
<FIGURE id=cyprus type=map>
<ARTWORK file=cyprus.map notation=GIF>
<CAPTION>Site of Limassol Forest Plutonic Complex
</FIGURE>
```

Note that neither the reference to the figure, in the `<FIG-REF>` element, nor the caption indicate the map number. The map number is obtained by counting how many preceding `<FIGURE>` elements there are whose type is `map`. The figure reference is a pointer to the unique identifier, `id`, of the `<FIGURE>` element that acts as a container for both the artwork and the associated caption.

Notice that the caption has been specifed after the artwork, though on the formatted page it appears above the map. This is another example of positioning being determined by the text-formatting process. For example, there could be a house-style rule that figures floated to the top of the page are to have captions below the artwork while those placed at the foot of a column have their captions above the artwork. SGML only specifies the logical relationship between the artwork and the caption, not the physical relationship.

2.2.5 The structure of books

Figure 2.5 shows how the divisional structure of a simple textbook can be illustrated in the form of a tree diagram. Six basic text divisions have been specified: parts, chapters, sections, subsections, sub-subsections and low-level divisions. Each division must be given a title, which can optionally be followed by some text before the next lower division of text is encountered.

Figure 2.6 shows the structure of a typical set of text elements within a textbook. Within each text section authors can identify:

- paragraphs of text;
- warnings and other forms of admonitory notes;
- list of items, definitions or other lists;
- tables and figures;
- special freestanding elements of text, such as long quotations, poetry, examples and equations.

The last of these options, when combined with the list of special elements, allows quotations and poems to be placed at the start of the text without a preceding `<P>` paragraph element. For example, a chapter might start:

```
<CHAPTER><TITLE id="three">Cold War: Provocation and Prevarication
<QUOTE>
<LINE><EMPHASIS>Words to the heat of deeds too cold breath gives
</EMPHASIS>
<SOURCE align=right>Macbeth II i 58</QUOTE>
<P>The discovery of the Spaniards ...
```

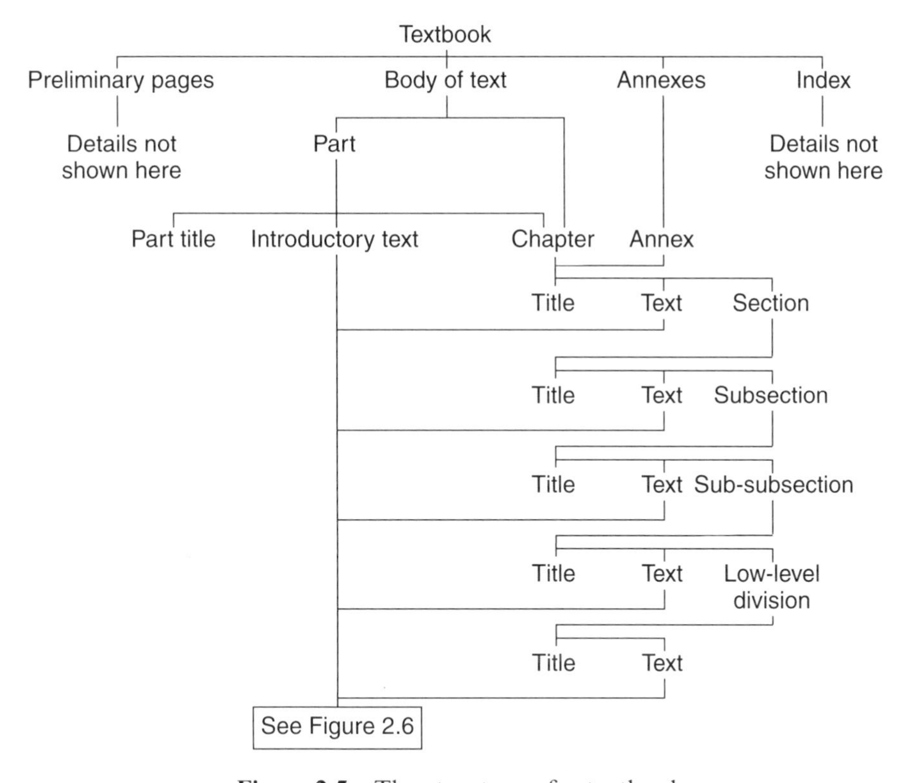

Figure 2.5 The structure of a textbook

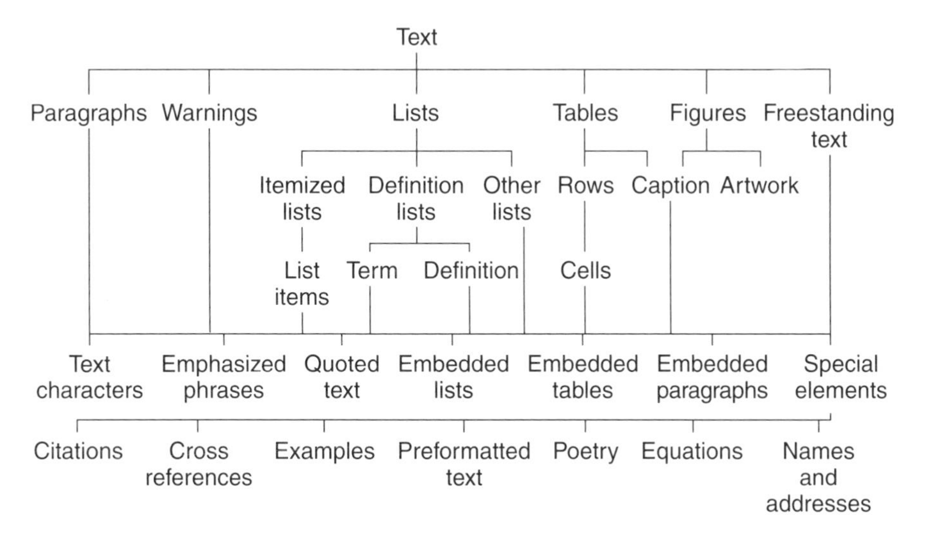

Figure 2.6 Text elements within a textbook

If quotations were not allowed at the main level a <P> would be needed in front of the <QUOTE> tag identifying the long quotation, though this may not be obvious to the author. (It is for this reason that definition of the structure of complicated documents will normally be left to specially trained document designers, whose job it is to design the element structure to fit the author's perceptions of the format of the text as exactly as possible.)

Figure 2.6 is not exhaustive, as the subelements associated with the lower levels of elements cannot be added without clouding the overall structure. Many elements have a similar substructure, consisting of text, emphasized phrases, embedded quotes, cross-references, embedded lists and so on. Fortunately, SGML allows users to define a commonly used group of elements as a referenceable **parameter entity**, the name of which can then be used in a number of places within other markup declarations as a shorthand identifier for shared elements.

It can be seen from the above analyses of the structure of documents that different structures are required for different types of documents, but that in many cases the basic textual elements will be shared by most types of document. Authors will not, however, normally be expected to analyze documents; this will be done by specially trained information analysts. An author will be provided with a previously defined document structure, which he may need to modify slightly to meet special requirements. The techniques used to interpret and modify existing document type definitions are described later in this book.

2.3 Formatting structured documents

Before we go into detail about the use of SGML, a word needs to be said about how the structure of documents is related to the appearance (format) of the final document.

A formatting program needs to know the format required for each element defined in the document type definition. Where an element can be used in more than one context, a different set of formatting rules may need to be applied in each context. The techniques employed for this will depend on the type of text formatter being used and the level to which it has been integrated with SGML.

At the simplest level, formatting will simply involve a replacement of each SGML tag with a set of markup codes relevant to the output device being used. In such cases a replacement string will need to be defined for each tagged element and for each attribute, or combination of attributes, that can be used to qualify the element.

At a slightly higher level, the formatting program may be given the names of one or more procedures (computer program macros) to be carried out when an element or attribute is encountered. These procedures may range in complexity from ones that position the element at the required point to procedures for extracting and numbering entries in the index or content list.

A fully featured SGML system will be able to use specifications coded using the *Document Style Semantics and Specification Language* (*DSSSL*) defined in ISO/IEC standard 10179 to control formatting. As this standard was only published in April 1996, however, there are currently no fully featured DSSSL formatters, though first-generation tools that process a subset of the DSSSL specifications are available. Alternative strategies include the adoption of the rules defined for the US Department of Defense's CALS Formatting Output Specification Instance (FOSI) for the interchange of formatting information.

SGML allows special, application-specific **processing instructions** to be added to the text to control the output format in those cases where the formatter cannot itself determine the correct formatting rules. This facility should, however, be used with extreme caution as it makes it difficult to move documents between platforms that use different text-formatting engines.

2.4 The difference between formatting and structure

Most word processors define the way in which text should be formatted using a mixture of explicit *formatting instructions* and named *styles*. A style name identifies a set of formatting instructions that have been predefined using one or more *style sheets*.

As word processors do not use a formal model to describe documents, they cannot use the context in which an element occurs to control its formatting. Word processor users have, therefore, to create different style sheets for each change of presentation. If, for example, paragraphs within an annex are presented in a smaller size than those within the main body of the text, a differently named style would need to be defined for the two types of paragraph.

The lack of a formal model also makes it impossible to confirm that headings are used in the correct sequence on word processors. While word processors often define headings in terms of numbered levels, there are no checks that, for example, a level 3 heading occurs before each level 4 heading, and after a level 2 heading.

To make it easier to import text from word processors many first-time users of SGML try to mimic the facilities of word processors in their initial DTDs. The most commonly cited example of this is provided by the HyperText Markup Language (HTML), which is described in detail in the latter part of this book (Chapters 12 to 15).

The first version of HTML was not an application of SGML – it was simply a way of describing the functions of a simple word processor in the form of interchangeable, ASCII-encoded, text. It contained markup tags to identify the start and end of six types of heading (`<H1>` to `<H6>`), the end of paragraphs

(<P>) and the start and end of italic, bold or fixed width, typewriter-style, text (<I>, <B> and <TT> respectively).

The concept of using SGML to formally describe HTML was introduced with version 2.0 of HTML. By this time it had been recognized that it was better practice to identify the role of elements rather than the way in which they were formatted. To make this possible, elements such as emphasis (<EM>), <STRONG> and <CODE> were introduced to replace the original, format-specific, definitions of italic, bold and typewriter.

Version 3.2 of the HTML DTD saw the introduction of other logically based elements. For example, a new division (<DIV>) element has been introduced so that, at long last, users can indicate which paragraphs and lists belong with which headings. In addition, the latest version of HTML has re-introduced a number of element control attributes, such as those used to define the way in which lists should be numbered and presented to users.

The development cycle of HTML is typical of the development cycle of many SGML-based systems, and indicates many of the pitfalls that normally occur through the failure to undertake full information analysis at an early stage in the development process. The typical development cycle for the formalization of documentation within a user community can be summarized as follows:

(1) A set of style sheets is developed to ensure that users follow an agreed house style.
(2) Style-sheet use is enforced to stop users from adding formatting instructions to override the defaults set by the house style.
(3) Users complain that style-sheet information is lost during transformation from one word processor to another (because most word processors interpret the style-sheet instructions immediately and only export the interpreted file).
(4) SGML is adopted to transfer information on style use between word processors – the original element set is based on a set of styles defined for word processors.
(5) Additional SGML elements are defined to allow logical grouping of elements so that partial documents can be interchanged.
(6) Realization that information management should be the key to identifying which role elements play leads to a full analysis of information processing requirements.

2.5 Information management

Information management is the key to good SGML practice. Information management involves both the identification of the role of each information element and the management of the relationship between elements.

For example, in a letter there is a relationship between the name used as the content of the <DEAR> element and the address that heads the letter. The first line of the address is normally a formalized version of the formal or informal name used to address the recipient of the letter at its start. Information management involves the recording of the relationships between these two information elements.

Another aspect of information management is ensuring the validity of data. For example, the logical role and structural position of an element such as <PART-NO> is not sufficient to validate a part number. To validate the entry the contents of the element must be checked against a parts database. If the part number is associated with a <PARTNAME> element, the validity of the entered name must also be checked through the part number reference if the name has not been generated automatically in response to the part number.

The relationships between elements form a vital part of information management. When a DTD is created, it is important that information relationships be properly recorded. Typically this will be done either by ensuring that related elements are placed within a container element that clearly shows their relationship or by assigning unique identifiers to key elements and ensuring that related elements make a formal reference to the relevant identifiers.

Containerization of related elements is one of the keys to the efficient storage and retrieval of parts of SGML documents. When the related elements in a set share a common parent, that parent element can be used to quickly identify and reposition all of its subelements. Most of the advanced uses to which SGML is put are based on this ability to create information containers. Many of the advances introduced in recent years by SGML-based standards, such as the *Hypermedia/Time-based Structuring Language* (*HyTime*) defined in ISO/IEC 10744, are based on SGML's ability to identify sets of related elements and define the relationships between these information elements.

The components of an SGML system

System components • Selecting an SGML document editor • The role of document analysis/design tools • The role of document conversion tools • The role of an SGML parser • Document databases and repositories • Printing SGML documents • Electronic delivery • The component parts of an SGML document

To set the scene for the following description of the facilities provided in the Standard Generalized Markup Language, this chapter provides an overview of how an SGML system can be built from a set of interrelated software components. The classification of components used in this chapter will follow that used in Steve Pepper's definitive *Whirlwind Guide to SGML Tools and Vendors* (Pepper, 1996), the latest version of which can be obtained over the WWW from `http://www.falch.no/people/pepper/sgmltool/`.

3.1 System components

Figure 3.1 shows the main component of a comprehensive SGML system. The central part of any SGML system is the **data repository**. This can take many forms, from a simple file store to a complex database of reusable SGML elements. Files to be placed into the repository must be validated by an **SGML parser**. Validation may also be required before documents are despatched from the repository to ensure that no referenced data has been omitted from the transmitted data set.

Input to the data repository can come from:

- **SGML document editors**;
- **document analysis tools** that create DTDs and associated control files;
- **data conversion tools** that turn existing file formats into SGML documents.

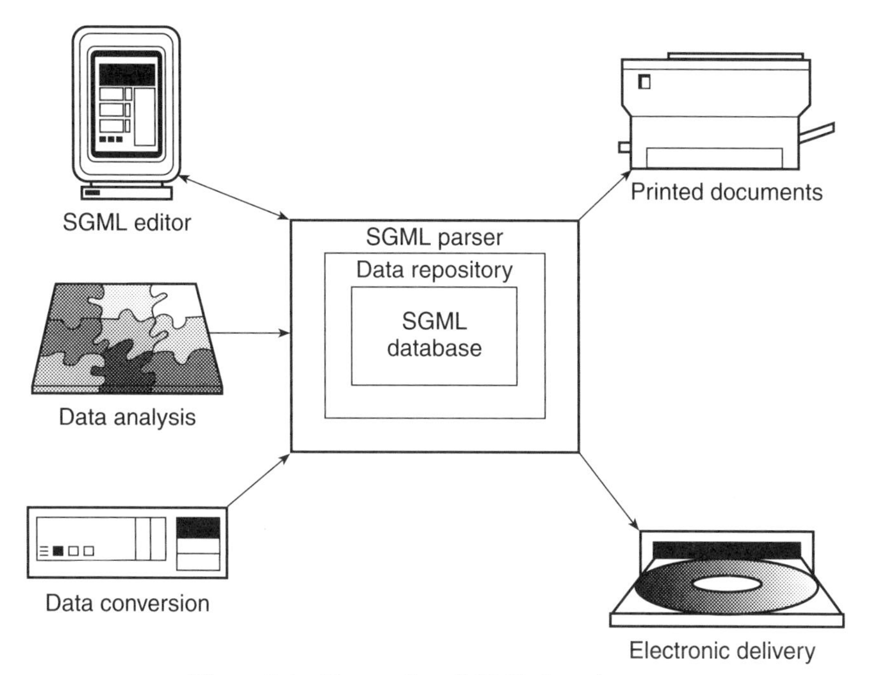

Figure 3.1 Parts of an SGML-based system

Data stored in the repository can be:

- sent to an SGML document editor for updating;
- formatted for printing;
- converted into a format suitable for electronic delivery.

3.2 Selecting an SGML document editor

SGML document editors fall into three main categories:

- editors that try to represent the printed page on the screen;
- editors that provide an unpaginated view of the text in the document;
- editors that provide a view of the file that does not attempt to match the printed result.

Editors that try to present the printed page as it is input normally hide SGML markup from users. If they do not provide a separate view of the marked-up file that allows users to edit the markup, they will have mechanisms for displaying details of the currently open elements, and their attributes, in well defined areas of the screen window, or in pop-up or pull-down windows.

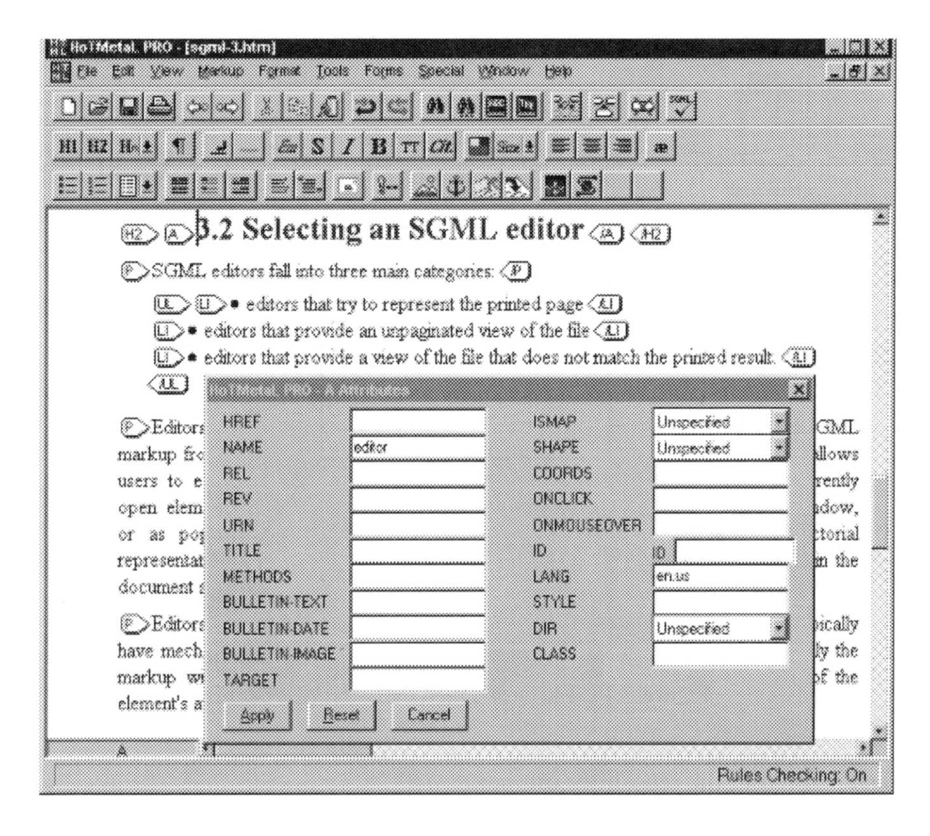

Figure 3.2 Example of a quasi-WYSIWYG editor screen

Alternatively, the editor may provide a pictorial representation of the document structure that helps users to understand where they are in the document structure.

Editors that show an unpaginated, quasi-WYSIWYG, view of the SGML file typically have mechanisms that allow the markup tags to be displayed as part of the text. Typically markup will be shown in the form of an icon. Often these icons will not contain details of the element's attributes, which can only be displayed in the form of a pop-up window. Figure 3.2 shows a typical view of the screen of such an editor when attribute editing is in progress.

As SGML concerns itself principally with the logical structure of data, rather than the way the data will be presented to end-users, there is no ideal way to display an SGML document during data capture. In many situations there are advantages in capturing the data on an editor that does not seek to represent a 'final view' of the data, but instead concentrates on making the SGML structure as clear as possible to the document creator. In such circumstances, an editor that displays the SGML markup as part of the document has advantages.

Of the many SGML-based text editors mentioned in *The Whirlwind Guide to SGML Tools and Vendors* the following are among the most popular:

- SoftQuad's Author/Editor (quasi-WYSIWYG)
- Arbortext's ADEPT editor (WYSIWYG)
- GRIF's SGML editor (WYSIWYG)
- InContext (quasi-WYSIWYG)
- TimeLux's EditTime (non-WYSIWYG).

3.3 The role of document analysis/design tools

There are a number of tools that are designed to make it easier for document analysts to create and validate their DTDs. Some of these are designed to work with specific editors or document parsers; others are designed as free-standing tools.

One class of document analysis tool takes existing DTDs and displays them in the form of a directed graph. The more advanced of such tools allow users to modify the displayed graph and then output a revised DTD. Where this is possible, it is normally also possible to create a DTD from scratch by drawing a graph of the required structure. A well known example of such a tool is Microstar's NEAR & FAR Designer.

One of the main strengths of SGML DTDs is their ability to define recursive structures, and to have rules for including and excluding certain parts of the document model in certain circumstances. Trying to display such rules graphically is extremely difficult. Where a DTD has been defined using a carefully controlled set of nested structures, it will often be impossible to display graphically the whole document structure in a viewable form. In such circumstances other forms of DTD analysis tools can help to identify, for example, all the places where a particular element can occur. An example of such a tool is SoftQuad's DTD Documentor.

Another category of useful data analysis tools allows users to scan a set of existing SGML and non-SGML documents to identify the elements they contain and the relationships between these elements. A typical example of such a tool is Avalanche's Document Analyzer.

3.4 The role of document conversion tools

While sophisticated text editors often include facilities for importing data from the more popular forms of word processors, they often do not have sufficient knowledge of data structures to be able to convert non-SGML documents into the format required for a specific SGML DTD. Stand-alone data conversion tools can provide fully programmable solutions to the problems of converting word-processor documents into SGML.

Data conversion tools can be categorized into two main classes:

- tools that can validate the SGML structure during conversion;
- tools that require the converted document to be validated by an SGML parser after conversion.

Tools that can validate the SGML structure during conversion typically use the output DTD as the starting point for describing the conversions to be made. As each element is identified, it is checked to ensure that it is valid at the current point in the document structure. If it is not, either an alternative conversion is attempted or an error is reported to the user.

Most existing data conversion tools fail to validate the SGML structure during conversion. They simply apply a set of programmed rules to the input document and then pass the unvalidated output file to an SGML parser for post-conversion validation.

Among the many data conversion tools listed in *The Whirlwind Guide to SGML Tools and Vendors* the following are possibly the most popular:

- Exoterica's Omnimark
- Electronic Book Technology's DynaTag
- Avalanche's FastTAG and SGML Hammer
- Zandar's TagWrite.

3.5 The role of an SGML parser

Before a converted, or new, SGML document is placed in a document repository it should be *parsed* to ensure that the structure of the completed document conforms to the rules specified in the associated document type definition. An **SGML parser** is defined in the SGML standard (ISO 8879) as:

> A program (or portion of a program or a combination of programs) that recognizes markup in SGML documents.
>
> NOTE – If an analogy were drawn to programming language processors, an SGML parser would be said to perform the functions of both a lexical analyzer and a parser with respect to SGML documents.

In practice, an SGML parser must do more than just recognize markup. It must also:

- expand any references to text entities, replacement text of which has been defined either as part of the DTD or by reference to one or more external files;

- identify any strings of data that form short references to entities and expand them appropriately;
- identify any numeric or named references to characters, or references to system-specific descriptions of characters or non-SGML data;
- identify the boundary of each piece of markup and its relationship to preceding or following markup;
- identify any missing attributes for which default or current values should be assigned;
- identify missing elements, the omission of which can be implied from the models defined in the DTD;
- ensure that rules for the inclusion or exclusion of elements have been correctly followed.

A validating SGML parser should be able to report errors and identify where the errors occurred. It should also be able to identify points at which the markup rules defined in the SGML declaration associated with each DTD have not been followed. For example, a validating SGML parser should:

- report the use of any invalid characters within SGML names;
- report when the document's name or string length limits have been exceeded;
- identify when the restrictions on memory storage capacity or the structure of formal public identifiers have been broken.

The most commonly used free-standing SGML parsers are those that form part of James Clark's set of public domain parsers (sgmls, nsgmls and SP). Commercially supported parsers include Exoterica's SGML Kernel and Sema's Mark-It.

3.6 Document databases and repositories

SGML documents can be stored in any type of data repository, including compressed file stores, encrypted file stores, and relational, hierarchical or object-oriented databases. The techniques used to identify the object to be stored, and the level at which stored objects can be reused, are heavily dependent on the storage manager that controls access to the storage facilities.

When documents are stored in a file store, rather than a database, an **SGML entity manager** can be used to control the way in which documents, and the entities they reference, are loaded into, and recalled from, the file store. An SGML entity manager should be able to convert documents from the coding format used for storage to that required for parsing. This can involve the application of algorithms for data compression/decompression, encryption/decryption and conversion from single-byte (8-bit) to multibyte (for example, 16-bit or 32-bit) formats. Where support is provided for bit-combination transformations, the entity manager can also provide facilities for converting from the encoding used for data storage to that used for document parsing/editing (for example, from EBCDIC to ASCII). Sophisticated SGML parsers, such as James Clark's SP, have built-in SGML entity managers.

Where databases are being used as the basic storage mechanism, documents can be split into separate elements for storage. The techniques used for identifying relevant storage units depend on the type of database being used and the sophistication of the database loading/unloading software.

When relational database management systems (RDBMSs) are being used for storage, it is not common practice to treat each element in the DTD as a storable object. Instead, the DTD is normally analyzed to identify reusable units, such as numbered sections or tables, that can be stored as binary large objects (BLOBs) within the database. An example of an RDBMS-based SGML document repository is IDI's Basis SGMLserver.

When object-oriented databases (OODBs) are being used, the SGML document structure provides a natural hierarchy of related objects that can be directly loaded into the database. By reading the DTD, a good SGML-based OODB will be able to determine automatically the relationships between elements, as well as between elements and their attributes. In ideal situations the OODB should be able to map the changes required to the document structure when a new variant of a DTD is introduced for a particular set of existing documents. An example of an OODB-based SGML repository is Electronic Book Technology's DynaWeb database.

There are some hybrid systems that combine object-oriented front ends with relational storage. As most RDBMS vendors are now developing object-oriented front ends, such systems are likely to become more common. An early example of the use of this approach can be seen in Texcel's ERIC data repository.

A good data repository will offer facilities over and above simple data loading and retrieval. A data repository should offer facilities for version control, data archiving and data sharing. An example of an RDBMS-based system that offers such facilities is CRI's Life*CDM. An example of a managed file-based data repository is Documentum's Astoria.

For many systems workflow management will form an integral part of the data repository. Such systems are able to assign tasks to specific users, set and monitor target dates for completion of specific processes, report on progress-to-date and route files and messages from one process to another. The degree of integration of the workflow management system with the data repository is often a key factor in the selection of an SGML data repository.

3.7 Printing SGML documents

Because of the background of SGML as a controlled method of documentation capture, most SGML systems are designed specifically for the production of printed documents. Where WYSIWYG text editors are being used for data capture, there may be no need for additional facilities for document formatting; printing the image shown on the screen may be sufficient.

Because SGML systems are specifically designed to divorce the document storage/interchange format from the document presentation format, SGML documents will typically have to be formatted when retrieved from storage. In many cases this will be done using a high-speed, high-quality formatting package. There are four main ways in which format control information can be assigned to the elements of a DTD:

- by use of SGML's LINK option to add formatting attributes to SGML markup;
- by converting SGML markup into formatter-specific coding;
- by associating a Formatting Output Specification Instance (FOSI) with the DTD;
- by associating a DSSSL formatting specification with one or more document instances.

SGML's LINK facility provides a number of techniques for enhancing the existing markup of an SGML document to provide the information required by a text formatter to format the text into columns and pages. Details of these techniques are given in Chapter 10.

Conversion of SGML markup into formatter-specific forms can often be undertaken using the same tools that are used to convert word-processor documents into SGML. Alternatively, conversion facilities may be offered as part of the text-formatting system. Examples of pagination systems offering such facilities include Datalogic's DL Composer and Advent's 3B2 system.

SGML systems that are specifically designed for use as part of the US Department of Defense's Continuous Acquisition and Life-cycle Support (CALS, 1993) program often support the interchange of formatting specifications in the form of FOSIs. While FOSIs only support a limited range of formatting options, they do provide a limited degree of specification transportability. A document composition system that supports the use of FOSIs is Arbortext's ADEPT Publisher.

April 1996 saw the publication of the long-awaited *Document Style Semantics and Specification Language (DSSSL)* as ISO/IEC 10179. Despite its recent release, many vendors have already committed themselves to upgrading their products to support at least a subset of the comprehensive set of data transformation and formatting options detailed in this exciting new standard. Those interested in developing long-term systems-development strategies should look carefully into the option of using this standardized mechanism for interchanging formatting specifications.

3.8 Electronic delivery

Whilst SGML was originally designed for the production of printed documents, one of its key roles today is for the electronic delivery of documents. Four main techniques for the electronic delivery of SGML documents can be identified:

- conversion of SGML documents into a browser-specific format;
- conversion of printer files into PDF (Portable Document Format) files;
- display of documents in an SGML document browser;
- conversion of documents to HTML for display using a standard WWW document browser.

Early examples of electronic delivery involved the processing of a set of SGML files to produce a binary format that could be displayed using a customized document browser. Typically such systems will fully index the text so that fast text searches can be performed on the stored data. One of the most comprehensive browsers to use this technique was Electronic Book Technology's DynaText system.

An alternative that is widely used by many publishers is to pass the PostScript files produced as part of the text-formatting process to Adobe's Acrobat Distiller program to produce PDF-encoded files that can be displayed using Adobe's Acrobat Reader.

Another approach is to store the data in its SGML form and then use an SGML document browser, such as SoftQuad's Panorama, to browse through the native SGML. In such cases, the formatting rules to be associated with the SGML files normally form part of a browser-specific information set that is associated with the SGML DTDs or document instances.

With the rapid spread of the Internet, many users are switching to HTML document browsers for presenting information over the Internet. In this case, conversion from the SGML storage format to the HTML transmission will be undertaken at the WWW server site as a transparent process. In this scenario, formatting is controlled by the set-up of the HTML browser. Where the browser supports the new Cascading Style Sheets (CSS) specification (World Wide Web Consortium, 1996), it may be possible for the server to control document formatting to a limited degree, although parameters set by the user should still be able to override the formatting specified by the document's creator.

3.9 The component parts of an SGML document

When documents are interchanged between, or within, SGML systems, three components must be interchanged in a predefined order:

- an **SGML declaration** specifying the character sets being used and the characters that are used to represent markup;
- a **document prolog** that contains the document type definitions (DTDs) and link process definitions (LPDs) required to process a specific set of documents, together with any files that are referenced in the prolog;
- the **document instance(s)** that contain data marked up using the DTDs defined in the prolog, together with files containing entities that are referenced in the document instances.

Not all SGML systems are able to process SGML declarations. Some systems have a built-in SGML declaration. Others rely on the default SGML declaration defined in ISO 8879:1986. In some cases facilities normally controlled via the SGML declaration have to be specified using menus within the program.

A good SGML system will be able to accept documents coded using different SGML declarations, and will be able to interpret files containing SGML declarations. Because the SGML declaration controls many of the functions of an SGML system, we will briefly cover its facilities in the next chapter. You should not, however, worry too much about understanding the role of the SGML declaration when you first come to grips with SGML. All you need to know initially is that the SGML declaration places certain restrictions on what can and cannot be done by an SGML system. A quick scan through the next chapter will start to give you some idea of what these restrictions are.

For most SGML systems, document prologs will be stored in the form of a set of files that can be referenced through `DOCTYPE` declarations at the start of a document instance. For some systems, however, the DTD will need to be stored in the form of a detached `DOCTYPE` declaration so that it can be precompiled before being associated with one or more document instances. Most document prologs consist of a single DTD. The reasons why multiple DTDs may be required, and the role of LPDs, will be explained in Chapter 10.

Where document instances are to be associated with precompiled prologs, they may simply start with a markup tag identifying the base document element. In most cases, however, the document instance will start with a `DOCTYPE` declaration that identifies the DTD to be used to process the document. When documents are moved from system to system, it is important to determine whether or not the `DOCTYPE` declaration needs to be attached to, or detached from, the document instance.

When SGML document sets are interchanged, it is important to ensure that all relevant files have been included. For products that conform to the specifications laid down by the SGML Open vendor consortium this will normally be achieved through the interchange of an **SGML catalog** that identifies the public and system names of all the files required to process a specific set of document instances.

The SGML declaration

The role of the SGML declaration • The Syntax clause • Other clauses in the SGML declaration • Alternative concrete syntaxes

This chapter explains briefly the component parts of the SGML declaration, and tries to give some idea of the role each part plays.

Many readers will find the concepts covered in this chapter difficult to grasp at first reading. Do not worry if you do not understand the role of any part of the SGML declaration at first reading. You are not meant to at this stage! The reason for asking you to read quickly through this chapter at the beginning of this explanation of SGML is that restrictions imposed by the SGML declaration are fundamental to understanding many of the rules in SGML. Terms introduced in this chapter will be used throughout the remainder of the book. When you return to this chapter to remind yourself of the concepts being referred to by these terms, you should find that the summary of the terms given in this chapter will explain the restrictions imposed on other SGML constructs.

4.1 The role of the SGML declaration

When interchanging documents it is important that each transmitted code has a well defined function. In addition it is important that document markup can be correctly distinguished from codes that form the text of the document.

The rules defining the meanings of the constructs used by a particular language are known as the **syntax** of that language. Two distinct types of syntax have been defined for SGML:

- An **abstract syntax** is used to specify how SGML markup should be constructed in terms of abstract concepts such as delimiter roles and character classes.
- A **concrete syntax** is used to define how these abstract concepts have been coded within specific sets of SGML documents.

This chapter will introduce you to many of the terms used to describe the SGML's abstract syntax. The use to which the abstract syntax is put will be explained in the following chapters.

```
<!SGML "ISO 8879:1986"
       -- Declaration for typical Basic SGML Document --
CHARSET BASESET "ISO 646:1983//CHARSET International
                Reference Version (IRV)//ESC 2/5 4/0"
        DESCSET 0     9    UNUSED
                9     2    9
                11    2    UNUSED
                13    1    13
                14    18   UNUSED
                32    95   32
                127   1    UNUSED
CAPACITY PUBLIC   "ISO 8879:1986//CAPACITY Reference//EN"
SCOPE    DOCUMENT
SYNTAX   PUBLIC   "ISO 8879:1986//SYNTAX Reference//EN"
FEATURES MINIMIZE DATATAG NO OMITTAG  YES RANK  NO SHORTTAG YES
         LINK     SIMPLE  NO IMPLICIT NO  EXPLICIT NO
         OTHER    CONCUR  NO SUBDOC   NO  FORMAL  NO
APPINFO  NONE
>
```

Figure 4.1 The SGML declaration for a basic SGML document

One particular concrete syntax, called the **reference concrete syntax**, has been formally defined within ISO 8879:1986 to provide a reference against which variant concrete syntaxes can be compared. It is a requirement of conforming SGML systems that they be able to parse documents conforming to the reference concrete syntax.

Each SGML document transferred to another system should be accompanied by a declaration, called the **SGML declaration**, which defines the coding scheme used in its preparation. Figure 4.1 shows the SGML declaration that should be used if a document is transmitted without an SGML declaration. (Such documents are referred to as **basic SGML documents**.)

The SGML declaration starts with a **markup declaration open** (MDO) sequence consisting of the codes `<!`. The declaration is closed by a matching **markup declaration close** (MDC) angle bracket (>) at the end of the declaration.

The rest of the first line of the SGML declaration consists of the letters SGML followed by a delimited string containing the number and date of the ISO standard in which SGML is defined (`"ISO 8879:1986"`). This statement indicates which version of the standard was used to prepare the following declarations.

The second line of the default SGML declaration contains some text bracketed by pairs of hyphens. Text entered in an SGML markup declaration between pairs of hyphens is treated as a **comment**. In this case the comment acts as a heading explaining the purpose of the following entries.

The names of the six main clauses that make up an SGML declaration are shown in the first column of the SGML declaration. They identify:

- character set description (CHARSET);
- capacity set details (CAPACITY);
- the scope of the concrete syntax (SCOPE);
- the concrete syntax to be used within the document (SYNTAX);
- optional SGML features used to process the document (FEATURES);
- application-specific information (APPINFO).

4.2 The syntax clause

A key part of the SGML declaration is the SYNTAX clause, which controls the codes that can be used for document markup. In Figure 4.1 the syntax has been entered as a formal public identifier which references the default syntax defined in ISO 8879:1986, which is shown in Figure 4.2.

4.2.1 The reference concrete syntax

The declaration for SGML's reference concrete syntax given in the SYNTAX clause shown in Figure 4.2 contains eight subclause definitions, each identified by a keyword. These define:

```
SYNTAX   SHUNCHAR CONTROLS 0 1 2 3 4 5 6 7 8 9 10 11 12 13
                  14 15 16 17 18 19 20 21 22 23 24 25 26
                  27 28 29 30 31 127 255
         BASESET  "ISO 646:1983//CHARSET International
                  Reference Version (IRV)//ESC 2/5 4/0"
         DESCSET  0 128 0
         FUNCTION RE          13
                  RS          10
                  SPACE       32
                  TAB SEPCHAR  9
         NAMING   LCNMSTRT    ""
                  UCNMSTRT    ""
                  LCNMCHAR    "-."
                  UCNMCHAR    "-."
                  NAMECASE    GENERAL YES
                              ENTITY  NO
         DELIM    GENERAL     SGMLREF
                  SHORTREF    SGMLREF
         NAMES    SGMLREF
         QUANTITY SGMLREF
```

Figure 4.2 Formal definition of the reference concrete syntax

- the decimal numbers of any codes which the program is to ignore because they are control characters (SHUNCHAR: **shunned characters**);
- the syntax character set, consisting of a **base character set** (BASESET) declaration, followed by a description of how these characters are to be used to define the concrete syntax (DESCSET: **described character set**);
- which codes represent **function characters** required by the syntax (FUNCTION);
- the **naming rules** to be applied when defining element, attribute and entity names (NAMING);
- the markup **delimiters** to be used in the document (DELIM);
- **reserved names** used within markup declarations (NAMES);
- the **quantity set** required for the document (QUANTITY).

The base character set used for the reference concrete syntax is that defined in international standard **ISO 646**. This 7-bit character set, known as the International Reference Version (IRV), is used as a starting point for all international standards that define character sets, for example, ISO 6937, ISO 8859 and ISO/IEC 10646.

Note: *A revision of ISO 646 took place in 1991. The revision (ISO 646:1991) matches the American Standard Code for Information Interchange (ASCII) used by many computer systems. (ISO 646 does allocate different names to some of the control characters, but these names do not affect the way these codes are used.) In addition, it has been identified that the ISO 2022 Escape sequence used for ISO 646 in the SGML reference concrete syntax was incorrect: it should have been* `ESC 2/8 4/0`*. Strictly speaking, therefore, the reference concrete syntax should be updated to read* `"ISO 646:1991//CHARSET International Reference Version (IRV)//ESC 2/8 4/0"`*. In practice, it is likely that the next revision of SGML will adopt the 16-bit version of ISO/IEC 10646:1993 as its default code set.*

The described character set portion of the reference concrete syntax character set description shows that 128 characters, starting from position 0 in the list, should be mapped to identical positions in the reference concrete syntax. Table 4.1 shows the 128 codes defined in ISO 646.

Codes with values less than 32, and that with a value of 127, have been allocated to control functions, while the 95 codes with values between 32 and 126 are associated with printable (data) characters. Note that the character numbers entered in the SHUNCHAR section of the syntax clause shown in Figure 4.2 are those defined as control codes within ISO 646:

```
SHUNCHAR CONTROLS 0 1 2 3 4 5 6 7 8 9 10 11 12 13
                  14 15 16 17 18 19 20 21 22 23 24 25 26
                  27 28 29 30 31 127 255
```

Table 4.1 The ISO 646 character set

Value		ISO (16-bit) representation	ISO name/ character	Purpose
Decimal	Hexadecimal			
0	0	0/0	NUL	Null code
1	1	0/1	TC1/SOH	Transmission code 1 / Start of header
2	2	0/2	TC2/STX	Transmission code 2 / Start of text
3	3	0/3	TC3/ETX	Transmission code 3 / End of text
4	4	0/4	TC4/EOT	Transmission code 4 / End of transmission
5	5	0/5	TC5/ENQ	Transmission code 5 / Enquire
6	6	0/6	TC6/ACK	Transmission code 6 / Acknowledge
7	7	0/7	BEL	Bell
8	8	0/8	FE0/BS	Format effector 0 / Backspace
9	9	0/9	FE1/HT	Format effector 1 / Horizontal tab
10	A	0/10	FE2/LF	Format effector 2 / Line feed
11	B	0/11	FE3/VT	Format effector 3 / Vertical tab
12	C	0/12	FE4/FF	Format effector 4 / Form feed
13	D	0/13	FE5/CR	Format effector 5 / Carriage return
14	E	0/14	SO	Shift out
15	F	0/15	SI	Shift in
16	10	1/0	TC7/DLE	Transmission code 7 / Data link escape
17	11	1/1	DC1	Device control character 1
18	12	1/2	DC2	Device control character 2
19	13	1/3	DC3	Device control character 3
20	14	1/4	DC4	Device control character 4
21	15	1/5	TC8/NAK	Transmission code 8 / Negative acknowledge
22	16	1/6	TC9/SYN	Transmission code 9 / Synchronize
23	17	1/7	TC10/ETB	Transmission code 10 / End of text block
24	18	1/8	CAN	Cancel
25	19	1/9	EM	End of media
26	1A	1/10	SUB	Substitute character
27	1B	1/11	ESC	Escape
28	1C	1/12	FS/DT/IS4	Frame separator / ISO 6937 document terminator
29	1D	1/13	GS/PT/IS3	Group separator / ISO 6937 page terminator
30	1E	1/14	RS/IS2	Record separator

(continued)

Table 4.1 *(continued)*

Value		ISO (16-bit) representation	ISO name/ character	Purpose
Decimal	Hexadecimal			
31	1F	1/15	US/IS1	Unit separator
32	20	2/0		Space
33	21	2/1	!	Exclamation mark
34	22	2/2	"	Quotation mark
35	23	2/3	#	Number sign
36	24	2/4	¤	General currency sign (Dollar in ISO 646:1991)
37	25	2/5	%	Percent
38	26	2/6	&	Ampersand
39	27	2/7	'	Apostrophe
40	28	2/8	(	Left parenthesis
41	29	2/9	)	Right parenthesis
42	2A	2/10	*	Asterisk
43	2B	2/11	+	Plus sign
44	2C	2/12	,	Comma
45	2D	2/13	-	Hyphen
46	2E	2/14	.	Full stop (Period)
47	2F	2/15	/	Forward slash (Solidus)
48	30	3/0	0	
49	31	3/1	1	
50	32	3/2	2	
51	33	3/3	3	
52	34	3/4	4	
53	35	3/5	5	
54	36	3/6	6	
55	37	3/7	7	
56	38	3/8	8	
57	39	3/9	9	
58	3A	3/10	:	Colon
59	3B	3/11	;	Semicolon
60	3C	3/12	<	Less-than sign
61	3D	3/13	=	Equals sign
62	3E	3/14	>	Greater-than sign
63	3F	3/15	?	Question mark
64	40	4/0	@	Commercial at
65	41	4/1	A	
66	42	4/2	B	
67	43	4/3	C	
68	44	4/4	D	
69	45	4/5	E	
70	46	4/6	F	
71	47	4/7	G	
72	48	4/8	H	
73	49	4/9	I	
74	4A	4/10	J	

(continued)

Table 4.1 *(continued)*

Value		ISO (16-bit) representation	ISO name/ character	Purpose
Decimal	Hexadecimal			
75	4B	4/11	K	
76	4C	4/12	L	
77	4D	4/13	M	
78	4E	4/14	N	
79	4F	4/15	O	
80	50	5/0	P	
81	51	5/1	Q	
82	52	5/2	R	
83	53	5/3	S	
84	54	5/4	T	
85	55	5/5	U	
86	56	5/6	V	
87	57	5/7	W	
88	58	5/8	X	
89	59	5/9	Y	
90	5A	5/10	Z	
91	5B	5/11	[	Left square bracket
92	5C	5/12	\	Backward slash (Reverse solidus)
93	5D	5/13	]	Right square bracket
94	5E	5/14	^	Circumflex accent
95	5F	5/15	_	Low line
96	60	6/0	`	Grave accent
97	61	6/1	a	
98	62	6/2	b	
99	63	6/3	c	
100	64	6/4	d	
101	65	6/5	e	
102	66	6/6	f	
103	67	6/7	g	
104	68	6/8	h	
105	69	6/9	i	
106	6A	6/10	j	
107	6B	6/11	k	
108	6C	6/12	l	
109	6D	6/13	m	
110	6E	6/14	n	
111	6F	6/15	o	
112	70	7/0	p	
113	71	7/1	q	
114	72	7/2	r	
115	73	7/3	s	
116	74	7/4	t	
117	75	7/5	u	
118	76	7/6	v	

(continued)

Table 4.1 *(continued)*

Value		ISO (16-bit) representation	ISO name/ character	Purpose
Decimal	Hexadecimal			
119	77	7/7	w	
120	78	7/8	x	
121	79	7/9	y	
122	7A	7/10	z	
123	7B	7/11	{	Left curly bracket
124	7C	7/12	|	Vertical line
125	7D	7/13	}	Right curly bracket
126	7E	7/14	~	Tilde
127	7F	7/15	DEL	Delete

There are, however, certain control codes that are significant within an SGML document, not as characters but as codes which serve particular functions. These codes are identified in the `FUNCTION` section of the syntax definition. In the case of the reference concrete syntax four functions are defined:

- Record End (`RE`);
- Record Start (`RS`);
- the space character (`SPACE`);
- the horizontal tab code (`TAB`).

The carriage return code (13) is used as the **Record End** code for the reference concrete syntax, with the line feed code (10) being used for the **Record Start**. The special rules that apply to the processing of these codes are explained in Section 11.4.

The **space** character (32) is treated as a function character because it has a special function as a **separator** within SGML markup declarations. The Tab code (9) can also be used as a separator, but, as it does not have exactly the same role as the space, it is placed into a special group of **separator characters** identified by the `SEPCHAR` control word.

Additional function codes can be specified by adding to the list a triplet consisting of:

- a **function name** of up to eight alphanumeric characters starting with a letter;
- a **function class** keyword;
- the decimal number of the code used to activate the function.

The types of function class that can be identified in SGML are:

- SEPCHAR – separator character;
- MSOCHAR – markup-scan-out character;
- MSICHAR – markup-scan-in character;
- MSSCHAR – markup-scan-suppress character;
- FUNCHAR – unspecified form of function character.

The most commonly used function classes are SEPCHAR, which is used for all codes that can separate the component parts of a markup declaration (in addition to RE, RS and SPACE), and FUNCHAR, which is used to identify system specific functions.

Note: *Markup scanning is suppressed between codes defined as markup-scan-out characters and codes defined as markup-scan-in characters, and for the code immediately following a markup-scan-suppress character.*

The NAMING section of the syntax clause identifies which characters can be used in tag or entity names and in SGML unique identifiers. By default SGML presumes that **names** can only start with alphabetic characters, in either shift (capital or lowercase), with subsequent characters being alphanumeric. The LCNMSTRT and UCNMSTRT entries in the syntax clause allow other, non-alphanumeric, characters to be defined as **name start characters**, the LCNMCHAR and UCNMCHAR entries defining which non-alphanumeric characters can be used as **name characters** after a name start character.

The reference concrete syntax only allows alphabetic characters to be used as name start characters, but within names the unaccented alphanumeric characters (a–z, A–Z and 0–9) can be supplemented by full stops and hyphens.

Note: *Digits cannot be used as the first character of an SGML name.*

Other characters that are required as parts of tag, attribute or entity names, or within unique identifiers, must be declared as valid name characters by putting the appropriate characters in the uppercase and lowercase name start or name character strings. The position of the entries in the string is important as characters in position *n* in the lowercase string may be replaced by the character in position *n* in the uppercase string during parsing. If there is no uppercase equivalent, the lowercase character must be repeated in the uppercase string (and vice versa).

The NAMECASE entries of the syntax clause show that, by default, the reference concrete syntax allows uppercase substitution of lowercase characters within an element name and related markup (GENERAL YES) but for entity names such substitution is not permitted (ENTITY NO). This allows different entity declarations to be defined for É and é, for example, while allowing <p> and <P> to be treated identically.

The GENERAL SGMLREF entry in the DELIM section of the syntax clause shows that the general default set of SGML delimiters is used in the reference

Table 4.2 Reference concrete syntax delimiter set

Character(s)	Name	Purpose
&	ERO	Entity reference open *or*
&	AND	And connector (within declaration group)
&#	CRO	Character reference open
%	PERO	Parameter entity reference open
;	REFC	Entity reference close
<	STAGO	Start-tag open
</	ETAGO	End-tag open
<!	MDO	Markup declaration open
<?	PIO	Processing instruction open
>	TAGC	Tag close *or*
>	MDC	Markup declaration close *or*
>	PIC	Processing instruction close
(	GRPO	Group open (within declaration)
)	GRPC	Group close (within declaration)
[	DSO	Declaration subset open *or*
[	DTGO	Data tag group open
]	DSC	Declaration subset close *or*
]	DTGC	Data tag group close
]]	MSC	Marked section close
"	LIT	Start or end of literal string
'	LITA	Alternative start or end of literal string
=	VI	Value indicator (within attributes)
--	COM	Start and end of comment
-	MINUS	Exclusion set identifier
+	PLUS	Inclusion set identifier *or*
+	PLUS	Required and repeatable occurrence indicator
*	REP	Optional and repeatable occurrence indicator
?	OPT	Optional occurrence indicator
|	OR	Or connector (within declaration group)
,	SEQ	Sequence connector (within declaration group)
/	NET	Null end-tag
#	RNI	Reserved name indicator

concrete syntax. Table 4.2 lists these default delimiters and shows the formal name assigned to each identifier.

Note that some codes are assigned more than one meaning. This is because the meaning of a markup delimiter is dependent on the context in which it is encountered. There are 10 different markup contexts:

(1) CON – Recognized in content, including marked section content

(2) CXT – Recognized within both CON or DSM context

(3) DS – Recognized only within a declaration subset

(4) DSM – Recognized within a declaration subset or a marked section

(5) GRP – Recognized within a group

(6) LIT – Recognized within a literal

(7) MD – Recognized within a markup declaration

(8) PI – Recognized within a processing instruction

(9) REF – Recognized within an entity or character reference

(10) TAG – Recognized within a start-tag or end-tag.

Table 4.3 shows which delimiters are recognized in which contexts.

The SHORTREF SGMLREF entry in the DELIM section of the syntax clause shows that the standard set of SGML short reference delimiters, shown in Table 4.4, can be used in conjunction with the reference concrete syntax.

In the concrete reference syntax most punctuation characters can be used as short reference delimiters, though tag delimiters (&, <, /, !, ? and >), and certain other significant symbols (for example, apostrophe, backslash, full stop and the general currency sign) are excluded. Six special code sequences are also defined, five of which allow common word-processor line ending conventions to be used as short reference strings.

The NAMES SGMLREF entry indicates that by default the standard SGML reference names for elements, entities, and so on, should be used. In the unlikely event of one of these names needing to be changed, the name to be altered should be followed by a delimited literal indicating the required replacement; for example, NAMES SGMLREF ENTITY "DING".

The QUANTITY entry at the end of the syntax clause also requires the presence of the SGMLREF keyword to indicate that, unless otherwise specified, the default **quantity set** will be used. Table 4.5 shows the default quantity limits.

The most restrictive entries in the default quantity set are:

- NAMELEN, which restricts the maximum length of entity and tag names used with the reference concrete syntax to eight characters;
- LITLEN, which restricts the maximum length of an entity replacement string to 240 characters;
- TAGLVL, which restricts the number of nested (open) tags to 24;
- GRPCNT, which restricts the number of elements within a single model group to 32.

These entries often need to be increased from their default values. When SGML is revised it is anticipated that the default values will be changed to 32, 2048, 32 and 64 respectively. Most SGML parsers already default to these, or higher, levels, though they should still warn users when the standard values have been exceeded.

Table 4.3 Contexts in which delimiters can be recognized

Context	Delimiters recognized
CON	CRO ERO STAGO ETAGO NET MDO MSC PIO and short reference delimiters
CXT	COM DSO GRPO MDC TAGC
DS	DSC
DSM	MDO MSC PERO PIO
GRP	GRPO GRPC LIT LITA PERO AND OR SEQ PLUS REP RNI DTGO DTGC
LIT	CRO ERO LIT LITA PERO
MD	COM DSO DSC GRPO LIT LITA MINUS PLUS PERO RNI
PI	PIC
REF	REFC
TAG	STAGO ETAGO TAGC VI LIT LITA

Table 4.4 Reference concrete syntax short reference delimiters

Character(s)	Number(s)	Purpose
&#TAB;	9	Horizontal tab
&#RS;	10	Record start (line feed)
&#RE;	13	Record end (carriage return)
	32	Space
"	34	Quotation mark
#	35	Number sign
%	37	Percent
'	39	Apostrophe
(	40	Left parenthesis
)	41	Right parenthesis
*	42	Asterisk
+	43	Plus sign
,	44	Comma
-	45	Hyphen
:	58	Colon
;	59	Semicolon
=	61	Equals sign
@	64	Commercial at
[	91	Left square bracket
]	93	Right square bracket
^	94	Circumflex accent
_	95	Low line
{	123	Left curly bracket
|	124	Vertical line
}	125	Right curly bracket
~	126	Tilde
--	45,45	Two hyphens
BB	66,66	Two or more blanks (spaces or tabs)
B&#RE;	66,13	Trailing blank(s) followed by record end
&#RS;B	10,66	Record start followed by leading blanks
&#RS;B&#RE;	10,66,13	Blank records (one or more blanks)
&#RS;&#RE;	10,13	Empty record

Table 4.5 Default quantities

Reserved name	Value	Purpose
ATTCNT	40	Maximum number of attribute names and name tokens in an attribute definition list
ATTSPLEN	960	Maximum length of a start-tag attribute specification
BSEQLEN	960	Maximum length of blank sequence mappable to a short reference string
DTAGLEN	16	Maximum length of data tag string
DTEMPLEN	16	Maximum length of data tag template or pattern template
ENTLVL	16	Maximum number of nesting levels for entities
GRPCNT	32	Maximum number of tokens in group (one level)
GRPGTCNT	96	Maximum number of tokens at all levels in a model group (data tag groups count as three tokens)
GRPLVL	16	Maximum number of nesting levels in a model group
LITLEN	240	Maximum length of a delimited literal (within delimiters)
NAMELEN	8	Maximum length of names, numbers, tokens, and so on
NORMSEP	2	Default separator length when calculating the normalized length of names, tokens, and so on
PILEN	240	Maximum length of processing instructions
TAGLEN	960	Maximum length of start-tags
TAGLVL	24	Maximum number of open elements

4.3 Other clauses in the SGML declaration

4.3.1 The character set description

The BASESET and DESCSET clauses in the **character set description** (CHARSET) that starts the SGML declaration are used to define the character set used within an SGML document. By default the ISO 646 character set used for markup is defined as the first component of the document's character set. This default document character set can be extended by referencing other ISO character sets. For example, the 96-character supplementary set of Latin accented characters, as defined in **ISO 8859/1**, could be added to the document's character set by placing the following entries underneath the standard DESCSET entry in the CHARSET clause at the start of the SGML declaration shown in Figure 4.1:

```
BASESET "ISO 8859-1:1987//CHARSET Right Part of
                                   Latin Alphabet No. 1//ESC 2/13 4/1"
DESCSET 128 32 UNUSED -- Control character positions --
        160 96 160 -- 96 characters in set --
```

The extra characters would be accessed by codes with values between 160 and 255, other codes greater than 128 being ignored.

Where the 16-bit **ISO 10646** code set is required, the default definitions for the base set, and its associated description, can be changed to read:

```
BASESET "ISO Registration Number 176//CHARSET ISO/IEC 10646-1:1993
       UCS-2 with implementation level 3//ESC 2/5 2/15 4/5"
DESCSET    0            9   UNUSED
           9            2   9
          11            2   UNUSED
          13            1   13
          14           18   UNUSED
          32           95   32
         127            1   UNUSED
         128           32   UNUSED
         160        65374   160
```

Note: *The first 128 codes of ISO/IEC 10646 are the 128 codes defined in ISO 646.*

To use the full 32-bit ISO 10646 UCS-4 code set this would be changed to read:

```
BASESET "ISO Registration Number 177//CHARSET ISO/IEC 10646-1:1993
       UCS-4 with implementation level 3//ESC 2/5 2/15 4/6"
DESCSET    0            9   UNUSED
           9            2   9
          11            2   UNUSED
          13            1   13
          14           18   UNUSED
          32           95   32
         127            1   UNUSED
         128           32   UNUSED
         160   2147483486   160
```

Note: *The above character set was proposed as the definition to be used for the internationalized version of the HyperText Markup Language (HTML) on the World Wide Web in August 1996.*

The described character set portion of the default document character set description shown in Figure 4.1 defines the purpose of the characters in ISO 646 more clearly than the matching entry in the syntax clause. It can be interpreted as:

- The nine control codes starting from 0 (0–8), the two control codes starting from position 11 (11 and 12), the 18 control codes starting from position 14 (14–31) and the control code in position 127 are not used within the document (they are, therefore, considered to be non-SGML characters).
- The two control codes starting at position 9 (Tab and Record Start) and the one in position 13 (Record End) have special significance within the document (they are SGML function codes).
- There are 95 data characters, starting from position 32 (the position of the space, which is also one of the special function characters).

4.3.2 The capacity set

The capacity set used with the reference concrete syntax is shown in Table 4.6. This **reference capacity set** restricts the total number of stored markup characters within an SGML document to 35 000 characters, but places no restrictions on the capacity of any one of the component parts of the markup, which can take up all 35 000 bytes of strorage if required. In some large documents it is possible for this default total capacity to be exceeded.

Note: *Most current SGML systems will ignore the default capacity set restrictions, perhaps providing a warning message to users if the default limits are exceeded. Modern large-memory systems do not have the memory restrictions that were typically found in desktop systems of the 1980s, where it was important to warn users of large documents that could exceed the program's memory allocation. Many of the existing restrictions defined in the capacity set clause will be removed when ISO 8879 is next updated.*

4.3.3 The scope clause

By default the `SCOPE` clause of an SGML declaration is the whole document – the syntax is used in both the document prolog and the document instance. If, however, the character set defined in the syntax section is only used to mark up the text (that is, all declarations have been coded using the reference concrete syntax) the default `SCOPE DOCUMENT` entry can be changed to read `SCOPE INSTANCE`.

4.3.4 The features clause

The `FEATURES` clause of the SGML declaration shows which of SGML's optional features are required to process the document. The optional features are:

- using data to identify the position of end-tags (`DATATAG`);
- omitting tags (`OMITTAG`);
- shortening tags (`SHORTTAG`);
- using a numeric suffix to the tag name to define the level of an element (`RANK`);
- linking document structures (`SIMPLE`, `IMPLICIT` or `EXPLICIT` links);
- defining more than one structure within a document (`CONCUR`);
- embedding subdocuments with different element structures within a document (`SUBDOC`);
- checking public identifiers assigned to external entities to ensure that they have the form required for formal public identifiers (`FORMAL`).

By default only the `OMITTAG` and `SHORTTAG` options are available, all other options being set to `NO`.

Table 4.6 Reference capacity set

Name	Default value	Points per unit	Purpose
TOTALCAP	35 000	All	Grand total of capacity points
ENTCAP	35 000	NAMELEN	Entity name capacity
ENTCHCAP	35 000	1	Number of entity replacement characters
ELEMCAP	35 000	NAMELEN	Element name capacity
GRPCAP	35 000	NAMELEN	Tokens within model groups (data tag groups count as three tokens)
EXGRPCAP	35 000	NAMELEN	Number of exception groups
EXNMCAP	35 000	NAMELEN	Tokens within exception groups
ATTCAP	35 000	NAMELEN	Attribute name capacity
ATTCHCAP	35 000	1	Attribute default values capacity
AVGRPCAP	35 000	NAMELEN	Attribute value token capacity
NOTCAP	35 000	NAMELEN	Data content notation name capacity
NOTCHCAP	35 000	1	Number of characters in notation identifiers
IDCAP	35 000	NAMELEN	Explicit or default ID value capacity
IDREFCAP	35 000	NAMELEN	Explicit or default IDREF value capacity
MAPCAP	35 000	NAMELEN	Short reference map declaration capacity
LKSETCAP	35 000	NAMELEN	Link set/type declaration capacity
LKNMCAP	35 000	NAMELEN	Link/document type name storage capacity

4.3.5 Application-specific information

The last clause in the SGML declaration can be used to transmit any **application-specific information** (APPINFO) needed to process the document. For example, a document that uses the ISO/IEC 10744 Hypermedia/Time-based Structuring Language (HyTime) application of SGML would have an entry reading APPINFO "HyTime". When no application-specific information needs to be exchanged, the default entry of APPINFO NONE applies.

4.4 Alternative concrete syntaxes

ISO 8879 also identifies some special sets of alternative concrete syntaxes. The most important of these are:

- the core concrete syntax;
- basic and core multicode concrete syntaxes;
- public concrete syntaxes.

The **core concrete syntax** is exactly the same as the reference concrete syntax, except that the SHORTREF entry in the DELIM section is followed by NONE rather than SGMLREF. A document prepared using the core concrete syntax is referred to as a **minimal SGML document**.

Where the code extension techniques defined in ISO 2022 are being used to extend the character set beyond the 95 characters available in the reference concrete syntax, the **multicode basic concrete syntax** defined in Annex D of ISO 8879 can be used. If the short reference facility is not required the equivalent **multicode core concrete syntax** can be used.

Where characters outside the standard ISO 646 unaccented Latin alphabet are required in markup, variants of the reference concrete syntax will be needed. Each such **variant concrete syntax** can be publicly declared as a **public concrete syntax** and given a **public identifier** that can be used to call it from within the SGML declaration. For example, a German variant concrete syntax might be identified as:

```
SYNTAX PUBLIC "ISO 8879:1986//SYNTAX Deutscher Hinweis//DE"
```

4.4.1 The HTML SGML declaration

The most famous variant concrete syntax is that used for the HyperText Markup Language (HTML). In the definition of Version 2.0 of this language, in Internet RFC 1866, the following SGML declaration was specified:

```
<!SGML "ISO 8879:1986"
-- SGML Declaration for HyperText Markup Language (HTML). --

 CHARSET BASESET  "ISO 646:1983//CHARSET
                  International Reference Version
                  (IRV)//ESC 2/5 4/0"
         DESCSET    0  9   UNUSED
                    9  2   9
                   11  2   UNUSED
                   13  1   13
                   14  18  UNUSED
                   32  95  32
                  127  1   UNUSED
         BASESET  "ISO Registration Number 100//CHARSET
                  ECMA-94 Right Part of
                  Latin Alphabet Nr. 1//ESC 2/13 4/1"
         DESCSET  128  32  UNUSED
                  160  96  32

 CAPACITY SGMLREF
          TOTALCAP 150000
          GRPCAP 150000
          ENTCAP 150000

 SCOPE DOCUMENT
```

```
SYNTAX SHUNCHAR CONTROLS 0 1 2 3 4 5 6 7 8 9 10 11 12 13 14 15 16 17 18
                         19 20 21 22 23 24 25 26 27 28 29 30 31 127
       BASESET  "ISO 646:1983//CHARSET
                International Reference Version
                (IRV)//ESC 2/5 4/0"
       DESCSET  0 128 0
       FUNCTION RE 13
                RS 10
                SPACE 32
                TAB SEPCHAR 9
       NAMING   LCNMSTRT ""
                UCNMSTRT ""
                LCNMCHAR ".-"
                UCNMCHAR ".-"
       NAMECASE GENERAL YES
                ENTITY NO
       DELIM    GENERAL SGMLREF
                SHORTREF SGMLREF
       NAMES    SGMLREF
       QUANTITY SGMLREF
                ATTSPLEN 2100
                LITLEN 1024
                NAMELEN 72 -- somewhat arbitrary; taken from
                              Internet line length conventions --
                PILEN 1024
                TAGLVL 100
                TAGLEN 2100
                GRPGTCNT 150
                GRPCNT 64

FEATURES MINIMIZE DATATAG NO
                  OMITTAG YES
                  RANK NO
                  SHORTTAG YES
         LINK     SIMPLE NO
                  IMPLICIT NO
                  EXPLICIT NO
         OTHER    CONCUR NO
                  SUBDOC NO
                  FORMAL YES
APPINFO "SDA" -- conforming SGML Document Access application -- >
```

This SGML declaration specifies the following changes to the default SGML declaration:

- The document character set is extended to include the 96 accented and special characters forming up the ECMA-94 Latin Alphabet Nr. 1 character set.

  Note: *As these characters have not also been specified as part of the SYNTAX clause they cannot be used within markup, only within the text of the document instance.*

- The total capacity to be reserved for SGML token storage has been increased to 150 000 octets, with the capacity for group and entity storage within this total capacity also extended to the same limit.
- The maximum length for an attribute specification has been extended from 960 to 2100 characters (to allow for long URLs within attribute specifications, for example); the maximum length of a markup tag, including its attribute specification, has also been increased to 2100 characters.
- The maximum length of literal strings has been increased to 1024 characters (again to allow for long URLs and other program parameters).
- The maximum length of names has been extended to 72 characters, the limit being determined by the preferred maximum line length for HTTP transmission, which requires that a space occurs at least every 72 characters).
- The maximum length of processing instructions has been increased to 1024 characters.
- The maximum number of nested tags has been increased to 100.
- The maximum number of tokens in a model group has been extended to 150, which must be split into no more than 64 groups.
- Formal public identifiers must conform to the formal rules for their definition.
- A special application for the use of SGML document access (SDA) attributes to identify types of HTML elements is associated with the document type definition via the `APPINFO` clause.

For the latest version of the HTML DTD, which supports multiple languages and the use of bidirectional texts, the following SGML declaration should be used to invoke the extended ISO/IEC 10646 character set:

```
<!SGML   "ISO 8879:1986"
--
         SGML Declaration for HyperText Markup Language version 2.x
         (HTML 2.x=HTML 2.0 + i18n).
--

CHARSET
         BASESET "ISO Registration Number 176//CHARSET
                 ISO/IEC 10646-1:1993 UCS-2 with
                 implementation level 3//ESC 2/5 2/15 4/5"
         DESCSET 0    9       UNUSED
                 9    2       9
                 11   2       UNUSED
                 13   1       13
                 14   18      UNUSED
                 32   95      32
                 127  1       UNUSED
                 128  32      UNUSED
                 160  65376   160
```

```
CAPACITY          SGMLREF
                  TOTALCAP   150000
                  GRPCAP     150000
                  ENTCAP     150000

SCOPE   DOCUMENT
SYNTAX
        SHUNCHAR CONTROLS 0 1 2 3 4 5 6 7 8 9 10 11 12 13 14 15
                 16 17 18 19 20 21 22 23 24 25 26 27 28 29 30 31 127
        BASESET "ISO 646:1983//CHARSET
                 International Reference Version
                 (IRV)//ESC 2/5 4/0"
        DESCSET 0 128 0

        FUNCTION
                 RE         13
                 RS         10
                 SPACE      32
                 TAB SEPCHAR 9

        NAMING   LCNMSTRT ""
                 UCNMSTRT ""
                 LCNMCHAR ".-"
                 UCNMCHAR ".-"
                 NAMECASE GENERAL YES
                          ENTITY NO
        DELIM    GENERAL  SGMLREF
                 SHORTREF SGMLREF
        NAMES    SGMLREF
        QUANTITY SGMLREF
                 ATTSPLEN 2100
                 LITLEN   1024
                 NAMELEN  72    -- somewhat arbitrary; taken from
                                   Internet line length conventions --
                 PILEN    1024
                 TAGLVL   100
                 TAGLEN   2100
                 GRPGTCNT 150
                 GRPCNT   64
        FEATURES
          MINIMIZE
                 DATATAG  NO
                 OMITTAG  YES
                 RANK     NO
                 SHORTTAG YES
          LINK
                 SIMPLE   NO
                 IMPLICIT NO
                 EXPLICIT NO
          OTHER
                 CONCUR   NO
                 SUBDOC   NO
                 FORMAL   YES
          APPINFO "SDA" -- conforming SGML Document Access application --
>
```

This chapter has only been able to give a brief overview of the key features of an SGML declaration. For a more in-depth description of the SGML declaration refer to Chapters 10 and 11 of *SGML: An Author's Guide* or to the annotated description of Clause 13 of the ISO 8879 provided in Part 3 of *The SGML Handbook* (Goldfarb, 1990).

Elements and attributes

Element roles • Element declarations • Using elements • Attributes • Declaring attributes • Using attributes • Specialized attributes • Controlling attribute values

This chapter explains how SGML document type declarations can be used to define which elements can occur in an SGML document instance, and the attributes that can be used to control the processing of each type of element.

5.1 Element roles

The role of an SGML element depends on the context in which it is found and on the form of markup used to enter it. The following roles can be identified:

- the base document element
- embedded elements
- qualified elements
- ranked elements
- minimized elements.

The first element specified in any SGML document is the **base document element**. This element must be formally *declared*, within the document type declaration, by entry of an element declaration whose name is the same as that of the document type declaration. The name of the base document element identifies the class of document to be created (for example, `<ACT>`).

Normally the last tag entered within an SGML document will be an end-tag, the name of which matches that used for the first tag (for example, `</ACT>`). This tag ensures that the end of the document is correctly identified by the SGML document parser.

Further elements can be *embedded* between the two tags identifying the limits of the base document element, up to the level specified by the current tag level quantity (TAGLVL). (In the reference concrete syntax this value is 24, so that up to 24 levels of embedded elements can be used within each base document element.)

Where necessary, elements can be *qualified* by attributes. An attribute is a named value that can be used during processing to control such things as the presentation or content type of the element with which it is associated. In the reference concrete syntax up to 40 different attributes can be associated with any element, provided that the total length of the attribute names and values does not exceed 960 characters.

Elements can optionally be *ranked* so that specific groups of elements are used at the same ranked element level. Ranked element level is specified by adding a number to the end of the element's generic identifier. When the RANK tag minimization option is being used, the current rank level can be implied from that of preceding elements.

Minimized elements are elements, the presence, name or attributes names of which can be implied by an SGML parser when the appropriate minimization options have been enabled in the FEATURES clause of the SGML declaration. Minimization techniques provided within SGML include:

- omitted tags
- empty tags
- unclosed tags
- NET-enabling start-tags and null end-tags (NET).

In addition, data tags can be used to identify references to end-tags that have been entered using pre-defined character strings.

5.2 Element declarations

Element declarations must be entered as part of a document type declaration subset. The reserved name ELEMENT (or its previously declared replacement) appears immediately after the **markup declaration open** (MDO) code that identifies the start of the markup declaration.

In its shortest form an element declaration takes the form:

```
<!ELEMENT name model>
```

where name is the **element name (generic identifier)** that uniquely identifies the element and model is either a formal declaration of the type of data that may be entered within the element or a **content model** showing which subelements can be embedded within the element. Each element declaration ends with a **markup declaration close** (MDC) code.

Where elements share a content model a bracketed **name group** can replace the element name. A name group consists of a set of connected element names bracketed by **group open** (GRPO) and **group close** (GRPC) delimiters. The element names are normally connected by an OR connector (| in the reference concrete syntax) to give an entry of the form:

```
<!ELEMENT (name-1|name-2|...|name-n) model>
```

The maximum length of an element name must not exceed the current value of the NAMELEN quantity. The first character of each element name must be alphabetic, or one of the additional name start characters defined in the syntax clause. Subsequent characters may be alphanumeric characters or one of the name characters declared in the syntax clause.

When the OMITTAG entry in the FEATURES clause of the current SGML declaration reads OMITTAG YES, two extra characters *must* be entered between the name and content of the element declaration to define the type of **omitted tag minimization** to be applied to the element. These extra characters define whether or not the start-tag and/or end-tag can be omitted if its presence can be unambiguously implied from the model of the element within which it is embedded. If the first character is O (the letter O, not the number zero) the start-tag for the element can be omitted at appropriate points. If it is - (hyphen) it can never be omitted. If the second character is O the end-tag can be omitted; otherwise it is - to show that the end-tag must never be omitted. The two characters must be separated from each other, and from the adjacent element name and content model, by at least one space. For example, an element whose end-tag may be omitted might be declared as:

```
<!ELEMENT artwork - O EMPTY >
```

This element declaration defines an **empty element**, <ARTWORK>, which has no embedded content. The element is simply a tag that marks the point at which an illustration is to be added to the document. The <ARTWORK> start-tag cannot be omitted but, as the element contains no text, the end-tag must be omitted for EMPTY elements, for which it would serve no purpose.

5.2.1 Model groups

When an element can contain embedded subelements the declaration's content model *must* be defined as a **model group**. Like name groups, model groups consist of one or more connected element names (called **element tokens** in this context) bracketed by group open (GRPO) and group close (GRPC) delimiter sequences, for example:

```
<!ELEMENT book - O (prelims, body, annexes) >
```

In this case a book is said to be made up of three nested subelements, <PRELIMS>, <BODY> and <ANNEXES>.

For model groups, unlike other name groups, the type of **connector** used is significant. Three types of connector are used in model groups to define the logical sequence in which elements are to appear are shown in Table 5.1.

Table 5.1 SGML connectors

<table>
<tr><th>Default character</th><th>Delimiter name</th><th>Meaning</th></tr>
<tr><td>,</td><td>SEQ</td><td>All must occur, in the order specified</td></tr>
<tr><td>&</td><td>AND</td><td>All must occur, in any order</td></tr>
<tr><td>|</td><td>OR</td><td>One (and only one) must occur</td></tr>
</table>

The **sequence connector** (a comma in the reference concrete syntax) connects elements that must occur in a predefined sequence. In the above example, therefore, the prelims must precede the body of the text, which must precede any annexes.

Where the sequence in which the elements are used is not fixed, subelement names should be connected with an **AND connector** (&). For example, the fields at the head of a memo could be defined using a model of the form:

```
<!ELEMENT heading O O (from & to & date) >
```

If only one element could be applicable *at a given point*, the relevant element names can be connected by an **OR connector** (|). For example, the following element could occur in the prelims of a book:

```
<!ELEMENT by O O (author|editor) >
```

Note: *The OR connector used in SGML is an exclusive OR rather than an inclusive OR.*

The use of each embedded subelement can be further qualified by the addition of an **occurrence indicator** immediately after the element name, or immediately after a group close delimiter linking a number of element names. The three types of occurrence indicator defined in SGML are shown in Table 5.2.

For example, to make optional the use of annexes in a book, you would extend the definition given above to read:

```
<!ELEMENT book - O (prelims, body, annexes?) >
```

An alternative, and somewhat better approach, would be to use an optional and repeatable <ANNEX> element:

```
<!ELEMENT book - O (prelims, body, annex*, index?) >
```

Table 5.2 SGML occurrence indicators

Default character	Delimiter name	Meaning
+	PLUS	Repeatable element(s) that must occur at least once
*	REP	Optional element(s) that may be repeated
?	OPT	Optional element(s) that can occur at most once

To allow more than one author or editor to be defined in the prelims you could extend the definition of the <BY> element shown above to read:

```
<!ELEMENT by O O (author+|editor+) >
```

Occurrence indicators have a higher precedence than connectors. For example, a model group such as `(author|editor)+` differs from one defined as `(author+|editor+)` because the first model permits any sequence of author and editor details to be entered, whereas the second model only permits a set of author details *or* a set of editor details to be entered within a <BY> element.

Model groups can be nested within each other up to the level indicated by SGML's GRPLVL quantity value. (The reference concrete syntax allows up to 16 levels of nested model groups.) Each nested model group can, if necessary, have its elements linked by a different connector. Each name in the group, each nested group and the whole content model can be qualified by an occurrence indicator. An example of a nested set of model groups is the element used for a Text Encoding Initiative (TEI) title statement, which is defined as:

```
<!ELEMENT titleStmt - O (title+, (author|editor|sponsor|funder|
principal|respStmt)*)
```

When parameter entities (see Chapter 6) are used to define the contents of model groups, a word of warning is required: *you cannot associate an occurrence indicator with a parameter entity*. If the elements, the names of which are listed in the replacement string of the parameter entity, are to be qualified by an occurrence indicator, then either:

- the occurrence indicator *and* its associated brackets must be included in the replacement string when the parameter entity is declared,

or:

- the name of the parameter entity must be enclosed in parentheses and the relevant occurrence indicator must be entered immediately after the closing parenthesis.

Note: *When using parameter entities to define part, or all, of a model group it is important to remember that the associated entity declaration must precede the entity reference. The safest way to ensure this is to place all parameter entity declarations at the start of the document type definition.*

5.2.2 Text elements

A special form of **primitive content token** is used in model groups to indicate points at which the element can contain text. This token consists of a **reserved name indicator** (RNI, # in the reference concrete syntax) followed by the reserved name PCDATA, which stands for **parsed character data**. #PCDATA indicates that, at that point in the model, the element can contain text which has been checked by the SGML parser to ensure that any embedded tags or entity references have been identified.

When the #PCDATA tag is present in a model group, the element's content is referred to as **mixed content**. If text is not permitted the model group is defined as having only **element content**. Different rules for processing record boundaries apply to mixed content. A typical example of an element defined using mixed content is:

```
<!ELEMENT para - O (#PCDATA|emphasis)+ >
```

A special feature of the #PCDATA keyword is that it is automatically assumed to have a repeatable (REP) occurrence indicator. All characters occurring between successive markup tags are considered to satisfy a single #PCDATA token (including any entered as character data in a marked section).

It is recommended that #PCDATA is only used when data characters are permitted anywhere in the content of an element, that is where #PCDATA is the only token in the model group or where it is a member of a repeatable model group whose members are connected using an OR connector.

Note: *This recommendation is made to avoid potential problems relating to the processing of record boundaries within mixed content.*

Where nested subelements cannot occur within an element, the element's contents can be declared to consist of one of the following types of **declared content**:

- **replaceable character data** (RCDATA), which can contain text, character references and/or general entity references that resolve to character data;
- **character data** (CDATA), which contains only valid SGML characters;
- **empty element** (EMPTY), having no contents or contents that can be generated by a presentation program.

A variant of the basic content model allows the reserved name ANY to replace an element declaration's model group. This tells the program that text or any element defined within the same document type declaration can be used as an embedded element.

For elements with declared content, or using the ANY reserved name, the keyword *replaces* the model group, including its brackets. Because, unlike #PCDATA, these reserved names cannot occur within a model group, they do not need to be preceded by the reserved name indicator.

A typical example of the use of declared content is shown in the following element declaration:

```
<!ELEMENT ISBN - - CDATA >
```

It should be noted that, in the case of elements defined using the replaceable character data and character data options, the program will ignore any requests to start a new element until such time as it encounters a valid end-tag open (ETAGO) delimiter, that is </ followed by any valid name start character. For this reason all elements declared using the CDATA or RCDATA declared content keywords should have compulsory end-tags and should not contain the ETAGO character sequence within their content.

5.2.3 Exceptions

Model groups can be qualified by the addition of lists of **exceptions**. There are two types of exceptions:

- **inclusions** defining elements that can be included at any point in the model group (that is, within the current element or within any element embedded in it);
- **exclusions** identifying embedded elements that cannot be used while the current element remains unclosed.

Exceptions are specified by entry of name groups immediately after the model group defining the permitted contents of the element. The group open (GRPO) delimiter at the start of each such name group must be preceded by a plus sign if the names identify inclusions, or a hyphen (minus sign) if they represent exclusions. Both sets may be present at the same time, provided that:

- they are separated from each other, and the preceding model group, by one or more spaces (or other valid SGML separators); and
- exclusions are specified before any inclusions.

Exclusions are not permitted that prohibit the use of embedded elements that are required as part of a model group.

Inclusions are typically associated with elements whose content model is #PCDATA, or are used at the start of a document to allow commonly occurring floating elements, such as footnotes, figures and tables, to occur anywhere in the text. For example, the definition given for a book above could be extended to read:

```
<!ELEMENT book - O (prelims, body, annexes?) +(footnote|figure|table)>
```

This model would allow footnotes, figures and tables to occur anywhere within a book.

It should be noted that inclusions are inherited by all the elements declared in the model, and any of their children. Where inclusions have been declared at a high level in the data structure, it will often become necessary to define exclusions at lower levels in the data model. For example, to prevent footnotes from containing embedded footnotes, or figures, the following declaration could be used for footnotes:

```
<!ELEMENT footnote - O (#PCDATA) -(footnote|figure) >
```

Note that this model would not prevent tables, or any other element that had been declared as an inclusion in a parent element of the footnote, from being entered within footnotes.

5.2.4 Comments within element declarations

Comments may be entered at most points where spaces are permitted within an element declaration, except within bracketed name or model groups. They must be preceded and followed by **comment delimiters** (a pair of hyphens in the reference concrete syntax). Comments can run over more than one line if necessary, for example:

```
<!ELEMENT position - O (#PCDATA|line+) -- one or more lines of text
describing position held -- >
```

It is recommended that comments within element declarations are placed after the model group.

5.2.5 Ambiguous content models

A content model cannot be ambiguous. Every element or character found in the document instance must be able to satisfy only one content token without looking ahead in the document instance. For example, an element whose content model is:

```
<!ELEMENT contact - O ((name, address?), company?, address)>
```

is ambiguous because it cannot be determined whether an <ADDRESS> element entered after a name satisifies the optional `address` in the nested subset or the compulsory one in the outermost group until it is known what markup tag follows the address. In most cases such content models can be easily avoided by introducing another level of container, for example:

```
<!ELEMENT contact - O (person, company?, address)>
<!ELEMENT person O - (name, address?) >
```

By making the end-tag of the container element (</PERSON>) compulsory you can ensure that the positions of the two <ADDRESS> elements can always be distinguished.

5.2.6 Analysing content models

The base document element, the name of which matches that of the document type declaration, provides the starting point for the analysis of any set of element declarations. The rules that should be applied when analysing a DTD are:

(1) Identify the element declaration that has the relevant document type name (which may be part of a name group or the replacement text of a parameter entity).

(2) Study the element's tag omission rules and its model group, including any exceptions.
(3) Find the element declaration for the first element listed in the model group.
(4) Repeat stages (2) and (3) until you come to one of the terminal keywords (#PCDATA, CDATA, RCDATA, EMPTY or ANY).
(5) Go back to the previous declaration and look for the declaration for the next element listed in its model group (or that of one of its parents).

To see the effect of these rules, we will use them to create a tree diagram for the following simplified DTD for a memorandum:

```
<!DOCTYPE memo [
<!ELEMENT memo                  O O (heading, body, signature?) >
<!ELEMENT heading               O O (from & to & copied-to? & date) >
<!ELEMENT (from|to|copied-to) - O (name, position?)+ >
<!ELEMENT name                  O O (#PCDATA) >
<!ELEMENT (position|date)       - O (#PCDATA) >
<!ELEMENT body                  O O (para+) +(artwork) >
<!ELEMENT para                  - O (#PCDATA|emphasis)+ >
<!ELEMENT emphasis              - - (#PCDATA) -(artwork) >
<!ELEMENT artwork               - O EMPTY >
<!ELEMENT signature             O O (salutation?, (name, position?)+)>
<!ELEMENT salutation            - O (#PCDATA) >
]>
```

The first thing that needs to be done is to identify the element declaration for the element, the name of which matches that of the document type declaration, memo in this case. The tag omission rules associated with this, the first, element declaration, tell us that both the start-tag and the end-tag can be omitted as their presence can be determined by the SGML parser from the presence of embedded elements. The model group for the memo element shows us that it contains only element content, and that three elements, heading, body and, optionally, signature must occur in a fixed sequence.

Following the third of the rules listed above, we find that the model for the first element in the initial model group, heading, shows that the start-tag and end-tag for this element can also be omitted. Again the model group consists solely of element content, but this time the four elements are connected by an AND connector to indicate that the order in which the elements are entered is not important (they have a fixed position on preprinted paper). Also one of the elements, the copied-to element, is optional.

When we look for the model for the first of these elements we find that it shares a declaration with two of the other components of the heading. The tag omission rules for this declaration tell us that the start-tag for these elements must be present, but that the end-tag is omissible. Each of these elements must contain an embedded name element, optionally followed by details of the position held by the named person. The PLUS occurrence indicator associated with the whole model group shows that multiple names, with or without positions, may be entered for each component of the heading if required.

The model for the name element shows that the both the start-tag and the end-tag can be omitted where their presence can be determined from the preceding and following elements. The content model consists of the special #PCDATA keyword showing that this is a terminal node that may contain parsed character data. At this point the fifth of our rules is invoked, so we need to return to the model group for the parent element, in this case the model shared by from, to and copied-to. The second element in the model group shared by this set of elements is the optional position element.

The only difference between the declaration for the position element, which is shared with the date element, and that for the name element is that the start-tag is not omissible. This is because the position element is always optional, while the position of the date element cannot be determined by the parser as it is part of an AND group. The presence of an optional component of a model, or an element within an AND group, must always be indicated by a start-tag.

As the model group for the position and date elements consists solely of the #PCDATA content token, we must return to the model of position's parent element(s), from, to and copied-to. As we have already seen the model for all the elements listed in this model group, we must immediately return to their parent element, heading. As all the elements in the model group for a heading share the same element declarations, the fifth rule requires us to return to its parent element, memo, and look at the second element listed in its model group, body.

The start-tag and end-tag for the body container can be omitted as the first paragraph in the memo will indicate the start of the body, and the presence of a signature will indicate the end of the body. The model group for the element shows that the body must contain one or more paragraphs (para). In this case the occurrence indicator has been placed adjacent to the element name, rather than being applied to the whole of the model group. In addition the inclusion added after the model group shows that artwork can be interspersed between paragraphs, or placed within any embedded text or subelements.

The model for the para element is an example of the use of mixed content. In this case the parsed character data (#PCDATA) can be repeatedly mixed with emphasis elements. It must be remembered, however, that this element inherits the inclusion specified for its parent element, para, so artwork can also be embedded within paragraphs. The tag omission rules show that start-tag of each paragraph must be present in the document instance.

The model for the emphasis element also indicates that it should contain parsed character data (#PCDATA), but in this case the model is qualified by the presence of an exclusion that prohibits the inheritance of the artwork inclusion from the model of the body element. Both the start-tag and the end-tag must be present to indicate the full scope of the emphasized text.

The model for the artwork element shows that this is an empty element that consists simply of a start-tag, with no end-tag. (The role of this element will be examined further shortly.)

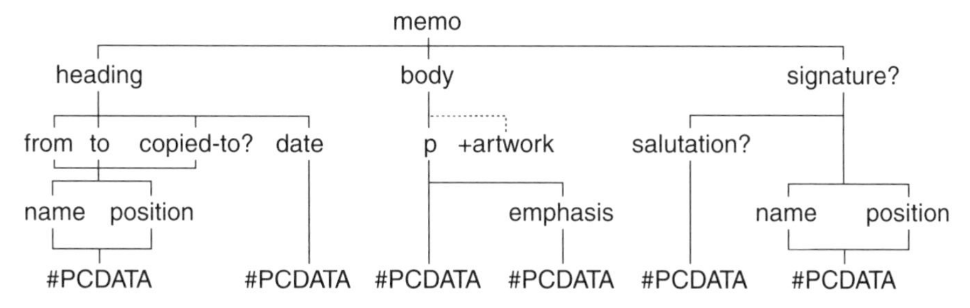

Figure 5.1 Graph showing the structure of the memo DTD

Now that all the elements in the model group for `body` have been identified, we must return to the model group of its parent, `memo`, and look at the next component of its model group, `signature`. Again both the start-tag and end-tag can be omitted from this element as their presence can be determined from the presence of its subelements or its parent's end-tags. The model group here is slightly more complex, consisting of the name of an optional element, `salutation`, followed by a repeatable model group that uses the same subelements as the header elements. There must be at least one `name` element within each `signature`.

The model for the `salutation` element shows that this consists simply of parsed character data. As this element is optional, its start-tag is always required, though its end-tag could be omitted. Figure 5.1 shows how a graph could be drawn to represent the model of a memo.

5.3 Using elements

Within a document instance the contents of elements are indicated by the use of **start-tags** and **end-tags**. A start-tag consists of the element's name between the currently declared **start-tag open** (`STAGO`) and **tag close** (`TAGC`) delimiters (< and > respectively in the reference concrete syntax). Optionally the tag close code can be replaced by a null end-tag (`NET`) delimiter (/ in the reference concrete syntax) so that a matching null end-tag can be used in place of the normal end-tag. Where appropriate, the element name can be qualified by the entry of one or more of the attributes declared for the element.

An end-tag consists of the element's name between the currently declared **end-tag open** (`ETAGO`) and **tag close** (`TAGC`) delimiters (</ and > in the reference concrete syntax). Where a null end-tag has been used to close the element's start-tag, the whole of the end-tag *must* be replaced by a single null end-tag code (/).

Not all tags need to be present in a document. If the `OMITTAG` feature has been enabled in the SGML declaration, tags can be omitted when their presence can be implied without ambiguity, provided they have been declared as omissible.

Element names can normally be entered in either uppercase or lowercase. (The NAMECASE section of the SGML declaration defaults to GENERAL YES. Where this entry is altered, DTD developers should take special care to warn users of the need to enter tags in the appropriate case.)

The main problem that can occur when using elements is that, unlike the style sheets used in uncontrolled word processors, SGML markup tags cannot be entered at a level for which they have not been declared. SGML-based text editors will be able to prevent users from entering invalid tags, but, if documents are prepared without the guidance of an SGML parser, errors can occur.

A more detailed example of the use of SGML elements can be found in the description of the HTML DTD in Chapter 13.

5.4 Attributes

An attribute is a named parameter value used to qualify an element's start-tag. Attributes are typically used to:

- identify the status of an element, for example `<BOOK status=draft>`;
- identify uniquely a particular occurrence of an element, for example `<FIGURE id="piechart1">`;
- cross-refer to a previously identified element, for example `<REFER to="piechart1">`;
- identify text to be generated by the application, for example `<INPUT value="100">`;
- define the size or source of data imported into the document, for example `<TEXTAREA rows=6 cols=70>` and `<FIGURE source="Reuters">`;
- control how text is to be presented, for example `<IMG src="new.gif" align=bottom>`.

There are two parts to an **attribute specification**: an **attribute name** and an **attribute value**. These two parts are joined by a **value indicator** (VI, = in the reference concrete syntax) to give an attribute specification of the form:

```
<element-name attribute-name=attribute-value ... >
```

Attribute values can be entered as **attribute value literals**. A literal is a string of characters recognized as a single unit by the system because the characters have been entered between a matched pair of **literal delimiters**. Two alternative sets of literal delimiters are provided in SGML. They are referred to within the standard as LIT (literal) and LITA (alternative form of literal). In the reference concrete syntax these are represented by the quotation mark (") and apostrophe (') respectively.

Note: *The choice of which set of literal delimiters should be used is a matter of user convenience. The only restriction is that the character chosen cannot appear in the entered attribute value.*

Only one type of literal delimiter can be used to delimit a particular attribute value, but the two types can be used interchangeably within the same tag, for example:

```
<A href='http://www.u-net.com/~sgml/piechart1.gif'
title="Martin's Work Breakdown">
```

As well as showing how changing the type of literal delimiter can allow you to use a literal delimiter within a string, the above example also exhibits the fact that line breaks can occur between attribute specifications in place of the normal space. This is particularly useful when the start-tag would otherwise be too long to fit on a line, as is the case in the example.

Where the FEATURE clause of the SGML declaration contains the statement SHORTTAG YES (as it does by default), the literal delimiters can be omitted if the only characters used in the value are ones currently declared as name characters. For example, a declaration of the form <INPUT name="field1" size="60"> could also be entered as <INPUT name=field1 size=60>.

When the entered attribute value has been declared as a member of a set of valid attribute values for the element, the attribute name, with the associated value indicator, can also be omitted when SHORTTAG YES has been specified. For example, an entry such as <H1 align="center"> can be shortened to give an attribute specification of the form <H1 center>. In this case the attribute value must *not* be entered within literal delimiters because, if it is, the program will be unable to identify the attribute referred to.

Attribute values can also consist of *delimited* lists of values, each part of which is separated from the others by a space, or another valid separator character (RE, RS or TAB).

Each attribute can be given a default value when it is declared. If either OMITTAG YES or SHORTTAG YES has been specified in the FEATURES clause, this default value will be used if a specific attribute value is not entered in the start-tag.

Where a default value cannot be specified, a special reserved name must be entered. For example, to tell the program that it should use internal rules for determining what value to assign to the attribute value the reserved name #IMPLIED is used. The reserved name #CURRENT can be used to tell the program to repeat the last value entered for that attribute of any element that shares the attribute list declaration in which it was declared.

Where an attribute value must be entered whenever the element is requested, the reserved name #REQUIRED can be used as the default value.

5.5 Declaring attributes

Attributes are declared in **attribute definition list declarations**. Each attribute definition list is a separate markup declaration, delimited by the currently defined markup declaration delimiters (<! and > in the reference concrete syntax). Declarations in the attribute definition list start with the reserved name ATTLIST (or its previously declared replacement), which is followed, after one or more separators (for example, space), by details of the element(s) the list is to be associated with. Once this **associated element type** specification has been entered, one or more **attribute definitions** can be entered before the closing delimiter, to give the attribute definition list the general form:

```
<!ATTLIST elements attribute-definition-1
                   ...
                   attribute-definition-n >
```

Where more than one element needs to be associated with a given list of attributes, the names of the associated element types are entered as a bracketed name group, individual names being separated by one of the SGML connectors to give an entry of the form:

```
<!ATTLIST (element1|...|elementn) attribute-definition-1
                                  ...
                                  attribute-definition-n >
```

Each attribute definition consists of an **attribute name**, a **declared value** and a **default value**. They are separated from each other by a **parameter separator** which is a separator character (for example, space, RE, RS or TAB), a system specific **entity end** code, a comment delimited by pairs of hyphens, or a parameter entity reference for an entity, the replacement text of which starts with a parameter separator.

Attribute names must start with a valid name start character and must contain only valid name characters. Their length must not exceed the current value of the NAMELEN quantity. This means that, when the default reference concrete syntax is being used because no SGML declaration has been transmitted for use with the document, attribute names must consist of not more than eight alphanumeric characters, full stops or hyphens, starting with a letter. (This is why many DTDs, unnecessarily, use cryptic short forms of attribute names: such short forms of names will be recognizable by any SGML parser.) An attribute name can only be used once in any declaration in an attribute definition list, but the same attribute name can be used in other declarations.

The declared value of an attribute is either a bracketed list of valid **attribute values** or a **reserved name** identifying the type of value(s) that can be entered. Where specific attribute values are defined, each listed attribute value must be unique to the attribute definition list, but, where reserved names are used, the same attribute value can be used for a number of different attributes.

Note: *This last rule can lead to problems where users need to assign Y/N values to more than one attribute in a list. Typically this is overcome by using a %boolean parameter entity whose replacement text is NUMBER in place of the token list, and then defining booleans in such a way that any number other than 0 is considered to be true (yes).*

Table 5.3 Reserved names for attribute declared values

Reserved name	Purpose
CDATA	Attribute value consists of character data (valid SGML characters, including markup delimiters)
ENTITY	Attribute value can be any currently declared subdocument or data entity name
ENTITIES	Attribute value is a list of subdocument or data entity names
ID	Attribute value is a unique identifier (ID) for the element
IDREF	Attribute value is an ID reference value (that is, a reference to a name entered as the unique identifier of an element elsewhere in the same document)
IDREFS	Attribute value is a list of ID reference values
NAME	Attribute value is a valid SGML name
NAMES	Attribute value is a list of valid SGML names
NMTOKEN	Attribute value is a name token (that is, contains only name characters, but in this case with digits and other valid name characters accepted as the first character)
NMTOKENS	Attribute value is a list of name tokens
NOTATION	Attribute value is a member of the bracketed list of notation names that qualifies this reserved name
NUMBER	Attribute value is a number
NUMBERS	Attribute value is a list of numbers
NUTOKEN	Attribute value is a number token (that is, a name that starts with a number)
NUTOKENS	Attribute value is a list of number tokens

Table 5.3 lists the reserved names that can be used for attribute types.

As tokens (NMTOKEN, NMTOKENS, NUTOKEN and NUTOKENS) provide a more flexible approach to checking attribute values, they are sometimes used in preference to their more specific equivalents (NAME, NAMES, NUMBER and NUMBERS), which place more restrictions on the characters that can be used in attribute values.

The default value entry of the attribute definition consists of either a specific value or one of the reserved names listed in Table 5.4. Notice that these reserved names are preceded by the reserved name indicator (RNI) to ensure that they are not mistaken for attribute values of the same name that have not been enclosed in literal delimiters.

The restrictions that apply to the use of the reserved names listed in Tables 5.3 and 5.4 are:

- The ID and NOTATION reserved names may be used only once in any attribute definition list.
- The NOTATION and #CONREF reserved names cannot be used for attributes associated with EMPTY elements.
- The same token cannot appear in two lists of valid attribute values in the same declaration.

Table 5.4 Reserved names for attribute default values

Reserved name	Purpose
#FIXED	The following value is a fixed default value (that is, it cannot be changed by entry of another value in the start-tag)
#REQUIRED	The attribute value must be entered within the start-tag of the element
#CURRENT	If no attribute value is specified in the start-tag, the value to be used is that entered for this attribute in the start-tag of the nearest preceding element that shares the declaration in the attribute definition list
#IMPLIED	If no attribute value is specified, the program may imply a value
#CONREF	The element may contain either specific cross-reference text or an attribute, the value of which is a recognized ID reference value (that is, a name that has been entered as the unique identifier for another element)

- The default value of an attribute declared using the ID reserved name must be either #REQUIRED or #IMPLIED.
- An empty default value literal can only be specified for attributes whose declared value is CDATA.

Further restrictions also apply to names associated with attributes declared using the ID and NOTATION reserved names, as will be explained when examples of the use of these reserved names are given.

5.6 Using attributes

5.6.1 Simple attributes

The simplest type of attribute is one with just two declared values, one of which is the default. For example:

```
<!ATTLIST book status (draft|final) draft >
```

This declaration shows that the two valid values (tokens) for the status attribute are draft and final. If a value of status="final" is not specified in the start-tag the default value of status="draft" will be applied. As both tokens only contain valid name characters, providing the concrete syntax contains the default SHORTTAG YES entry, then:

- Literal delimiters do not need to be used around the default value, or entered attribute values.
- The attribute name and value indicator can be omitted from the start-tag so that a short form of <BOOK final> is all that is required to identify that a book that has moved from draft to final status.

A list of declared values can contain as many names as required. For example, acts presented to the European Parliament use the following set of attributes:

```
<!ATTLIST act leg.val (agr|dec|rec|rec.ecsc|dir|reg|dec.ecsc|
dec.eea|proc|opin|prot|com.pos|other) #REQUIRED
ld (da|de|el|en|es|ga|fi|fr|it|nl|pt|sv|ml) #REQUIRED >
```

5.6.2 Using tokens

Where the list of possible values is liable to change regularly, or cannot be fully defined, the list of declared values can be replaced by a declared-value reserved name that identifies names or name tokens. For example, elements conforming to the rules specified by the Text Encoding Initiative (TEI) can have an attribute associated with them that identifies which TEI element type form they are. The default definition for this attribute is:

```
TEIform NAME #IMPLIED
```

The value to be implied by the program, if no value is specified, is the name of the element with which the attribute is associated.

When a element that is not part of one of the TEI standard DTDs is required, it should be associated with one of the predefined TEI forms. To do this you simply add a `TEIform` attribute to its definition, for example:

```
<!ELEMENT special-para - O (heading, text) >
<!ATTLIST special-para TEIform NAME #FIXED "p" >
```

By using `NAME` as the declared value, this declaration ensures that the name must conform to the rules used for naming elements in the DTD without having to list all the TEI element names as permitted values in a very long list.

Where more than one value may be required, the declared value can be changed to `NAMES`.

Where names required for an attribute may need to begin with a digit, or another name character not defined as a valid name start character (say, a hyphen), the `NMTOKEN` or `NMTOKENS` declared values can be used in place of `NAME` and `NAMES`. The values entered for such **name token** attributes will be parsed to ensure that they only contain name characters and that their length does not exceed the limit specified by the `NAMELEN` quantity.

Numeric attributes

The only difference between the `NUTOKEN` and `NUTOKENS` **number token** declared value keywords and the name token keywords (`NMTOKEN` and `NMTOKENS`) is that the first character of any number token *must* be numeric. As the following declaration for an `<ARTWORK>` element shows, the two declared value types can be used together:

```
<!ELEMENT artwork       - O  EMPTY              >
<!ATTLIST artwork    width   NMTOKEN colwidth
                     depth   NUTOKEN #REQUIRED >
```

In this case the horizontal size (width) of the artwork defaults to a special parameter value (colwidth) known to the formatting program, unless a specific value is entered for the attribute. As this special name starts with a letter, rather than a number, the NMTOKEN keyword has been used for the declared value. For the depth attribute the declared value has been defined as NUTOKEN to ensure that the first part of the compulsory vertical size value is always a number.

To see the differences between these two definitions compare these valid tags:

```
<ARTWORK width=150mm depth=100mm>
<ARTWORK depth=8in>
<ARTWORK width="30-picas" depth='4-in'>
```

with these invalid ones:

```
<ARTWORK>
<ARTWORK width=mm150 depth=mm100>
<ARTWORK depth=8 in>
<ARTWORK width="30 picas" depth="4 in">
<ARTWORK colwidth depth=24pi>
<ARTWORK depth=6">
```

Many of the entries in the invalid list may seem at first sight to be valid. You need to understand why they are invalid if you are to make full use of the checks provided when number tokens are being used in place of name tokens.

In the first of the invalid examples an error occurs because the compulsory depth attribute has not been entered. (Remember that attributes whose default value is #REQUIRED must have their value entered as part of the start-tag.)

The second example is invalid because the value entered for the depth attribute does not start with a number. When the declared value is NUTOKEN the attribute value must start with a digit, rather than a letter. It should be noted, however, that the value for the width attribute, which has been a declared value of NMTOKEN, is valid as it begins with a letter and only contains name characters.

The faults in the third and fourth invalid examples relate to the use of spaces in the value. Spaces may only occur within delimited literals. With the third invalid example the SGML parser would accept depth=8 as a valid entry, but would then be required to treat in as the value of the width attribute. However, as only tags that have lists of permitted values can be entered without an attribute name and value indicator, this format would be invalid for the width attribute.

The fourth invalid entry will be treated as incorrect because the presence of a space identifies the entry within the literal as a list of tokens rather than a single token. This is invalid because the attributes have been declared using NMTOKEN and NUTOKEN rather than NMTOKENS and NUTOKENS.

For the fifth of the invalid entries an attempt has been made to minimize the entry by omitting the attribute name and value indicator (width=). As mentioned above, this technique of shortening a tag is only valid where a specific set of valid name tokens has been entered as the declared value.

The final example illustrates another subtle fault. Here an attempt has been made to use the quotation mark (") to represent inches. However, unless otherwise instructed by a change in the document's set of delimiter characters, the parser should treat the symbol as an unmatched literal delimiter and so flag the entry as invalid.

One way of simplifying the attribute definition list for the artwork element would be to treat both values as part of a single number token list by use of a declaration of the form:

```
<!ATTLIST artwork size NUTOKENS #REQUIRED >
```

In this case a valid start-tag for the artwork element might take the form:

```
<ARTWORK size="100mm 5in">
```

Note how the only space separates the two entries.

Where only one unit of measurement is being used in the output system, the NUTOKEN and NUTOKENS keywords can be replaced by NUMBER or NUMBERS to restrict attribute values to numeric values only.

There is, however, one danger with the NUMBER keyword. Only integers can be entered for attributes declared in this way; decimal values cannot be defined. If decimal values are likely to be needed, the NUTOKEN or NUTOKENS options must be used, as these will allow periods to be used as decimal points at any point other than the first character (values less than one must be entered with a zero in front of the decimal point). If negative values are required, however, NMTOKEN or NMTOKENS must be used as, while a hypen is a valid name character, it is not a number.

5.7 Specialized attributes

The following special types of attribute values are catered for by SGML:

- attributes referring to entities;
- unique identifiers;
- references to unique identifiers.

5.7.1 Entity attributes

The declaration given for the artwork element above said nothing about the source of the artwork. (It only defined the size of the space to be left for the image.) If the illustration was one that could be processed by a pagination system, the file containing the coded picture could be declared as an external entity in the DTD. It might be declared in a declaration of the form:

```
<!ENTITY fig1 SYSTEM "fig1.gif" NDATA GIF>
```

To allow this picture to be processed at the appropriate point, the declarations for the artwork element could be extended to read:

```
<!ELEMENT artwork     - O  EMPTY                >
<!ATTLIST artwork width    NMTOKEN  colwidth
                  depth    NUTOKEN  #IMPLIED
                  file     ENTITY   #REQUIRED  >
```

The attribute definition list shows that the <ARTWORK> element must have its start-tag qualified by an attribute, called file, whose value is the name of an entity declared in the DTD referenced by the document instance. Using this definition, the illustration can be referenced using a start-tag of the form:

```
<ARTWORK file="fig1">
```

When using ENTITY as the declared value, it is important to remember that the associated element must be declared as EMPTY and, therefore, requires no end-tag. It should also be noted that, if the program encounters an <ARTWORK> start-tag without a file name, the program will report an error.

Entities do not have to contain non-SGML data. They could equally well contain an SGML subdocument or text which does not contain SGML markup instructions (for example, CDATA or SDATA entities). Entities referenced using attributes may not, however, contain markup or other text that requires parsing.

5.7.2 Unique identifiers

The ID declared value allows a unique identifier to be associated with specific start-tags. Once a start-tag has been given a unique identifier, it can be cross-referenced by other attributes declared using the IDREF or IDREFS declared value.

The default value associated with an attribute that has the ID keyword as its declared value must be either:

- #REQUIRED, indicating that a unique identifier *must* be entered; or
- #IMPLIED, indicating that the identifier can be implied by the system if not present.

Because each identifier must be unique to the document, the SGML standard recommends that the same attribute name (for example, id) is used for all identifiers. This recommendation is not, however, compulsory. The <ARTWORK> element could be assigned a unique identifier that could be referenced from the text by extending its definition to read:

```
<!ELEMENT artwork    - O  EMPTY                >
<!ATTLIST artwork width  NMTOKEN  colwidth
                  depth  NUTOKEN  #IMPLIED
                   file  ENTITY   #REQUIRED
                     id  ID       #REQUIRED >
```

Each SGML identifier (known as an **id value**) must be a valid SGML name, starting with a letter. This means that identifiers such as `<ARTWORK file=fig1 id=1>` are invalid. If you do want to use numbers as identifiers you must place at least one letter in front of the first digit, for example, `<ARTWORK file=fig1 id=f1>`.

Unique identifiers can be entered in either case, any lowercase characters being converted to uppercase before the uniqueness of the identifier is determined (unless the SGML declaration has been altered to contain the statement `NAMECASE GENERAL NO`). This means, for example, that a start-tag of the form `<ARTWORK FILE=fig1 ID=F1>` would be treated as identical to the tag shown above. Note, however, that a start-tag reading `<ARTWORK FILE=FIG1 ID=F1>` would not be identical to its predecessors because entity names are normally case sensitive. This means that `fig1` and `FIG1` refer to different entities.

5.7.3 References to unique identifiers

An attribute with a declared value of `IDREF` or `IDREFS` can be used to refer to a unique identifier within the same document instance. Normally only one unique identifier will be involved, so the attribute can be declared using the singular keyword (`IDREF`). Typically the declaration will take the form:

```
<!ELEMENT figref - O   EMPTY              >
<!ATTLIST figref to    IDREF     #REQUIRED
                 page (yes|no) no         >
```

In this case the figure reference element (`<FIGREF>`) has been declared as an empty element because its contents are automatically generated by the program. It has a compulsory attribute (`to`), which must be a reference to a unique identifier used in the same document instance.

At the point where the artwork is to be referred to within the text a figure reference should be entered in the form `<p>As shown in <FIGREF to=f1>, ...`. This might generate a cross-reference of the form `As shown in Figure 3.1, ...`.

If the start-tag was changed to read `<FIGREF to=f1 page=yes>`, the generated text might be extended to read `As shown in Figure 3.1 on page 94, ...`.

While attributes using the `IDREF` or `IDREFS` keywords will normally have a default value of `#REQUIRED`, there are circumstances in which entries whose default value is `#CONREF` may apply.

The **content reference** (#CONREF) default value reserved name is particularly useful where documents are being prepared as a number of individual files, which will be linked together as subdocuments to a master document prior to output. Because cross-references can only be made to identifiers entered in the same (sub)document, cross-references to identifiers used in other subdocuments will need to be entered specifically by the author. To allow for this, the #CONREF default value option permits references to be made in two ways:

- By entering the wording required for the cross-reference as the contents of the element;
- By using a cross-reference attribute.

To see how this works, consider the following declaration for a figure reference:

```
<!ELEMENT figref - O   (#PCDATA) >
<!ATTLIST figref to    IDREF              #CONREF
                 page (yes|no)            no        >
```

Because the to attribute has, in this case, been given a default value keyword of #CONREF the contents of the associated element cannot be declared to be EMPTY. Instead the element declaration has been given a content model that allows parsed character data to be entered.

Cross references to a unique identifier can still be made in the format used for the last example. When, however, the reference is to a figure in another subdocument, the relevant entry should be entered as text within a start-tag and end-tag, for example:

```
<p>As shown in <FIGREF>Figure A.1 in Appendix A</FIGREF> ...
```

When the content reference attribute is present in the start-tag, the element is treated as an EMPTY element (without content) and, therefore, no end-tag is present. When the attribute value is not specified, however, the element's end-tag must be entered to identify the end of the reference. Because the end-tag is present in some cases and not in others, the second of the tag omission indicators for any element associated with an attribute whose default value is #CONREF should be O.

Only one attribute should be defined using the #CONREF default value in any attribute definition list declaration. If the attribute list were, for some unusual reason, to contain two #CONREF default value keywords, the parser must be able to imply values for *both* attributes because, if either attribute is present, the element will automatically become an empty one.

5.8 Controlling attribute values

Two other keywords can be used to control entered values:

- #FIXED when a **fixed attribute value** is required;
- #CURRENT when the **current attribute value** is to be used as the default value.

If an entered default value is preceded by the reserved name #FIXED, its value can never be changed. An example of an element with a fixed attribute value is the version attribute associated with the <HTML> element (see Chapter 12).

When the SGML declaration contains both SHORTTAG YES and OMITTAG YES the #CURRENT default value keyword can be used. This keyword tells users that, for the first occurrence of the associated element, a value must be entered (as if #REQUIRED had been used), but, if no value is entered for subsequent occurrences of the element, the last entered value will be used as the current default value.

It should be noted, however, that only one current value is associated with each attribute. If an attribute declaration is shared by a number of elements, the value used as the current value will be the last value entered for the named attribute in *any* of the associated elements. For example, if the following attribute definition was added to the document type declaration subset:

```
<!ATTLIST (p|note) indent NUTOKEN #CURRENT>
```

and a section of text was coded as:

```
<P indent=0>This is an example of a normal, unindented paragraph of
text. Notice that, because the paragraph tag was the first one that
used the indent attribute a value had to be entered, even though no
indent was required.
<NOTE indent=36pt>This note has been set with a 36pt indent.</NOTE>
<P>Because no specific indent value has been stated this paragraph
has also been indented by 36pt as this is the value currently
associated with the indent attribute.
<P indent=0>To cancel the indent applied to the note it is necessary
to enter a new value for the indent attribute as part of the
paragraph's start-tag.
```

the set text might appear in the form:

```
This is an example of a normal, unindented paragraph of text. Notice
that, because the paragraph tag was the first one that used the indent
attribute, a value had to be entered even though no indent was
required.

        NOTE: This note has been set with a 36pt indent.

        Because no specific indent value has been stated this
        paragraph has also been indented by 36pt as this is the
        value currently associated with the indent attribute.

To cancel the indent applied to the note it is necessary enter a new
value for the indent attribute as part of the paragraph's start-
tag.
```

Notice that, until the indent is specifically restated, the value entered at the start of the <NOTE> element remains in force for the <P> element as well.

Entity declaration and use

Types of entity • Entity references • Entity declarations • External entities • Character references • Entity sets

6.1 Types of entity

An **entity** is defined in ISO 8879 as 'a collection of characters that can be referenced as a unit.' SGML places no constraints on the maximum size of an entity.

An entity that contains a complete SGML document is known as an **SGML document entity**. SGML document entities have three main sections:

- an optional **SGML declaration** defining the markup syntax and character set used within the document;
- a **prolog** containing declarations defining the structure of the document (the **document type definition**) and related information;
- the text of the **document instance**.

SGML document entities can contain embedded references to other entities. There are two main types of entity:

- **general entities** that contain data that is to form part of a document: they can only be referenced in the document instance;
- **parameter entities** that contain characters required as part of one or more SGML declarations: they are referenced within the prolog or within markup declarations embedded in the document instance.

Both of these categories can be further subdivided into:

- entities whose replacement text is defined within the prolog (internal entities)
- entities whose replacement text is stored in a separate file (external entities).

Where the replacement text of a general entity should not be parsed when being incorporated into the document, it can be declared as a character data entity (`CDATA`). Where the replacement text is defined in a manner that is system-specific it can be defined as a specific character data entity (`SDATA`). Where the replacement text contains codes intended to control processing it can be defined as a processing instruction entity (`PI`).

There are three main types of external entity that would be stored in a separate file:

- An SGML text entity contains text that conforms to the declarations defined for a document type definition in the prolog.
- SGML subdocument entities are used to incorporate SGML-coded text that has been defined as a separate document, with its own document type definition, into another document.
- Graphics, and data marked up using notations other than SGML, can be declared in the form of a non-SGML data entity (`NDATA`).

Character data (`CDATA`) and specific character data (`SDATA`) can also be stored in external entities.

Embedded entities are the key to understanding SGML. Each embedded entity has two components: an entity declaration and one or more entity references. The entity declaration defines the name and contents of the entity; the entity references identify the points at which those contents are to be incorporated into the document.

Entity declarations form part of the document type declaration. Parameter entity references are used within document type and link type declarations to identify the points at which the replacement text of parameter entities is to be read and interpreted. General entity references are used within the document instance to identify the points at which the replacement text or external file defined in the entity declaration are to be incorporated into the text.

Closely associated with SGML entities are character references and short references. Character references allow authors to enter characters that are not available on the keyboard by reference to a character number or a function name. Short references allow single characters, or specially defined groups of characters, to act as a shorthand reference to an entity.

6.2 Entity references

An **entity reference** is entered into an SGML document to indicate each point at which the contents of a previously defined entity are to be incorportated into the document. There are two types of entity reference:

- general entity references;
- parameter entity references.

6.2.1 General entity references

A **general entity reference** consists of:

- an **entity reference open** (ERO) delimiter;
- an **entity name**;
- a **reference end**.

When the reference concrete syntax is being used the entity reference open delimiter is &. The length of the entity name must not exceed the current NAMELEN quantity, and the name must start with a valid name start character and be followed by valid name characters.

A reference end is either:

- a **reference close** (REFC) delimiter (a semicolon by default);
- a record end (RE) function code;
- a character, such as a space, which is not part of a valid entity name.

A typical general entity reference will, therefore, take the form `&name;`, or just `&name` if immediately followed by a space or record end code.

A special entity, known as the default entity, can be declared in a document type definition. If such a default entity has been declared its contents will be output whenever an otherwise undeclared name is encountered within an entity reference. Normally the default entity will contain a message warning that an unrecognized entity name has been encountered at that point in the document, for example:

```
*** Reference to undeclared entity found here ***
```

6.2.2 Parameter entity references

Parameter entity references may only occur within SGML markup declarations. A distinction is made between general entities and parameter entities to avoid the possibility of an author accidentally trying to declare an entity whose name has already been used by a DTD developer. By distinguishing between the uses to which the two types of entity are put, it is possible to unambiguously use the same name for a parameter entity and a general entity.

Parameter entities can also be referenced within markup declarations, such as those used to identify the role of marked sections, which can occur within document instances.

A parameter entity reference consists of:

- a **parameter entity reference open** (PERO) delimiter;
- an entity name;
- a reference end.

When the reference concrete syntax is being used, the parameter entity reference open delimiter is %. When the length of the parameter entity reference open delimiter and the parameter entity name are added together their length may not exceed that currently specified for the NAMELEN quantity (the delimiter is treated as part of the entity name).

A typical parameter entity reference will, therefore, have the form %name;.

6.3 Entity declarations

Entity declarations form part of a document type declaration subset (or a link type declaration subset) defined within the document prolog.

Within the document type declaration subset, each individual entity declaration is entered between its own set of markup declaration delimiters. The reserved name ENTITY (or its previously declared replacement) follows the markup declaration open (MDO) delimiter to identify the declaration as an entity declaration. The rest of the declaration consists of the **entity name** followed by the replacement **entity text** to give an entity declaration the general form:

```
<!ENTITY name "replacement entity text">
```

In its simplest form the replacement text will consist of a string of characters delimited by a matched pair of either quotation marks (") or apostrophes ('). A typical **SGML text entity** might be declared as:

```
<!ENTITY OPOCE "Office for Official Publications of the European
Communities">
```

This entity can be referenced by entering &OPOCE; at points in the text of relevant document instances at which the replacement text is to appear.

The replacement text of SGML text entities can include markup codes, including start-tags, embedded entity references, character references, short references and data tags, which will be interpreted as the entity text is added to the document. For example, a general entity declaration might take the form:

```
<!ENTITY en-reg "<em lang=fr>en r&egrave;gle</em>" >
```

When this entity is called, by entering &en-reg; in the text, the program will recognize the embedded text as a French emphasized phrase, bracketed by an <em lang=fr> start-tag and an </em> end-tag. Before outputting this highlighted phrase in the appropriate font the program will expand the reference to the entity called è to obtain the system-specific code needed to generate a lowercase e with a grave accent.

One word of warning: you cannot reference an entity within its replacement text as this will create a recursive loop. For this reason, the replacement string cannot contain any characters which might be treated as short references that should be mapped to the entity being defined.

6.3.1 Declaring parameter entities

A parameter entity declaration is distinguished from a general entity declaration by having a parameter entity reference open (PERO) delimiter, such as %, and one or more spaces immediately in front of the required name to give it the form:

```
<!ENTITY % name "replacement text" >
```

Typically the replacement text for a parameter entity will consist of a series of element names separated by the relevant SGML model group connectors, for example:

```
<!ENTITY % heading "H1|H2|H3|H4|H5|H6">
```

It is important to remember that parameter entities must be declared before the entity is referred to within the document type definition. In most prologs you will find that all parameter entities are declared at the start of the document type declaration subset. Where parameter entities are used to define the replacement text required for other parameter entity declarations, care must be taken to ensure that the declarations always precede the references. For example, the following declarations are used in the July 1996 experimental version of the HTML DTD:

```
<!ENTITY % font    " TT | B | I | U | S | BIG | SMALL | SUB | SUP " >
<!ENTITY % phrase  " EM | STRONG | DFN | CODE | SAMP | KBD | VAR |
                   CITATION | Q " >
<!ENTITY % special " A | IMG | APPLET | OBJECT | FONT | BR | SCRIPT |
                   STYLE | MAP | SPAN | BDO " >
<!ENTITY % form    " INPUT | SELECT | TEXTAREA | LABEL " >
<!ENTITY % text    " #PCDATA | %font; | %phrase; | %special; | %form; "
>
```

It is important to ensure that the definitions of the parameter entities referenced in the replacement text for the `text` parameter entity are declared before they are referenced, as in the case of the above sequence of declarations.

6.3.2 Comments

The purpose of an entity can be explained by incorporating **comments** within the definition. The start and end of each comment must be indicated by entering comment (COM) delimiters (a pair of consecutive hyphens in the reference concrete syntax). Like the replacement entity text, comments can take up more than one line, for example:

```
<!ENTITY disclaim "Users should note that all International
Standards undergo revision from time to time and that any reference
made herein to any other International Standard implies its latest
edition, unless otherwise stated." -- Must appear in the Foreword of
                                      each ISO standard -- >
```

6.3.3 Special forms of general entity declaration

Variations on the basic declaration allow users to specify the following special forms of general entities:

- a default entity that can be used in place of any entity for which replacement text has not otherwise been defined in the DTD;
- entities consisting entirely of character data that should not be parsed for markup;
- entities containing system-specific replacement text;
- entities containing a delimiter-independent representation of a start-tag or an end-tag;
- entities defining marked sections, processing instructions or markup declarations.

A special **default entity** can be declared by using the reserved word #DEFAULT in place of an entity name, for example:

```
<!ENTITY #DEFAULT
"*** Reference to undeclared entity found here ***">
```

The replacement text for this default entity will be used for any general entity reference, the name of which is not recognized as one of the entities declared in the currently active DTD.

The CDATA keyword can be placed between the entity name and its replacement text to tell the program that the replacement text is to be treated as a **character data entity**. This means that any characters within the string that could possibly be interpreted as markup codes will be ignored. For example, the declaration:

```
<!ENTITY para CDATA "<P>" >
```

would allow a ¶ entity reference to generate the characters <P> rather than the start-tag for a paragraph (which would be output if CDATA was not used).

Where a document, such as this one, contains a lot of text that may be mistaken for markup, it is better to declare special entities that can be used to generate SGML delimiter sequences. The characters most likely to need treating in this way are the less-than sign (<) used at the start of many types of markup declaration and the entity reference open (ERO) delimiter (&). The following declarations could be used to set up entities that would meet this need:

```
<!ENTITY lt CDATA "<" >
<!ENTITY amp CDATA "&" >
```

Using this definition, code for a paragraph start-tag (<P>) could be entered as <P>. (This would not be recognized as a valid start-tag because tags and entity references are only recognized if they are contained within the same entity.) Similarly, the general entity reference &SGML; could be entered as &SGML; to ensure that it is not recognized as an entity called SGML (or the default entity if no such entity has been declared in the DTD).

It should be noted that the semicolon is a compulsory part of both the < and & entity references because they are immediately followed by a name character. If the semicolon had been left out of the first example, the program would have tried to find an entity whose declared name was ltp. In the case of the second example, the program would look for an entity called ampSGML. If entities with these names had not previously been declared, and no default entity had been defined, the parser should flag the entity reference as invalid.

Another approach to this problem, and the one most commonly used in such situations, is to use the reserved word SDATA to identify the declaration as a **specific character data entity**. For example, the following entity declarations are provided in ISO 8879:

```
<!ENTITY lt SDATA "[lt ]" --=less-than sign-->
<!ENTITY amp SDATA "[amp ]" --=ampersand-->
```

Most SGML-based programs would automatically expand standard ISO entity references such as these to give the code sequence required to generate the character during formatting because the convention of enclosing the entity name in square brackets is one used for all ISO entity sets. However, where users have defined their own, system-specific, replacement codes in entity replacement text, the inclusion of the SDATA reserved name in the entity definition will allow the receiving program to request the command sequence needed to generate the requested character(s) on the local text formatter.

Note: *While characters defined as valid in the document's character set, but as invalid in the document's concrete syntax, can be included in SDATA entities, non-SGML characters that have been declared as unused in the document's character set cannot be entered as part of the replacement text of an SDATA entity.*

When short references are being used, the replacement text for some entities will consist solely of an element start-tag or end-tag. In such cases the role of the entity can be unambiguously defined by preceding the *undelimited* element name, and any associated attributes, with a STARTTAG or ENDTAG reserved name. For example, the declaration:

```
<!ENTITY refstart STARTTAG "sub align=left" >
```

will cause the program to replace &refstart; with <sub align=left>, while:

```
<!ENTITY refend ENDTAG "sub" >
```

will cause it to replace &refend; with </sub>.

Alternatively the two entities could have been defined as:

```
<!ENTITY refstart "<sub align=left>" >
<!ENTITY refend "</sub>" >
```

but in this case the program would not know that the replacement text contained a markup tag which needed further processing until it had added the replacement text to the main text stream. In addition, while the first pair of definitions would work irrespective of what definition is used for markup delimiters, the second pair of definitions will only work while the reference concrete syntax definitions for STAGO, ETAGO and TAGC are in force.

Other keywords can be used to identify parameter or general entities, the replacement text for which defines an embedded SGML markup instruction. The reserved words that are placed between the entity name and the replacement text to identify such entities are:

- MS to identify the replacement text as a marked section;
- MD to identify the text as a markup declaration (bracketed by MDO and MDC);
- PI to identify the text as a processing instruction (bracketed by PIO and PIC).

Typically these keywords will be used in entity declarations such as:

```
<!ENTITY special MD "USELINK special">
```

This declaration allows the entity reference &special; to be used to generate a <!USELINK special> markup declaration in the text at a point where special processing of embedded elements is required.

6.4 External entities

External entities are declared with an **external entity specification** in place of the replacement text. The external entity specification indicates the source of the data to be added to the document and, optionally, the type of entity being defined.

Two types of external entity are recognized by SGML:

- entities of which the location identifier is specific to the system preparing the document;
- publicly declared entities, the purpose of which is known to more than one system.

Each of these main types can be further subdivided into one of three **entity types**:

- SGML subdocument entities;
- SGML text entities containing SGML marked-up text;
- data entities containing text that should not be parsed, or non-SGML data.

6.4.1 System-specific external entities

The simplest way of declaring a **system-specific external entity** that is known only to the systems it is used on is to use the reserved name `SYSTEM` in place of the replacement text in the entity declaration, in a declaration of the form:

```
<!ENTITY file1 SYSTEM >
```

where `file1` is a valid entity name that is also recognized by the system as a reference to a file on the local storage system.

Note: *Experience has shown that the use of this simplified form of referencing external entities leads to problems when interchanging documents between systems. For this reason the use of this shortened form for the identification of external entities within distributed systems is discouraged.*

More typically, however, the `SYSTEM` keyword in an entity declaration will be qualified by a **system identifier** that uniquely identifies the source of the required entity. In many instances the system identifier will consist of a file name, optionally qualified by a pathname, for example:

```
<!ENTITY module4 SYSTEM "c:\SGML\course\module4.sgm" >
```

When the program encounters a `&module4;` entity reference within the text, it will call the file identified by the system identifier and parse its contents as SGML-encoded text at the point identified by the entity reference.

In 1997 a new annex to ISO/IEC 10744, the *Hypermedia/Time-base Structuring Language (HyTime)* introduced the concept of **formal system identifiers** (FSIs) to SGML. A formal system identifier has a structured form that identifies both the file required and the source of the file. For example, an FSI could be used to identify that a file has been referenced through an Internet **Uniform Resource Locator** (URL) using a system identifier of the following form:

```
<!ENTITY chapter4 SYSTEM
      "<url FSIbase='http://www.u-net.com/~sgml/'>sgml-4.htm" >
```

6.4.2 Alternative markup notations

When a system-specific external entity contains data that has been coded using a form of markup that differs from that used in the main document, the system identifier can be qualified by an **entity type** statement. Four entity types are recognized within SGML:

- subdocuments that contain text coded in SGML using an alternative document type definition, which is clearly identified at the start of the file;
- character data (`CDATA`) entities that contain only valid SGML characters which do not require parsing;
- specific character data (`SDATA`) entities that contain characters, the interpretation of which is specific to the system;
- non-SGML data (`NDATA`) entities that contain codes outside the set declared to be valid SGML characters for the document.

If an external entity contains a complete SGML-coded document, including the appropriate document type declaration, it can be declared as a system-specific **SGML subdocument entity** by placing the reserved word `SUBDOC` after the entity's system identifier, for example:

```
<!ENTITY table1 SYSTEM "table1.sgm" SUBDOC >
```

Note: *This feature can only be used if the SGML declaration has a `FEATURES` clause containing a `SUBDOC YES` entry. It should be noted, however, that the `FEATURES` clause defaults to `SUBDOC NO`.*

When an SGML program that has received the above entity declaration encounters a `&table1;` entity reference, it will store its current parsing state before calling up the file called `table1.sgm`. While it is processing this file it will use the document type declaration identified at the start of the subdocument file, rather than the one previously being used. When the end of the subdocument is reached, the parsing state stored when the entity reference was encountered will be restored.

Where the retrieved entity contains data that is not coded in SGML, the entity must be declared as a **data entity**. This is done by entering a reserved word (`CDATA`, `SDATA` or `NDATA`) immediately after the system identifier. A **notation name** identifying the type of coding used within the data entity must follow the keyword, optionally followed by any data attributes that are required to process the contents of the referenced file.

If an Encapsulated PostScript file has been created, it could be incorporated into a document by adding an entity declaration of the form:

```
<!ENTITY fig1 SYSTEM "fig1.eps" NDATA postscript >
```

A reference of the form `&fig1;` will cause the parser to pass the file called `fig1.eps` in the current working directory to the process identified in the notation declaration that has been given the name `postscript`.

6.4.3 Notation declarations

Notation declarations have the general form:

```
<!NOTATION name identifier >
```

where name is the **notation name** (used after NDATA in the entity declaration) and identifier is a valid **notation identifier**, which is either system-specific or publicly declared.

If the notation identifier is system-specific, it will consist of the reserved word SYSTEM, followed by a system identifier which identifies the process control file that needs to be activated to parse the non-SGML data, for example:

```
<!NOTATION postscript SYSTEM "eps.bat" >
```

When the system has finished processing the data, it will transmit a special, system-dependent, signal, known as an **entity end** signal, to the SGML parser.

Note: *This signal is output by the system at the end of each entity to tell the parser that it can continue processing the rest of the text now that the entity reference has been satisfied. The entity end signal is not a control code and need not be one of the codes declared within the document's character set. It can be any signal recognized by the operating system as an indication that the end of an entity's replacement text has been reached.*

Where an external entity contains character data, or other system-specific information, its declaration must also be qualified by a suitable notation name, for example:

```
<!ENTITY example1 SYSTEM "example1.dtd" CDATA SGML >
<!ENTITY our-logo SYSTEM "our-logo.out" SDATA "logo" >
```

where the associated notation declarations could take the form:

```
<!NOTATION SGML SYSTEM "newstream.in">
<!NOTATION logo SYSTEM "Logo.bat" >
```

Data attributes

When a notation declaration has been associated with a data entity, the notation name can optionally be qualified by **data attributes**. These data attributes can either be passed to the system as parameters associated with the commands that activate the required notation interpreter or they can be used to determine which commands should be sent to the system.

Data attributes are declared in the same way as other attributes except that the associated element type statement is replaced by the name(s) of the notation(s) with which the attributes are to be associated. To indicate the changed role of the attribute definition the reserved name #NOTATION must precede the notation name(s).

To see how data attributes can be used in practice, consider the following data attribute definition:

```
<!ATTLIST #NOTATION (postscript|TeX) width NUTOKEN #IMPLIED
                                     depth NUTOKEN #IMPLIED >
```

Here two data attributes, `width` and `depth`, have been associated with the notation declarations whose names are `postscript` and `TeX`. If no values are entered for these attributes, the width and depth of the illustration will be as supplied. If the width or depth of the illustration to be processed is to be altered during processing, the entity declaration can be extended to read:

```
<!ENTITY fig1 SYSTEM "fig1.eps" NDATA postscript [width="5in"
depth="3in"]>
```

Notice that, within the entity declaration, the **data attribute specification** uses the currently defined **declaration subset open** (DSO) and **declaration subset close** (DSC) codes to delimit the entered list of attributes. In the reference concrete syntax these are the open and close square brackets respectively.

Like other attributes, data attributes can be minimized if the permitted values have been defined as a name token group. For example, if the attribute list was extended to read:

```
<!ATTLIST #NOTATION (postscript|TeX) width NUTOKEN #IMPLIED
                                     depth NUTOKEN #IMPLIED
                                     align (left|right|centre) left >
```

the entity declaration could take the form:

```
<!ENTITY fig1 SYSTEM "fig1.eps" NDATA
                  postscript [width="5in" depth="3in" centre]>
```

Note: *When defining attributes for use with notations the `ENTITY`, `ENTITIES`, `ID`, `IDREF`, `IDREFS` and `NOTATION` keywords must* ***not*** *be used, as these keywords can only be used as declared values for attributes associated with elements. Similarly the `#CURRENT` and `#CONREF` default value options cannot be used.*

6.4.4 Publicly declared external entities

Publicly declared external entities are external entities that contain declarations, text or other data designed to be used on more than one SGML system.

Many publicly declared entities consist solely of a predefined set of markup declarations which can be used to extend document type declaration subsets defined within the prolog. When the relevant parameter entity reference is encountered in the document type declaration, the program will add the declarations it has previously stored as a publicly declared entity to any local declarations.

The advantage of using publicly declared entities is that the declarations do not need to be transmitted between systems when the receiving system is already known to have access to them. Instead, all the user needs to do is add the necessary public entity declarations, with the associated references, to the document to tell receiving systems which sets of declarations will be referenced in transmitted documents.

Publicly declared external entities are said to be 'publicly declared' because the relevant declarations have been assigned names known by receiving systems, but the declarations can be 'private' in the sense that the associated definitions are only provided to a closed user community.

There are, however, certain publicly declared entities that may truly be called 'publicly declared'. These contain sets of declarations that have been defined by one of the organizations authorized by the International Organization for Standardization (ISO) to keep registers of declarations used in more than one document. Once a declaration set has been registered in this way it will have a unique name by which it can be recognized by all systems referencing the standardized data.

The International Organization for Standardization has defined entity sets to identify most commonly used Latin, Greek and Cyrillic characters, as well as other constructs defined in international standards. Such sets are identified by special ISO owner identifiers. ISO owner identifiers start with the letters `ISO` followed by the number and date of the standard referred to, for example, `"ISO 8879:1986"`.

Note: *Before requesting any publicly declared entity it is important to check that the relevant declarations will be available to any system receiving the marked-up SGML document. The fact that an entity has been publicly declared does* **not** *mean that it will be known to all SGML systems, it simply means that its definition does not need to be transmitted between systems that already know the definition.*

Requesting publicly declared external entities

Publicly declared external entities which just contain text can be requested by entering a declaration of the form:

```
<!ENTITY name PUBLIC "public identifier" >
```

This entity can be recalled at any point in the text by entering a general entity reference of the form `&name;`.

Optionally the public identifier can be followed by the filename used to store the entity contents on the local system, for example:

```
<!ENTITY name PUBLIC "public identifier" "filename.ext" >
```

Because this makes the entity declaration less portable, however, this form of external entity declaration is discouraged.

Note: *With the development of the concept of entity catalogs by the members of the SGML Open vendors' consortium there is nowadays little need for this form of qualified public identifier.*

If the external entity contains SGML markup declarations that are to be added to the document type declaration subset, it must be declared by entering a parameter entity declaration of the form:

```
<!ENTITY % name PUBLIC "public identifier">
```

the entity then being recalled by entering the relevant parameter entity reference (in this case `%name;`) at some point between the entity declaration and the declaration subset close character (`]` in the reference concrete syntax) marking the end of the document type declaration subset.

The public identifier used in the entity declaration of the above external entities is either a formal public identifier or a name agreed between users.

Note: *If the `FEATURES` clause of the current SGML declaration contains the entry `FORMAL YES` the public identifier must be a formal public identifier.*

ISO 8879 restricts the characters that may be used in public identifiers to a special set of **minimum data characters** consisting of the uppercase and lowercase alphabetic letters, spaces (or `RE` and `RS` codes), numbers and the following characters, which are declared to be part of a special character class:

```
' ( ) + , . - / : = ?
```

Note: *This list of special characters cannot be extended or otherwise altered in the SGML declaration. If you wish to use an agreed name to identify a set of declarations, you must make sure that your name consists only of characters mapped in the current document character set to these special characters or one of the ISO 646 (ASCII) alphanumeric characters.*

Formal public identifiers

Formal public identifiers fall into one of three categories:

- those defined by ISO or a standards body affiliated to ISO;
- those allocated to registered declaration sets;
- unregistered declarations.

The rules for defining ISO assigned public identifiers are defined in ISO 9070, *Information Processing – SGML Support Facilities – Registration Procedures for Public Text Owner Identifiers.* A typical ISO registered entity set will be identified by a declaration, within the document type declaration subset, of the form:

```
<!ENTITY % ISOlat1 PUBLIC
  "ISO 8879:1986//ENTITIES Added Latin 1//EN" >
```

This declaration must then be invoked by incorporating the parameter entity `%ISOlat1;` into the document type declaration subset before the closing square bracket, for example:

```
<!DOCTYPE docname [
  <!ENTITY % ISOlat1 PUBLIC
    "ISO 8879:1986//ENTITIES Added Latin 1//EN" >
  .
  .      -- other required declarations --
  .
  %ISOlat1; ]>
```

ISO assigned public identifiers have three components, separated from each other by a pair of solidus strokes (slashes). The three components are:

- an **ISO owner identifier** which shows the number and date of the standard being referred to;
- a public text class (for example, `ENTITIES`) and an associated public text description (for example, `Added Latin 1`)
- a public text language code (for example, `EN` for English).

Entity sets registered by bodies other than ISO will use a **registered owner identifier** in place of the ISO owner identifier. The registered name is preceded by `+//` to identify the following identifier as one applying to a registered set. A typical declaration might be:

```
<!ENTITY % EC-acts PUBLIC
  "+//OPOCE//DTD for European Community Acts//EN">
```

One special class of registered owner identifier that is of special interest to book publishers is that assigned to the International Standard Book Numbering Agency in ISO 9070. This special identifier allows publishers to be identified by reference to the group and publisher identifiers that form the first part of the ISBNs assigned to their books. For example, a set of entity declarations for use in European Commission publications could be assigned an identifier of the form:

```
<!ENTITY % OPOCE PUBLIC "+//ISBN 93 826::Office for Official
  Publications of the European Communities//ENTITIES Accented
  Characters//EN">
```

Companies can apply to register their own ISO 9070 owner names through the Graphic Communications Association, which is located at 100 Dangerfield Road, Alexandria, Virginia, USA.

Where the declarations have not been formally registered, an **unregistered owner identifier** should be used as the owner identifier. This has the same form as a registered owner identifier, except that a hyphen is used in place of the initial plus. The name used to identify the owner must consist of only the minimum data characters (alphanumeric or special) allowed in public identifiers. A typical declaration might take the form:

```
<!ENTITY % SGMLdoc PUBLIC
  "-//The SGML Centre//DTD for Manual Production//EN">
```

The **public text class** name that follows the owner identifier may have one of the following values:

- `TEXT` when text for the document instance (including any element tags and entity references) is stored in the external entity;
- `DOCUMENT` when the external entity contains an SGML declaration, a document type declaration and text;
- `SUBDOCUMENT` when the external entity contains the document type declaration and the text for a subdocument to be referenced within the current document;
- `DTD` when the external entity contains a document type declaration subset containing declarations defining the document's structure and entities;
- `ELEMENTS` when the external entity only contains element, attribute or notation declarations, with their associated parameter entities, comments, processing instructions and marked sections;
- `ENTITIES` when the external entity only contains entity declarations;
- `SHORTREF` when the external entity only contains the short reference, entity and map use declarations making up a short reference set;
- `LPD` when the external entity only contains the link set, link attribute and entity declarations making up a link type declaration subset;
- `CHARSET` when the external entity only contains details of the base character set to be used within an SGML declaration;
- `SYNTAX` where the external entity only contains details of the concrete syntax to be used in the SGML declaration;
- `CAPACITY` when the external entity only contains capacity set declarations to be referenced in the SGML declaration;
- `NOTATION` when the external entity identifies the process to be used when processing non-SGML data;
- `NONSGML` when the stored data contains non-SGML characters.

Note: *All public text class keywords must be entered using capital letters only.*

Only one keyword can appear in any formal identifier, though most of the keywords can be used more than once in a document. (Only one syntax or capacity declaration can be made in any SGML declaration.)

Where the `TEXT`, `NONSGML` or `SUBDOCUMENT` public text class keywords are used in a public identifier, the entity must be defined as a general entity. The `ELEMENTS`, `ENTITIES` and `SHORTREF` keywords may only be used in parameter entity declarations because they refer to files that contain markup declarations that need to be added to any local declarations within the document type declaration subset. The `DTD` and `LPD` keywords must be associated with document type declarations and link process definitions respectively. The `CHARSET`, `SYNTAX` and `CAPACITY` keywords may only be used in the relevant section of an SGML declaration.

The `NOTATION` keyword differs slightly from the other public text class keywords in that it is only used to qualify notation declarations. It is typically used in the form:

```
<!NOTATION postscript PUBLIC "-//my-system//NOTATION EPS
  Processor//EN">
```

This declaration defines a notation called `postscript` as a locally recognized notation that will be used to process Encapsulated PostScript files.

Each public text class keyword is qualified by a **public text description** explaining the purpose of the publicly declared entity. (This description is restricted to the alphanumeric and special minimum data characters used for public identifiers.) Where the entity consists of declarations that are not generally available to the public, the public text description should be preceded by an **unavailable text indicator** (`-//`) to give the identifier the form:

```
<!ENTITY % name PUBLIC
        "-//owner//class -//description//language" >
```

The **public text language** parameter that normally ends a formal public identifier must be one of the two-character codes for identifying languages defined in ISO 639. This language code tells the system which language the public text has been prepared in. The most commonly encountered codes are:

- `EN` for English
- `FR` for French
- `DE` for German
- `GR` for Greek
- `IT` for Italian
- `NL` for Dutch
- `ES` for Spanish
- `PT` for Portuguese
- `AR` for Arabic
- `HE` for Hebrew
- `RU` for Russian
- `CH` for Chinese
- `JA` for Japanese.

Codes have also been defined for most European languages, including 'dead' languages such as Latin, and for international languages such as Esperanto, Interlingua and Interlingue.

Notice that the language codes are all defined as a pair of *capital* letters. These codes cannot be replaced by the equivalent lowercase letters within the formal public identifier, even if the name case rules in the SGML declaration permit general substitution of tag characters, because the standard specifically states that the uppercase form must be used for all public text language values.

Where the public text class keyword is `CHARSET` the public text language code is replaced by a **public text designating sequence**. This sequence of codes uniquely identifies the selected character set by using techniques defined in ISO 2022. Each sequence starts with an escape code (1/11, hexadecimal 1B) followed by a number indicating the type of code set being described. This number is further qualified by one or more numbers identifying the required set of characters.

The types of code that can be indicated by the first code after the escape code include:

- 2/1 to identify the set as defining a C0 standard control code set (32 characters, starting at 0/0);
- 2/2 to identify the set as defining a C1 supplementary control code set (32 characters, starting at 8/0);
- 2/4 to identify the set as a multiple-byte 94 character code set;
- 2/5 to identify the set as one not defined by ISO 2022;
- 2/8 to identify the set as a standard 94 character G0 set (starting at position 2/1);
- 2/9 to identify the set as a 94 character G1 supplementary character code set (starting at 10/1);
- 2/10 to identify the set as a G2 alternative 94 character supplementary code set (overlaying G1 at 10/1);
- 2/11 to identify the set as a G3 alternative 94 character supplementary code set (overlaying G1 at 10/1);
- 2/13 to identify the set as a 96 character G1 supplementary character code set (starting at 10/0);
- 2/14 to identify the set as a G2 alternative 96 character supplementary code set (overlaying G1 at 10/0);
- 2/15 to identify the set as a G3 alternative 96 character supplementary code set (overlaying G1 at 10/0).

Note: *ESC 2/5 4/0 is a special sequence used to return to the basic G0 character set from a character set defined outside ISO 2022.*

A typical use of a public text designating sequence to define a document's character set in an SGML declaration would be:

```
CHARSET DESCSET "ISO6937:1994//CHARSET Latin Alphabet//ESC
2/14 4/1"
```

The 96 character set required is that specified in the 1994 version of ISO/IEC standard 6937, which, in this instance, is being used as a G2 code set.

Where a publicly declared entity consists of entity declarations that contain system-specific data (that is, they use the SDATA option) the associated formal public identifier can be further qualified by the addition of a **public text display version** description. This description identifies the types of device by which the entities will be recognized.

A typical extended entry might take the form:

```
<!ENTITY % Ventura PUBLIC
  "-//The SGML Centre//ENTITIES Dingbats used in
  Ventura//EN//Ventura">
```

Note: *When creating a formal public identifier it is important not to split the literal string immediately after one of the slashes (solidii) used to identify the start of a new component within the public identifier, because the start of a new line in the delimited string will be treated as if a space had been entered, and spaces are not permitted immediately after a slash.*

The way in which formal public systems are resolved into local system identifiers is system dependent. Software conforming to the rules laid down by the SGML Open consortium will use exchangeable SGML Open **catalogs** to record these mappings. If you receive a document without receiving a catalog with it, you will need to create your own mapping between formal public identifiers and local files. If you receive a catalog with the files you will need to ensure that the filenames shown in the catalog are available at the specified location. If your versions of the referenced files are stored at other locations you will need to change the location shown in the catalog. If you do not have copies of any of the files listed in the catalog you will need to obtain them prior to parsing the document or DTD.

6.5 Character references

Keyboards can only provide keys for a limited range of characters. While many systems provide a menu option that can be used to select characters that are not directly available on the keyboard, these menus do not always provide access to all the characters that are accessible on a printer. For characters that are not part of the SGML character set a mechanism is needed for referencing them that only requires the use of characters known to be in the character set.

Characters that cannot be entered by use of a dedicated keystroke can be entered either as a reference to a previously declared system-specific (SDATA) entity or as a **character reference**, or by using a combination of both techniques.

A character reference is a reference entered within the text that specifies the required character either by entry of its *decimal value* or by reference to the *function name* it has been allocated in the currently defined concrete syntax (for example, `RE`, `RS`, `TAB` or `SPACE`).

A special **character reference open** (`CRO`) delimiter is used to identify character references. In the reference concrete syntax `CRO` is defined as `&#`, giving a typical character reference the form `µ` or `&#RE;`.

Character references can be used within the replacement text of an entity declaration. For example, the entity declaration:

```
<!ENTITY microns "&#181;m">
```

could be defined to allow `µns;` to be entered to generate the characters µm.

Character references are often used when a markup character, such as a double quote, is required in the replacement text of an entity. For example, to define a piece of quoted text within an entity it could be declared as:

```
<!ENTITY OPOCE
  "&#34;Office for Official Publications of the European
  Commission&#34;">
```

Alternatively the entity could be defined within single quotes as:

```
<!ENTITY OPOCE
  '"Office for Official Publications of the European Commission"'>
```

If an apostrophe needs to be included in replacement text surrounded by single quote delimiters it must be entered in the form of a character reference to the code whose decimal number is 39 (`'`).

Numeric character references are always treated as data (that is, the character they resolve to is not checked to see if it could be part of a markup delimiter). Characters referenced via a function name, however, will be treated as markup if entered at an appropriate point. For example, `
` will always be output as a carriage return, whereas `&#RE;` might be interpreted as the end of an entity reference if placed at the end of an entity name, rather than as a code to be sent to the printer.

One point to remember about numeric character references is that their numbers may need to be altered if the document's character set is changed or if the document is passed to a system using a different character set. For this reason special characters should, wherever possible, be given function names, or be defined as `SDATA` entities, within a document's character set.

6.6 Entity sets

An **entity set** is a set of entity declarations that are designed to be used together in a number of prologs. As such they are often stored in a separate file that can be referenced using a publicly declared external entity.

Entity sets are typically used to declare:

- standardized sets of characters used to extend the basic ISO 646 character set;
- system-specific character sets;
- text to be used in a number of documents.

Entity sets may also contain:

- parameter entity declarations;
- comment declarations;
- processing instructions;
- marked section declarations

which complement the entity declarations within the set.

As with all external entities, there are two basic types of entity set:

- publicly declared entity sets that are known by many systems;
- private, system-specific, entity sets.

6.6.1 Publicly declared entity sets

Publicly declared entity sets are typically used to define sets of characters that are not part of the main ASCII character set or the document character set. The standardized entity names defined in such sets can be converted (once) by any receiving system to the local equivalent by use of appropriate system-specific (`SDATA`) replacement text.

ISO has defined (in ISO 8879 and in ISO/IEC TR 9573) character sets for:

- accented latin characters:
  - `ISOlat1` for accented and dipthong characters used in Western Europe;
  - `ISOlat2` for accented and dipthong characters using in Eastern and Northern Europe;
- stand-alone diacritical accents (`ISOdia`);
- Greek characters (`ISOgrk1` and `ISOgrk2`), together with an alternative set typically used in maths (`ISOgrk3` and `ISOgrk4`);
- Cyrillic (`ISOcry1` and `ISOcry2`);
- standard graphical symbols (including punctuation) and fractions (`ISOnum`);
- standard publishing characters (`ISOpub`);
- box and line drawing (`ISObox`);
- technical symbols (`ISOtech`);
- mathematical symbols (`ISOamso`, `ISOamsb`, `ISOamsr`, `ISOamsn`, `ISOamsa`, `ISOmfrk`, `ISOmopf` and `ISOmscr`);
- chemistry (`ISOchem`).

Wherever possible entity set declarations should start with a comment declaration indicating the purpose of the set and how it should be invoked. For example, the ISOlat1 set starts with the following comment declarations:

```
<!-- (C) International Organization for Standardization 1986
     Permission to copy in any form is granted for use with
     conforming SGML systems and applications as defined in ISO
8879,
     provided this notice is included in all copies.
-->
<!-- Character entity set. Typical invocation:
     <!ENTITY % ISOlat1 PUBLIC
       "ISO 8879:1986//ENTITIES Added Latin 1/EN">
     %ISOlat1;
-->
```

To invoke this entity set on a system that has a copy of the relevant entity declaration file users need only add the entity declaration and parameter entity reference specified in the comment to their document type declaration subset.

6.6.2 Private entity sets

Private entity sets can be used to define entities that are to be used in a number of locally produced documents. Each entity set should be prepared as a separate file. Each set of entity declarations making up the entity set should be preceded by a comment declaration indicating the purpose of the set and how it should be invoked.

A document type definition can call any number of different entity sets, and contain its own entity declarations. The sequence in which the sets are called may be important. Normally, entity sets will be called after the document's entity declarations to ensure that any locally declared entities having the same name as one of the entities in an entity set will retain their local declarations. (The first definition found for an entity name is the one used by the system.) If, for some reason, the same entity name is used in two or more entity sets, the declaration used will be the one in the set whose parameter entity reference was encountered first.

Short references

Introduction to short references • Short reference mapping declarations • Short reference use declarations • Using short references

7.1 Introduction to short references

Short references are characters, or strings of characters, that provide a shorthand reference to an SGML entity. In the reference concrete syntax most non-alphanumeric characters not used as markup delimiters are defined as valid short reference delimiters (see Table 4.4). Within short reference strings SGML uses the letter B to indicate a sequence of one of more blanks (separator characters). The reference concrete syntax defines five strings of function character and special character sequences that are commonly used at line ends when preparing text on a word processor as possible short references:

```
&#RS;&#RE;  10,13     Empty record
&#RS;B&#RE;10,66,13 Blank records (one or more blanks)
B&#RE;      66,13     Trailing blank(s) followed by record end
&#RS;B      10,66     Record start followed by leading blanks
BB          66,66     Two or more blanks (spaces or tabs)
```

These strings allow blank lines, indents and other occurrences of multiple spaces to be identified and processed as appropriate.

Other characters declared in the document's character set can be added to this set by entering them as part of the DELIM section of the SYNTAX clause of the SGML declaration. Each additional short reference string required is declared, between literal delimiters ("), at the end of the SHORTREF entry in the SGML declaration. Typically the extended entry will take the form:

```
DELIM GENERAL  SGMLREF
      SHORTREF SGMLREF "<{" "<{/" "}>" "&{" "};"
```

In the above example five new short reference sequences have been added to the default set shown in Table 4.4.

If one or more of the standard short reference delimiters is not to be identified as a short reference delimiter string the standard set of delimiters can be disabled by replacing SGMLREF with NONE, for example:

```
DELIM GENERAL  SGMLREF
      SHORTREF NONE "<{" "<{/" "}>" "&{" "};"
```

If no strings are entered after this keyword, short reference mapping will be prohibited.

Short references are mapped to entities in short reference mapping declarations. More than one mapping declaration can be defined in a document, but only one map will be in force at any one time.

The current short reference map is determined by use of short reference use declarations. Where these are declared in the document type definition, they are activated automatically whenever a particular element, or group of elements, is encountered in the document instance. Alternatively, a short reference map declaration can be entered at the point in the document instance at which the map is to be invoked.

Where multiple DTDs are associated with a document (see Chapter 10) only the base document type can have short references associated with it.

7.2 Short reference mapping declarations

Short reference mapping declarations are identified by an initial keyword of `SHORTREF` (or its declared replacement) immediately after the markup declaration open sequence, for example, `<!SHORTREF`. This is followed by a unique **map name** which is used to identify the mapping declaration in short reference use declarations.

The map name is followed by a set of definitions associating short reference delimiter strings that have been defined as valid in the SGML declaration with an entity which has been defined *earlier* in the same document type definition. Within the short reference map, short references are entered as parameter literals, between matched pairs of quotation marks or apostrophes. This string is followed by a space and the name of the entity containing the replacement text for the specified short reference character(s).

The following short reference map has been suggested as a mechanism for providing short cuts within mathematical data in a proposed extension to the HTML DTD:

```
<!SHORTREF MAP1   "^" REF1
                  "_" REF3
                  "{" REF5 >
```

The three entities referred to are declared, before the short reference map, as:

```
<!ENTITY REF1 STARTTAG "SUP">
<!ENTITY REF3 STARTTAG "SUB">
<!ENTITY REF5 STARTTAG "BOX">
```

A short reference delimiter character (or string) can be used only once in any particular mapping declaration. If the entered short reference delimiter is not one of those defined in the SGML declaration currently in force, the mapping will not take place and the short reference will be treated as part of the text. (At least one valid short reference string must be specified in each short reference mapping declaration.)

7.3 Short reference use declarations

There are two ways in which a short reference map can be activated: automatically or manually. Automatic mapping of short references is achieved by entering **short reference use declarations** within a document type definition. Manual mapping occurs when a short reference use declaration is entered as part of document instance.

An automatically actioned short reference use declaration has the general form:

```
<!USEMAP map-name element-list>
```

where map-name identifies a map defined in an associated short reference mapping declaration and element-list contains the names of the elements that are to activate the map.

The map declared in Section 7.2 can be invoked by the declaration:

```
<!USEMAP MAP1 MATH >
```

This declaration tells the program that the map declared with the name of MAP1 is to be used whenever an element called MATH is being processed. This map will stay in force until the end-tag for the element (</MATH>) is encountered, unless it is overridden by another map that has been set up to apply to a valid subelement of the table element.

If more than one element is to activate a particular map, the element names must be entered as a *name group*. When the reference concrete syntax is being used a typical declaration will take the form:

```
<!USEMAP quotes (p|footnote) >
```

If either of the listed elements is started, by entry of an appropriate start-tag, the quotes map will automatically become the current map, overriding any existing map until the associated end-tag is identified.

Maps may be activated from within the text of a document by entry of a declaration of the form:

```
<!USEMAP map-name >
```

In this case no element name is stated because the map will be associated with the currently open element, remaining in force until its end-tag is identified. As with automatically actioned maps, the requested map will be used for any embedded subelements for which separate maps have not been specified. However, but if an embedded subelement is associated with another map, that map will override the previous map until such time as the end-tag for the subelement is identified.

A special variant of the short reference use declaration can be used to declare an **empty map** that temporarily disables any map currently being used. The empty map is specified by replacing the map name with the reserved word `#EMPTY` to give a declaration of the form:

```
<!USEMAP #EMPTY >
```

for a short reference use declaration within the document instance, or:

```
<!USEMAP #EMPTY element-list >
```

for a map declared within the document type definition.

Note: *Please do not confuse the use of the SGML `USEMAP` keyword with the use of the HTML `usemap` attribute.*

7.4 Using short references

The following example shows how nested short references could be used within mathematical formulae:

```
<!ENTITY REF1 STARTTAG "SUP">
<!ENTITY REF2 ENDTAG   "SUP">
<!ENTITY REF3 STARTTAG "SUB">
<!ENTITY REF4 ENDTAG   "SUB">
<!ENTITY REF5 STARTTAG "BOX">
<!ENTITY REF6 ENDTAG   "BOX">

<!SHORTREF MAP1      "^" REF1
                     "_" REF3
                     "{" REF5 >

<!SHORTREF MAP2      "^" REF2
                     "_" REF3
                     "{" REF5 >

<!SHORTREF MAP3      "_" REF4
                     "^" REF1
                     "{" REF5 >

<!SHORTREF MAP4      "}" REF6
                     "^" REF1
                     "_" REF3 >

<!USEMAP MAP1 MATH>
<!USEMAP MAP2 SUP >
<!USEMAP MAP3 SUB >
<!USEMAP MAP4 BOX >
```

To understand how these maps interrelate, we will consider the way in which an HTML system should process the following boxed formula:

```
<MATH>{&int;_0_^n^f(x) dx}</MATH>
```

The processing sequence for this string will be:

(1) The start-tag for the <MATH> element will activate MAP1.

(2) The { will be replaced by the entity called REF5, which will generate a start-tag for a <BOX> element.

(3) The <BOX> start-tag will activate MAP4.

(4) The ∫ entity reference will generate an integral sign.

(5) The first underline (_) will be replaced by the entity called REF3, which will generate a start-tag for a <SUB> (subscript) element.

(6) The <SUB> start-tag will activate MAP3.

(7) The zero (0) will be treated as the data for the <SUB> element.

(8) The second underline will be replaced by the entity called REF4, which will generate an end-tag for the subscript (</SUB>).

(9) Once the end of the subscript element has been identified, MAP3 will be deactivated and MAP4 will be reactivated.

(10) The first circumflex (^) will be replaced by the entity called REF1, which will generate a start-tag for a <SUP> (superscript) element.

(11) The <SUP> start-tag will activate MAP2.

(12) The letter n will be treated as the data for the <SUP> element.

(13) The second circumflex will be replaced by the entity called REF2, which will generate an end-tag for the superscript (</SUP>).

(14) Once the end of the superscript element has been identified MAP2 will be deactivated and MAP4 will be reactivated.

(15) f(x) dx will be treated as data for the <BOX> element.

(16) The } code will be replaced by the entity called REF6, which will generate an end-tag for the box (</BOX>).

(17) Once the end-tag for the box element has been identified MAP4 will be deactivated and MAP1 will be reactivated.

(18) When the end-tag for the math container (</MATH>) is identified MAP1 will be deactivated.

Although short references provide a very useful method of reducing the number of tags that need to be entered by authors, a word of caution is required. *When choosing suitable short reference delimiters you must make sure they are unique.* For instance, if you choose the apostrophe as the delimiter used to start and end quoted text, how will quote delimiters be distinguished from other apostrophes within the text? It might be possible to declare short reference delimiters consisting of a space and an apostrophe that could be used to identify the start of a quote provided it does not occur at the start of a paragraph. A matching short reference delimiter consisting of an apostrophe followed by a space could be used to generate the end-tag for an embedded quote, but this sequence would not recognize the end of quoted text where the quotation mark is followed by other punctuation symbols, while an apostrophe on its own might be identified erroneously if the text contained any embedded plural possessive words such as those found in the phrase `'the bosses' toilet'`. While further short reference delimiters can be defined to cover most situations, this can lead to fairly complicated maps which could be avoided by careful choice of short reference delimiters

A similar problem can occur if two short reference strings start with the same sequence of characters. For example, if the SGML declaration contained the entry:

```
SHORTREF SGMLREF "##"
```

both a single hash code `(#)` and a pair of hash codes would be valid short reference delimiters. If the map currently being used only contained a mapping for the single variant, for example:

```
<!SHORTREF newmap "#" hash >
```

a string of three hashes (`###`) would be interpreted as `##&hash;`. In this case, the first two hashes have been recognized as a valid SGML short reference string that is currently unmapped, so the characters have been passed through as they are, while the final hash has been recognized as the single hash short reference which is to be mapped to the entity whose name is `hash`.

Before we leave the subject of short references, it should be noted that short reference strings are never recognized within markup.

Marked sections and processing instructions

The role of marked sections • Marked section declarations • Using marked sections • Processing instructions • Using processing instructions in marked sections

8.1 The role of marked sections

Marked sections can be used to identify sections of text that need special processing. There are two principal reasons for marking sections of text:

- because the text includes character sequences that could accidentally be interpreted as markup;
- because the text may not be needed in all versions of the document.

Where examples of SGML markup need to be included in a document, they can be entered as part of a marked section to ensure that they are not misinterpreted as markup. Using this approach obviates the need to convert the initial characters (such as < and &) of markup sequences used in examples to references to `CDATA` or `SDATA` entities (for example, `<` and `&`).

Where a single document contains more than one version of the text, marked sections allow users to determine which sections should be processed during a particular parse. Text which may or may not appear in the printed version can also be entered as marked sections so that users can determine, for example, when such text should be included in drafts or proofs, or when it should be left out of final versions. Marked sections can also be used to identify text that has been added to a document on a temporary basis.

Marked sections can be used within the document prolog to identify variants of document type definitions. For example, they are used extensively in Text Encoding Initiative (TEI) DTDs, and within later versions of the

HTML DTD, where they identify elements that have been retained to ensure backward compatibility but whose use in new documents is deprecated.

8.2 Marked section declarations

Marked section declarations are enclosed between special **marked section start** and **marked section end** delimiter sequences within the document instance or prolog. The marked section delimiter sequences are both made up of a combination of two other delimiters. The marked section start delimiter sequence consists of the markup declaration open (`MDO`) delimiter immediately followed by a declaration subset open (`DSO`) delimiter. This initial `DSO` is followed by a **status keyword specification** identifying the type of marked section required, which is followed by a second `DSO` delimiter that identifies the start of the marked section text.

The end of each marked section is indicated by a special **marked section close** (`MSC`) delimiter sequence, which is immediately followed by a markup declaration close (`MDC`) delimiter. The marked section close delimiter will consist of two matching characters that are obviously linked to the `DSO` delimiters used for the marked section start sequence. For example, in the reference concrete syntax the opening square brackets used for the two `DSO` delimiters in the marked section start sequence are matched by two closing square brackets (`]]`) in the `MSC`. This gives a marked section the form:

```
<![ status-keywords [ ... marked section ... ]]>
```

There are two special points to notice about this declaration format:

- Status keywords *must* be preceded by, and can be followed by, a space or another valid parameter separator, such as a comment or parameter entity reference.
- No other spaces are allowed within the delimiter sequences used to identify the start and end of a marked section.

The five **status keywords** that can be used in the status keyword specification are:

- `CDATA` to indicate that the contents of the marked section are to be treated as **character data** that does not contain any resolvable SGML markup;
- `RCDATA` to indicate that the contents of the marked section are to be treated as **replaceable character data** in which any character references, `CDATA`, `SDATA` or text entity references are to be resolved before the marked section is output;
- `IGNORE` to indicate that the contents of the marked section are to be ignored during parsing;

- INCLUDE to indicate that the contents of the marked section are to be parsed;
- TEMP to indicate that the section is a temporary part of the document.

Where no keyword is specified the INCLUDE keyword is assumed.

Where multiple keywords have been entered, and where marked sections are embedded within other marked sections, the order of precedence/inheritance that applies to the entered keywords (highest priority shown first) is:

- IGNORE
- CDATA
- RCDATA
- INCLUDE

Embedded marked sections are only recognized where INCLUDE, IGNORE and TEMP are the only keywords used in the status keyword specification. Marked sections cannot be embedded within sections defined using the CDATA or RCDATA keywords because, within such sections, the parser only looks for the next marked section end delimiter sequence (]]>). As soon as it encounters this sequence it will terminate the section that started with CDATA or RCDATA, rather than any embedded marked section.

It should also be noted that marked sections can only contain valid SGML characters as non-SGML data must always be called as part of an NDATA external entity. The fact that a marked section is flagged to be ignored does not mean that it may contain non-SGML (shunned) characters.

8.3 Using marked sections

The CDATA and RCDATA keywords are typically used in situations where the author wishes to output SGML tags as part of his text. Only one of these two keywords should be used in any marked section keyword list.

To include an example such as:

```
<EM>emphasized phrase</EM>
```

within a paragraph (without using an entity reference) you could enter it as:

```
<![ CDATA [<EM>highlighted phrase</EM>]]>
```

The CDATA keyword tells the parser that the contents of the marked section are to be sent directly to the parser's output stream, without being checked for embedded markup.

If the section of text to be marked contains characters which cannot be entered directly (for example, because they are not part of the document's character set and so have to be defined as character references) the RCDATA keyword can be used in place of CDATA. This will tell the parser that it must resolve any general entity or character references within the marked section of text during parsing. For example, to generate the sequence:

```
<SIZE>12μm</SIZE>
```

you could enter:

```
<![ RCDATA [<SIZE>12&micro;m</SIZE>]]>
```

to ensure that the character reference will be correctly resolved to the μ character while the start-tag and end-tag of the highlighted phrase are retained as part of the text.

The sequence]]> cannot be entered directly within a marked section when the reference concrete syntax is being used. When preparing examples of marked sections, remember to change at least one character of the current markup section close delimiter. Normally the last character of the nested marked section will be changed to >, and the first to <, to ensure that the example will not be treated as a marked section, giving it the form:

```
<![ CDATA [&lt;![ RCDATA [<SIZE>12&micro;m</SIZE>]]&gt;]]>
```

8.3.1 Ignored sections

The IGNORE and INCLUDE status keywords are normally used to identify marked sections of text that belongs to different versions of a document. To allow users to control which version is to be output, the relevant status keywords are normally defined as parameter entities in a *document type declaration subset* at the start of the document so that they can be quickly redefined when the job is reprocessed. (Marked section keyword definitions are one of the few places where a parameter entity reference is valid within a document instance.)

In a typical application the necessary parameter entities might be defined as:

```
<!ENTITY % mark1 "IGNORE" -- Identifies text specifically for Mark 1 -- >
<!ENTITY % mark2 "INCLUDE" -- Identifies text specifically for Mark 2 -- >
```

The associated parameter entity references, %mark1; and %mark2; can be used within a marked section declaration in the text to identify text that applies to a particular version of the product, as the following example illustrates:

```
<P>To install the card:<UL>
   <LI>switch off the power supply
   <![ %mark1; [<LI>unscrew the retaining bolts holding the cover]]>
   <![ %mark2; [<LI>unclip the cover]]>
   <LI>select a spare card slot ...
```

Normally, the first of the marked sections would be ignored so that the later, Mark 2, version is printed. If, however, it became necessary to reprint the Mark

1 version of the instructions, the only parts of the document that need to be changed are the two entity declarations in the document type declaration subset, which would be changed to read:

```
<!ENTITY % mark1 "INCLUDE" -- Identifies text specifically for Mark 1 -- >
<!ENTITY % mark2 "IGNORE" -- Identifies text specifically for Mark 2 -- >
```

The above technique can be extended to any number of versions, affecting many sections of text, provided that care is taken not to overlap marked sections.

The IGNORE keyword can also be used to prevent notes added to the text as reminders from being printed. While such notes can be flagged directly with the `IGNORE` keyword, so that they are never processed, it is better practice to use a parameter entity to control when they should be parsed. For example, the parameter entity:

```
<!ENTITY % comment "IGNORE" >
```

could be used in conjunction with a declaration of the form:

```
<![ %comment; [Remember to say something about Marked Sections.]]>
```

If such notes are to appear in a draft all the author needs to do is change the entity declaration to read:

```
<!ENTITY % comment "INCLUDE" >
```

or even:

```
<!ENTITY % comment "" >
```

(Remember that when no keyword is specified the `INCLUDE` keyword is assumed.)

8.3.2 Temporary sections

There are occasions when part of a document may only be required temporarily. For example, you may need to add the phrase 'in preparation' to a citation until such time as the cited work is published. In this case the `TEMP` keyword can be used to identify the marked section as one that will need to be removed later. Typically the entry will take the form:

```
<CITATION>Bryan, M. T. (1997) <EM>SGML and HTML Explained</EM>
<![ TEMP [(in preparation)]]></CITATION>
```

The `TEMP` keyword is only a flag; it does not affect the way in which the text is processed. In the above example the program treats the marked section in exactly the same way that it would treat a section for which no keyword has been entered; it acts as if `INCLUDE` had been entered alongside `TEMP`. The only difference between the above declaration and a declaration of the form:

```
<CITATION>Bryan, M. T. (1997) <EM>SGML and HTML Explained</EM>
<![[(in preparation)]]></CITATION>
```

is that requesting the removal of the section when it is no longer required will be easier when the TEMP keyword is present because the program can identify such marked sections as ones that may need to be discarded.

8.3.3 Combining keywords

More than one keyword can appear at the start of a marked section declaration. For example, once the publication mentioned in the above citation has been published, the word IGNORE could be added to the marked section declaration to avoid having to delete the text. The stored citation could then have the form:

```
<CITATION>Bryan, M. T. (1997)
<EM>SGML and HTML Explained</EM>
<![ IGNORE TEMP [(in preparation)]]>
</CITATION>
```

By retaining the temporary section in this case, any future users of the citation will be able to see that it was prepared before the book was published, which should act as a warning that the citation may not be complete.

8.3.4 Storing marked sections as entities

Where a marked section is likely to be used more than once in a document it can be stored as an entity. To speed up identification of the text as a marked section, the MS keyword should be used in the entity declaration. The parser will then automatically add the marked section open and close delimiter sequences to the replacement text entered for the entity. For example, if the temporary 'in preparation' marked section declaration defined above was to be used in a number of citations it could be declared as an entity by entering:

```
<!ENTITY inprep MS " TEMP [(in preparation)" >
```

Once the entity has been defined in this way the citation can be altered to read:

```
<CITATION>Bryan, M. T. (1997) <EM>SGML Explained</EM> &inprep;</CITA-
TION>
```

When storing marked sections as entities, however, it is important to remember that all of the delimiters of the marked section must be defined within the same entity. For example, the entity references:

```
<!ENTITY ignore "<[IGNORE ["
> <!ENTITY message "Remember to check this before publication" >
```

could *not* be used to create a marked section by entry of a definition such as:

```
&ignore;&message;]]>
```

8.3.5 Nested marked sections

SGML allows marked sections to be nested up to the level defined by the currently active TAGLVL quantity. By default, up to 24 different levels of marked sections can be active at any point in the document. Only sections defined using the INCLUDE, IGNORE and TEMP keywords can contain nested marked sections.

To see how nesting works, consider the following example:

```
<!DOCTYPE book SYSTEM "my-book.dtd" [
<!ENTITY % bibliog "INCLUDE" >
<!ENTITY % comment "IGNORE" >
<!ENTITY inprep MS " TEMP [(in preparation)" > ]>
<book>
...
<![ %bibliog; [<H1>References</H1>
<CITATION>Bryan, M. T. (1997) <EM>SGML Explained</EM> &inprep;</CITATION>
<![ %comment; [Need to cite Burn's paper here &inprep;]]>
...
]]>
```

Here the bibliography is to be included in the document, but, because in some cases it will not be required, it has been treated as a marked section, the presence of which can be controlled by use of the %bibliog; parameter entity. Within the bibliography further marked sections have been used to define temporary additions to the citation (for example, the comment) and to add a note for the author. Notice that, within the note, the &inprep; entity reference has been used as a reminder of why the details still need to be added. This reference to an embedded marked section will, however, only be expanded if the keyword stored in the %comment; parameter entity reference is changed to INCLUDE.

If the entity declaration for the %bibliog; entity reference is changed to:

```
<!ENTITY % bibliog "IGNORE" >
```

all the marked sections embedded within the bibliography will be ignored because the IGNORE keyword in the outermost marked section has precedence over all other embedded keywords.

8.4 Processing instructions

Processing instructions are instructions to the local system telling it, in its own language, how to process the document. Typically processing instructions are used to define how the following text should be formatted. Because such instructions are system specific, and often also application dependent, they need to be specially identified so that, for example, when the document is sent to another system, or its format is changed, any processing instructions incorporated in the document, or its document type declaration, can be changed accordingly.

Because processing instructions are normally written in a language that is known only to the current system, or to systems using a similar set of instructions, the instructions cannot be entered as part of the generalized coding used for SGML. To distinguish the processing instructions from other markup, therefore, they are enclosed in a special set of delimiters known as the **processing instruction open** (`PIO`) and **processing instruction close** (`PIC`) delimiters. In the reference concrete syntax `PIO` is <? and `PIC` is >.

The format of the data within the processing instruction is determined by the processing system. The only restrictions placed on the format of processing instructions by SGML is that:

- They may only contain characters recognized as SGML characters.
- They may not contain the character used as the processing instruction close delimiter.

It should be noted that, once a processing instruction has been started, the SGML parser will ignore all characters up to and including the currently defined processing instruction close sequence.

The maximum length of individual processing instructions is controlled by the `PILEN` quantity in the SGML declaration. In the reference concrete syntax `PILEN` is set to 240.

8.5 Using processing instructions in marked sections

Where two different systems may to be used to format a document, the marked section facility can be used to control the processing instructions used on each system. For example, two sets of processing instructions could be entered in the text as:

```
<![ %systema; [<?processing instruction for System A>]]>
<![ %systemb; [<?processing instruction for System B>]]>
```

While the document is being processed on System A the associated parameter entities would be defined as:

```
<!ENTITY % systema "INCLUDE" >
<!ENTITY % systemb "IGNORE" >
```

When the document is transferred to System B the processing instructions used can be quickly changed by altering the entity declarations to read:

```
<!ENTITY % systema "IGNORE" >
<!ENTITY % systemb "INCLUDE" >
```

Tag minimization

Types of minimization • Tag omission • Short tags • Tag grouping (rank) • Automatic tag recognition (data tags)

This chapter explains the rules provided in SGML to reduce the number/size of markup tags that need to be entered by users.

9.1 Types of minimization

SGML provides four main techniques for minimizing the number and length of a document's markup tags:

- tag omission (OMITTAG);
- tag shortening (SHORTTAG);
- tag grouping (RANK);
- automatic tag recognition (DATATAG).

The intention to use tag minimization features must be indicated by activating the appropriate MINIMIZE options in the FEATURES clause of the SGML declaration. By default only the OMITTAG and SHORTTAG options may be used.

9.2 Tag omission

The most commonly used form of minimization is **tag omission**. This optional SGML feature allows tags to be omitted when their presence can be *unambiguously* implied by the program from the structure of the document declared in the document type definition.

Whenever the FEATURES clause of the SGML declaration contains the entry OMITTAG YES, all element declarations in the document type definition *must* contain two characters defining the type of **omitted tag minimization** permitted for the declared element(s). The first of these two characters is set to O (the letter O rather than the number 0) if the element's start-tag can be omitted; otherwise a hyphen is entered. If the element's end-tag can be omitted the second character is set to O; otherwise a hyphen is entered. The two characters must be separated by a space (or any other valid separator character) and must be separated from the preceding element name, and the following model for the element's contents, by further spaces or separator characters.

Note: *If tag omission has not been permitted in the SGML declaration the two tag omission characters can still be present in the element declaration. It is, therefore, standard practice to put tag omission rules into DTDs even when the* `MINIMIZE` *section of the* `FEATURES` *clause contains an entry of* `OMITTAG NO` *in the SGML declaration.*

9.2.1 Start-tag omission

Start-tags can only be omitted from a document when both of the following apply:

- The element concerned is contextually required (that is, it must occur at that position).
- Any other element that could occur at the same point, such as an element specified as an inclusion, is contextually optional.

Start-tag minimization should, therefore, only be used where the elements in the currently active model group are connected with sequence (`SEQ`) connectors. (If the `AND` or `OR` connectors are used, the parsing program will not be able to determine uniquely which element's tag has been omitted.) Similarly, elements whose start-tags may be omitted should not be optional, that is, have an `OPT` (`?`) or `REP` (`*`) occurrence indicator next to the element name, as such indicators make it impossible to identify which element should occur next.

Start-tags cannot be omitted for elements whose content type has been declared using the `RCDATA`, `CDATA` or `EMPTY` reserved names. Start-tags should also not be omitted where the first character in the element with the omitted tag is one of the short reference characters associated with the element in a short reference (`SHORTREF`) declaration that has been associated with the element through a short reference use (`USEMAP`) declaration, especially where the short reference would be associated with a different entity if the start-tag were not present.

When the presence of an omitted start-tag is implied by the parser, the currently defined default values will automatically be used for any attributes associated with the element. It is important, therefore, before start-tag omission is permitted, to ensure that the default values of any attributes associated with elements that may have their start-tags omitted are checked carefully. If any of the attributes associated with the element has a required attribute, either because its default value has been declared using the

#REQUIRED keyword or because the default value is #CURRENT and the element has not yet been used, the start-tag cannot be omitted. In such cases the full tag, including all compulsory attributes, must be added to the text.

9.2.2 End-tag omission

The rules governing the omission of end-tags are much less restrictive than those for start-tags. End-tags can be omitted wherever the tag is followed by the end-tag of another currently open element (one started at a higher level than the current element) *or* when the tag is followed by an element, or data character, that is not a permitted part of the element's content model. End-tags can also be omitted if their presence can be implied by the end of an SGML document or subdocument.

9.2.3 Omitting tags

The following elements will be used to illustrate the effect of tag omission:

```
<!ELEMENT section - O (title, p+, subsection*) >
<!ELEMENT title   O O (#PCDATA) >
<!ELEMENT p       - O (#PCDATA|%phrases;|q)+ >
```

If tag omission is not permitted by the current concrete syntax (that is, OMITTAG NO has been specified in the SGML declaration), a section defined using this model would need to be coded as:

```
<SECTION><TITLE>Section Headings</TITLE>
<P>Section headings should indicate ...
... end of the paragraph.</P>
<P>An alternative use for section headings ...
... at the end of the section.</P></SECTION>
```

Here each start-tag is matched by an equivalent end-tag, the start of each compulsory element in the model group always being required.

When tag omission is allowed, however, the coding can be simplified to:

```
<SECTION>Section Headings
<P>Section headings should indicate ...
... end of the paragraph.
<P>An alternative use for section headings ...
... at the end of the section.</SECTION>
```

In this example the tag minimization option has led to a halving of the number of tags that need to be added to the text. Let us look at how this was achieved.

The most important saving occurred in the section title, where both the start- and end-tags have been omitted. The start-tag can be omitted because the absence of this compulsory first embedded subelement could be implied by the parser from the content model of the section element (<SECTION>). The parser knows from the content model that, before it can accept any data for the section, it must receive a start-tag for the <TITLE> element . As soon as it sees a character other than a start-tag delimiter (<) it will recognize that the character should be preceded by <TITLE>.

The end-tag for the title can be omitted because the <P> used to identify the start of the first paragraph in the section is not valid within the content model of the section title. As the section title can only consist of text the parsing program will automatically recognize that a </TITLE> tag should precede the first of the <P> tags.

The two paragraph end-tags (</P>) have been omitted from the minimized version of the coded text for different reasons. At the end of the first paragraph the tag can be omitted because the content model for the paragraph element does not allow other paragraphs to be directly embedded within a paragraph. As soon as the parsing program sees the second <P> it knows it can infer the presence of the end-tag of the preceding paragraph.

The second of the paragraph end-tags has been omitted because it is immediately followed by the end-tag of an element at a higher level in the document's structure. Providing the OMITTAG option has been activated, the parsing program will automatically close any currently open embedded element that has been declared as having omissible end-tags when it encounters an end-tag for a higher level element. (If an embedded element whose end-tag cannot be omitted is still open, however, the program will report an error in the coding.)

It should be noted that the presence of the </SECTION> tag is not compulsory. If the section shown in the above example was immediately followed by another section its end-tag could be omitted to give an entry of the form:

```
<SECTION>Section Headings
<P>Section headings should indicate ...
... end of the paragraph.
<P>An alternative use for section headings ...
... at the end of the section.
<SECTION>Omitting Tags
<P>When specified in an element's declaration ...
```

When an SGML parser analyzes this part of the document, the presence of the start-tag (<SECTION>) for the second section will cause it to infer the presence of an </SECTION> tag at the end of the first section. From the presence of this implied end-tag the program will also be able to identify the need for a </P> tag to close the last paragraph of the preceding section.

9.3 Short tags

Shortened versions of tags can be used whenever the FEATURES clause of the SGML declaration contains the statement SHORTTAG YES. There are four ways in which element tags can be shortened:

- empty tags created by omitting the generic identifier (element name) from the tag;
- unclosed tags created by omitting the closing delimiter of the tag;
- null end-tags created by using the **null end-tag** delimiter in place of a tag close delimiter;
- tags with attribute names omitted.

9.3.1 Empty tags

Empty tags are tags from which the element's name (and any attributes) has been omitted. In its simplest form an **empty start-tag** consists of the currently defined start-tag open and tag close symbols (< and > respectively in the reference concrete syntax), without an intervening space. Similarly an **empty end-tag** consists of the currently defined end-tag open and tag close delimiters (</ and > in the reference concrete syntax).

Empty tags can only be associated with the base document type, that is, they apply to the first document type defined in the prolog. For empty end-tags the generic identifier added by the program is always the name of the last element to be opened in the base document type.

The way in which the program interprets an empty start-tag depends on whether or not tags can also be omitted from the document. If `OMITTAG YES` has been specified in the SGML declaration, the parser will give an empty start-tag the generic identifier of the most recently started element in the base document type. Otherwise, the generic identifier used will be that of the most recently ended element in the base document.

Where tag omission is permitted, the first of the above rules allows the program to infer which generic identifier it should use before determining whether or not a tag has been omitted from the markup. By presuming that the last-opened element is to be repeated, the parser has a value which it can use to check for the omission of end-tags. It can then determine whether the last element used should be closed by the addition of an implied end-tag, or whether the new tag represents a further level of nesting within the document's structure.

When tags cannot be omitted, the last element to be closed is presumed to be the one to be repeated, even if the element is not a repeatable element. This can, unfortunately, lead to errors where the last element used is not repeatable, because the program can report an empty start-tag as an error, even when the content model unambiguously defines which element must occur next. For this reason it is better not to allow short tag minimization while tag omission is forbidden.

Typically a piece of text coded using empty tags will take the form:

```
<P>This paragraph contains two lists. The first has four
entries:<OL>
```

```
<LI>item 1
<>item 2
<>item 3
<>item 4</></>
while the second only has two:<UL>
<LI>first item
<>second item.</></>
<>Multiple lists ...
```

In this example the first three empty start-tags, and the first empty end-tag, will be given a generic identifier of LI as this was the last element to be started. Once the last of the items in the first list has been formally closed by the first empty end-tag, the ordered list (<OL>) becomes the currently active element. This list then is closed by the next empty end-tag (the second one of the first pair) before the second part of the paragraph element can be processed. The next empty start-tag and the first of the two empty end-tags are assigned LI as their element name. The last end-tag will close down the unordered list (UL) .

Provided OMITTAG YES has been specified in the SGML declaration, and tag omission has been allowed for all end-tags, the last empty start-tag will cause the currently open element, the paragraph element, to be closed before the element name is reused as the name of the new element. The final result of parsing will be a file of the form:

```
<P>This paragraph contains two lists. The first has four
entries:<OL>
<LI>item 1</LI>
<LI>item 2</LI>
<LI>item 3</LI>
<LI>item 4</LI></OL>
while the second only has two:<UL>
<LI>first item</LI>
<LI>second item.</LI></UL></P>
<P>Multiple lists ...
```

9.3.2 Unclosed tags

Where two or more consecutive tags are required in a document, the end delimiters of all tags but the last one in the sequence can, if SHORTTAG YES has been specified in the SGML declaration, be omitted. No restriction is placed on whether the next tag in the sequence is a start-tag or an end-tag: end-tags can be followed by start-tags, and vice versa. The four permissible combinations are illustrated by the following examples:

```
<P<EM>
</EM</P>
</TITLE<P>
<ARTWORK sizey=120mm</P>
```

In the first case a new paragraph is to start with an emphasized phrase. An **unclosed start-tag** has been used for the first of the tags. The second example shows how the tags could be minimized by using an **unclosed end-tag** if a paragraph ended with an emphasized phrase. The third example shows a paragraph starting immediately after a title. The final example shows how the tags might be combined when the first tag has attributes associated with it.

Note: *The use of unclosed tags is deprecated by the SGML community, but it can be useful in overcoming keying errors in environments that do not use SGML-sensitive editors for data capture.*

9.3.3 Null end-tags

Null end-tags provide a means of specifying the end of an element in the base document type with a single character. In the reference concrete syntax the character defined as the **null end-tag** (NET) delimiter is the solidus (slash), but any code not defined as a name character can be assigned to this role within the SGML declaration.

Two stages are involved in activating the null end-tag option. The first step involves creating a **net-enabling start-tag** by replacing the tag close (TAGC) delimiter at the end of an element's start-tag with a NET delimiter. The second step involves replacing the whole of the element's end-tag with a matching NET code. Let's see how this works in practice by looking at the use of an <ISBN> element which can be defined as:

```
<!ELEMENT ISBN - - CDATA -ISBN number- >
```

Instead of entering an ISBN as:

```
<ISBN>0 201 17535 5</ISBN>
```

we can use the null end-tag option to enter the element in the form:

```
<ISBN/0 201 17535 5/
```

Notice that, by replacing the end delimiter of the start-tag with the special NET code, we have been able to reduce the end-tag to a single, matching, character. This feature is particularly useful when the content of the model has been declared, as in the above case, using the reserved name CDATA, or RCDATA, where the presence of an end-tag is compulsory.

Null end-tags can be used for any element declared in the base document that does not require the character assigned to the null end-tag role in its contents, or those of any embedded elements. However, because care is needed to ensure that the relevant element is not prematurely ended by entry of the character assigned as the NET code, null end-tags are normally only used for elements that do not contain embedded subelements.

Null end-tags can be nested to any level permitted for elements (typically the default value of 24 levels). Each null end-tag identified by the program closes down the last element defined using a net-enabling start-tag (one whose tag ends with a NET code). The following example shows how null end-tags can, with care, be embedded within each other:

```
<P/Nested <EM/net-enabling start-tags/ are permitted, as this
   example shows./
```

The main point to notice about this example is that the number of net-enabling start-tags exactly matches the number of individual null end-tags in the paragraph.

The following is an example of an illegal use of a null end-tag:

```
<P/Paragraphs cannot contain either/or choices if
started with a net-enabling start-tag./
```

A program receiving this would terminate the paragraph after the word 'either'. It would then place the rest of the paragraph in the next higher open element, if permitted to, treating the slash intended to end the paragraph as a normal text character (unless the element concerned had been opened using a null end-tag!).

One way of avoiding this problem is to use a character reference, or an entity reference, to generate the embedded slash. In this case the paragraph could be amended to read:

```
<P/Paragraphs cannot contain either&#47;or choices if
started with a net-enabling start-tag./
```

or:

```
<P/Paragraphs cannot contain either&sol;or choices if
started with a net-enabling start-tag./
```

where / has been defined as:

```
<!ENTITY sol CDATA "/">
```

9.3.4 Omitting attribute names

As mentioned in Section 5.4, there are two ways in which attribute specifications can be shortened when the default SHORTTAG YES entry in the SGML declaration has been left unchanged:

- The literal delimiters can be omitted if the only characters used in the value are ones currently declared as *name characters*.
- When the entered attribute value has been declared as a member of a set of valid attribute values for the element, the attribute name and the immediately following value indicator (=) can both be omitted.

For example, a start-tag of the form <ARTWORK width="40mm" align= "center"> could be shortened to read <ARTWORK width=40mm center>.

9.4 Tag grouping (rank)

When the current SGML declaration contains the statement `RANK YES` in the `FEATURES` clause, elements can be declared as **ranked elements**. When an element declaration contains a **rank stem** and a **rank suffix**, the element's start-tag can be shortened by omission of the rank suffix, provided that the element concerned has been entered in full (that is, with a numeric rank suffix) at some preceding point in the document. A typical declaration might take the form:

```
<!ELEMENT HEADING 1 - - (#PCDATA) >
```

Where a single element declaration has been used for a ranked group of elements, the rank suffix that is added to the end of a minimized ranked element is the last rank number entered for any member of that ranked group. For example, headings and related paragraphs could share the following model:

```
<!ELEMENT (HEADING|P) 1 - - (#PCDATA) +(%phrases;) >
```

Note: *As the rank option has been found to be confusing to users use of this option will be deprecated in the next edition of ISO 8879. For this reason this optional SGML feature is not covered in any depth in this book. A more in-depth discussion of this feature can be found in Chapter 5 of* SGML: An Author's Guide to the Standard Generalized Markup Language *(Bryan, 1988).*

9.5 Automatic tag recognition (data tags)

Data tags are sequences of characters which, as well as forming part of the document, also mark the *end* of an element. Whenever the data tag option has been activated by entry of `DATATAG YES` in the `FEATURES` clause of the SGML declaration, the parser will check the content of those elements, the declarations of which contain data tag definitions, to see if it can identify the end of the element from the presence of a specified string of characters.

Data tags are declared within the *content model* of an element in the base document's DTD by replacing the name of one or more of the embedded elements with a **data tag group**. Each data tag group is enclosed within a special pair of delimiters known as the **data tag group open** (DTGO) and **data tag group close** (DTGC) delimiters. In the reference concrete syntax these delimiters are the open and close square brackets. The declaration within these delimiters has two main parts: the **generic identifier** of the element concerned and the **data tag pattern**, which the parser searchers for whenever the specified element has been opened. The data tag pattern can also consist of two parts. Each pattern must start with a **data tag template**, or a **data tag template group**, which defines the character sequence(s) the parser is to look for. This can optionally be followed by a **data tag padding template** that identifies one or more characters which should be skipped if they occur immediately after a data tag. Each part of the data tag group is separated from the others by the currently defined sequence indicator (SEQ, a comma in the reference concrete syntax).

To see how data tags work consider the following set of declarations:

```
<!ELEMENT  mission   - - (delegate+) >
<!ELEMENT  delegate O O ([name, ", ", " "], for) >
<!ELEMENT  name      O O (#PCDATA) >
<!ELEMENT  for       O O (#PCDATA) >
<!ENTITY   entry     STARTTAG "delegate" >
<!SHORTREF map1      "&#RS;" entry >
<!USEMAP   map1      mission >
```

A data tag template, consisting of a comma followed by a space, has been associated with the element called <NAME> that forms the first element within the <DELEGATE> element's content model. Optionally this template can be followed by more spaces, which the program should treat as part of the data tag. The short reference map associated with the <MISSION> element shows that a record start code (RS) will be recognized as the start of a new <DELEGATE> entry.

To see how the these declarations affect the coding of a document consider the following list of members on a mission:

```
<MISSION>
James D. Mason,        ANSI
Charles F. Goldfarb, ANSI
James Clark,           BSI
Martin Bryan,          BSI
Yushi Komachi,         JIS</MISSION>
```

As soon as the parser encounters the start-tag for the <MISSION> element it will invoke the short reference map (map1) that will identify the start of each line as the start of a <DELEGATE> entry.

Each <DELEGATE> element starts with the <NAME> of a delegate, the end of the name being indicated by a comma and at least one space. When the parser sees this data tag sequence it will automatically infer the presence of a </NAME> end-tag. As the comma, and any immediately following spaces, are not part of the delegate's name, or part of the <FOR> element, the program automatically treats the data tag as an implied #PCDATA element, so that the <DELEGATE> element is considered to be defined as:

```
<!ELEMENT delegate (name, #PCDATA, for) >
```

where #PCDATA can only consist of a comma followed by one or more spaces.

Because data tags act as real end-tags, rather than omitted end-tags, once the parser has identified the end-tag for the <NAME> element, it will also be able to infer the presence of the start-tag immediately after the data tag template because the declaration for the <DELEGATE> element tells it that a <FOR> element must follow.

The combination of the data tag and the short reference for the <MISSION> element means that the program would treat the uncoded text as if it had been coded:

```
<MISSION>
<DELEGATE><NAME>James D. Mason</NAME>,       <FOR>ANSI</FOR>
<DELEGATE><NAME>Charles F. Goldfarb</NAME>, <FOR>ANSI</FOR>
<DELEGATE><NAME>James Clark</NAME>,          <FOR>BSI</FOR>
<DELEGATE><NAME>Martin Bryan</NAME>,         <FOR>BSI</FOR>
<DELEGATE><NAME>Yuchi Komachi</NAME>,        <FOR>JIS</FOR></MISSION>
```

It is important to realize the difference between the role of the data tag and the short reference in the above example. While the short reference *replaces* the record start character it is linked to, the characters defined in the data tag template are *retained as a special piece of (implied) parsed character data*. It should also be realized that the data tag is looked for only whilst the <NAME> element remains the currently open element, while the short reference applies to any embedded elements as well (unless they invoke their own short reference map).

When declaring data tag templates, it is important to ensure that the length of the data tag template, or data tag padding template, does not exceed that declared as the DTEMPLEN quantity in the SGML declaration. Similarly the data tags entered in the text, including any padding characters, must not exceed the DTAGLEN quantity. In the reference concrete syntax both of these quantities are set to 16 characters.

Data tag templates cannot include *numeric* character references to non-SGML characters or SGML function characters, though these are permitted in entity strings. This prohibits the use of the 	 sequence to identify a Tab code in a data tag, though it would be a valid part of the replacement text of an entity. If, for example, the Tab code had been used within the above example to position the second column, the declaration for the <DELEGATE> element would need to be altered to:

```
<!ELEMENT delegate - O ([name, ",&#TAB;", "&#TAB;"], for) >
```

It should, however, be noted that if this declaration is to be used, all entries must be keyed without any spaces between the comma and the Tab code. If there is a likelihood that the typist may key a space after the comma, the range of permitted data tags should be extended by defining all the valid templates in a data tag template group. As with other groups within the content model, the data tag template group is enclosed by group open and group close symbols (left and right brackets in the reference concrete syntax). In the case of data tag template groups, the entries within the group must be separated by OR connectors. This gives the entry the form:

```
<!ELEMENT delegate - O ([name, (",  "|",&#TAB;"|", &#TAB;"),
                                   "&#TAB;"], for) >
```

Unfortunately, groups are not permitted for the data tag padding template, so, if Tab codes are used to move to the start of the next column, any following spaces will not be recognized as a part of the template and so will not be removed from the data stream.

Multiple document structures (SUBDOC, CONCUR and LINK)

Types of multiple document structures • SGML subdocuments • Concurrent document structures • Linking document structures

This chapter explains some of the optional SGML features that are provided by a few advanced SGML tools.

10.1 Types of multiple document structures

More than one document structure may be required to cope with the varying roles of the data stored in an SGML document. Sometimes the different document structures are used individually; at other times concurrent multiple roles can be allocated to a single piece of text. Three different techniques for relating document structures are provided in SGML:

- embedding files that are coded using an alternative document structure (SUBDOCuments);
- marking up documents using multiple CONCURrent DTDs;
- Creating automatically processable LINKs between the structures declared in different DTDs.

Where a document is made up from a number of previously prepared subsections, each of which may have its own document structure, the individual subsections can be created as externally stored subdocuments of the main document. Subdocuments must be declared as external entities in the document type declaration that is used by the calling document. At the appropriate point in the text an entity reference is used to call the previously declared subdocument into the main document.

Concurrent document structures can be used, for example, to distinguish between the different purposes to which data may be put (for example, for book production, CD-ROM delivery or on-line database retrieval), or to identify structures generated during the processing of a document (for example, the layout structure of a formatted book). Each concurrent structure used within the document must be declared in the document's prolog using a separate document type declaration.

Note: *The concept of concurrent structures is particulary important to the Association for Computing in the Humanities' Text Encoding Initiative (TEI), where it is used for recording the way in which particular editions of a work have been paginated or edited.*

Where it is possible to create one structure automatically from another, the parser can be instructed to create the alternative structure automatically using SGML's explicit link (`EXPLICIT`) feature. Simpler controls on processing are provided by the simple link (`SIMPLE`) option, to control the processing of the whole document, and the implicit link (`IMPLICIT`) option, to control the processing of individual elements.

Note: *Links cannot be used at the same time as concurrent markup structures, because concurrent document types cannot be activated when link types are active.*

10.2 SGML subdocuments

SGML **subdocuments** are self-contained, externally stored, entities that consist of a document type declaration followed by text marked up with the entities, elements and attributes defined in the local declaration.

SGML subdocuments are particularly useful where a document contains special sections of data that are, typically, produced from different sources. If, for example, complex tables are to be generated from a spreadsheet package, the DTD used to validate tables produced by the package can be transmitted with the table when it is exported to another document, avoiding the need to ensure that the table structure in the receiving document matches that of all the programs supplying it with information.

Before preparing text for use as a subdocument of another document, it is important to ensure that the same SGML declaration will be used for each subdocument in the overall document. *It is the SGML declaration of the main document that applies to an SGML subdocument, because subdocuments may not contain their own SGML declarations.* If a local SGML declaration has been added to the subdocument while it is being prepared, it will need to be removed before the file can be used as a subdocument within another document.

If subdocuments are to be used, the `SUBDOC NO` entry in the `OTHER` section of the `FEATURES` clause of the SGML declaration must be changed to `SUBDOC YES n`, where `n` indicates the maximum number of subdocuments that will be open at any point in the document.

Once a subdocument file has been prepared, it must be declared as an external entity before it can be called. If the subdocument is stored locally it can be declared as a system-specific entity by entry of an entity declaration such as:

```
<!ENTITY paper1 SYSTEM "c:\pub\captured.txt" SUBDOC>
```

If the system can recognize the name of the file automatically from the entity's name, the optional **system identifier** (for example, `"c:\pub\captured.txt"`) can be omitted to give an entity declaration such as:

```
<!ENTITY captured SYSTEM SUBDOC>
```

Where the subdocument's contents are already known to all systems likely to receive the document, the entity can be publicly declared by entry of a declaration such as:

```
<!ENTITY copyrite PUBLIC "-//OPOCE//DOCUMENT Copyright notice
//EN" SUBDOC >
```

It should be noted that, even though they contain markup declarations, SGML subdocuments are defined as general entities rather than parameter entities. This is because the entity reference for the subdocument must occur at the appropriate point within the text of the document instance, rather than within the document prolog.

A previously defined subdocument should be called by entering an entity reference, such as `©rite;`, at the appropriate point in the text. Before requesting a subdocument from the system, an SGML parser will record the current state of the processor for recall after the subdocument has been processed.

A typical document instance referencing stored subdocuments might look like this:

```
<!DOCTYPE SUP PUBLIC "-//OPOCE//DTD OJ Supplement//EN" [
 <!ENTITY rec94372 SYSTEM "rec94372.cat" SUBDOC>
```

```
 <!ENTITY txt94372 SYSTEM "al94-372.enc" SUBDOC>
]>
<SUP><RECORD ID="FXAL94372ENC">&rec94372;&txt94372;</sup>
```

Within a subdocument only locally defined markup declarations apply. This means that you cannot cross-refer to an identifier declared in the main document from within a subdocument, or vice versa.

Note: *ISO/IEC 10744, the Hypermedia/Time-based Structuring Language (HyTime), shows how SGML can be extended to allow references in one document to reference identifiers in another document, which could be an embedded subdocument.*

10.3 Concurrent document structures

Where two or more 'views' of a document's contents can exist concurrently, more than one document type declaration can be specified at the start of a document. For example, if data is to be stored in a controlled document database and also displayed on the World Wide Web, it may be necessary to indicate two different roles for a piece of text in its markup, as the following (somewhat simplified) example shows:

```
<(TEI.2)TEI.2><(HTML)HTML>
<!--TEI header elements omitted here for simplicity-->
<(TEI.2)BIBL><(TEI.2)MONOGR><(HTML)HEAD>
<(TEI.2)AUTHOR><(HTML)TITLE>Shirley,          James</(HTML)TITLE></
(TEI.2)AUTHOR>
</(HTML)HEAD><(HTML)BODY>
<(TEI.2)TITLE type=main><(HTML)H2>
The Gentlemen of Venice
</(HTML)H2></(TEI.2)TITLE>
<(TEI.2)TITLE type=subordinate><(HTML)H3>
A tragi-comedie presented at the private house in Salisbury Court
by Her Majesties servants
</(HTML)H3)</(TEI.2)TITLE>
<(TEI.2)IMPRINT><(HTML)ADDRESS>
<(TEI.2)PUBLISHER>H. Moseley</(TEI.2)PUBLISHER><(HTML)BR>
<(TEI.2)PUBPLACE>London</(TEI.2)PUBPLACE></(HTML)ADDRESS>
<(TEI.2)DATE><(HTML)P><(HTML)STRONG>
1655
</(HTML)STRONG></(HTML)P)</(TEI.2)DATE></(TEI.2)IMPRINT>
<(TEI.2)EXTENT><(HTML)P>78pp</(HTML)P></(TEI.2)EXTENT>
</(TEI.2)MONOGR></(TEI.2)BIBL></(HTML)BODY>
</(TEI.2)TEI.2></(HTML)HTML>
```

Notice how the names of the elements have been qualified by a bracketed **document type specification** to indicate which of the DTDs declared in the document prolog they are associated with. In this case two well known industry standard DTDs have been used, that of the Text Encoding Initiative (TEI) and that of the HyperText Markup Language (HTML) used on the World Wide Web.

Note: *For simplicity's sake I have omitted the TEI header elements that should precede the start of the bibliographic entry (<BIBL>) information. The reasons for this omission will be explained shortly.*

It is important to note that there is not, in this example, a one-to-one correspondence between the occurrences of elements within the two DTDs. For example, within the address element of HTML there is no equivalent of a line element. Instead the HTML linebreak (<BR>) empty element is associated with the end-tag of the TEI publisher element.

More than one element may sometimes need to be used in one structure to obtain the correct result in another structure. For example, to print the TEI date in a bolder typeface and on a separate line within HTML it is necessary to associate the <(TEI)DATE> element with two HTML elements, <(HTML)P> and <(HTML)STRONG>.

Normally such concurrent document structures will not be entered directly by authors but will be created through automatic processes. The concurrent structures produced by these processes will be used to tell the system how it should present data to different processes without having to maintain a separate copy of the file for each process.

Concurrent document structures can also be used to record intermediate stages in a process, or the final state of a file when processing has been completed. For example, in a typical publishing application a document will pass through a number of production stages to produce galley proofs, paginated text, imposed sheets and so on. Traditionally, each of these stages has resulted in an output file that is coded to suit the use to which it will be put. The problem with this is that, if changes are required to the text, more than one version of the file may have to be updated. To avoid having to create different files at each stage in the production process, SGML allows the details required for each structure to be stored in the same file. SGML marked sections can then be used to identify text that is specific to a particular version of the file, other structures defining the relevant parameter entities as IGNOREd text.

When the FEATURES clause of the SGML declaration has been altered to contain a CONCUR YES n entry, where n indicates the maximum number of document structures that can be used concurrently, DTDs can be declared in the document's prolog *in addition to* that of the **base document type** (which is always the first DTD declared in the prolog). Each document structure must be declared by entry of a document type declaration.

Typically a document with two concurrent document structures might start:

```
<!SGML    "ISO 8879:1986"
  BASESET "ISO 646:1983//CHARSET
          International Reference Version (IRV)//ESC 2/5 4/0"
```

```
  .
  .
  .
  FEATURES MINIMIZE DATATAG NO   OMITTAG  YES  RANK       NO SHORTTAG YES
           LINK     SIMPLE  NO   IMPLICIT NO   EXPLICIT NO
           OTHER    CONCUR YES 2 SUBDOC   NO   FORMAL   NO
  APPINFO NONE
>
<!DOCTYPE TEI.2 SYSTEM "tei2.dtd"
  [<!ENTITY % TEIonly   "INCLUDE">
   <!ENTITY % HTMLonly "IGNORE" >]>
<!DOCTYPE HTML PUBLIC  "-//IETF//DTD HTML 2.0//EN"
  [<!ENTITY % TEIonly   "IGNORE" >
   <!ENTITY % HTMLonly "INCLUDE">]>
```

The first element entered after the above declarations is that for the TEI P3 DTD. As the locally stored file identified in this declaration is the first DTD in the prolog, it is the base document type for the document, which is automatically taken by the SGML parser as the DTD name to be associated with any tag that does not have a DTD specified.

When the document is processed to create the equivalent HTML file, the second structure, which is aimed at presentation of the information on a screen, can be *added* to the TEI logical structure used to capture and store the data.

The above example also illustrates how parameter entity definitions can be added to the document type declaration subset to allow users and applications to identify data that is specific to a particular structure. The definitions given above could be used to extend the earlier example as follows:

```
<(TEI.2)TEI.2><(HTML)HTML>
 <![ %(HTML)TEIonly; [
 <!--TEI header elements-->
 <!(TEI.2)TEIHEADER> ... </(TEI.2)TEIHEADER>
]]>
<(TEI.2)BIBL><(TEI.2)MONOGR>
<![ %(TEI.2)HTMLonly; [
 <(HTML)HEAD><(HTML)TITLE>TEI Monograph Catalogue</(HTML)TITLE>
 <(HTML)BASE href="http://www.u-net.com/~sgml/TEI">
 <(HTML)LINK rel=translation title="Fran&ccedil;ais" href="Bibl-FR.htm">
 </(HTML)HEAD>
]]>
<(HTML>BODY>
<(TEI.2)AUTHOR><(HTML)H1>Shirley, James</(HTML)H1></(TEI.2)AUTHOR>
<(TEI.2)TITLE type=main><(HTML)H2>
The Gentlemen of Venice
</(HTML)H2></(TEI.2)TITLE>
<(TEI.2)TITLE type=subordinate><(HTML)H3>
A tragi-comedie presented at the private house in Salisbury Court
by Her Majesties servants
</(HTML)H3)</(TEI.2)TITLE>
<(TEI.2)IMPRINT><(HTML)ADDRESS>
<(TEI.2)PUBLISHER>H. Moseley</(TEI.2)PUBLISHER><(HTML)BR>
<(TEI.2)PUBPLACE>London</(TEI.2)PUBPLACE></(HTML)ADDRESS>
```

```
<(TEI.2)DATE><(HTML)P><(HTML)STRONG>
1655
</(HTML)STRONG></(HTML)P)</(TEI.2)DATE>
</(TEI.2)IMPRINT><(TEI.2)EXTENT> <(HTML)P>78pp</(HTML)P></(TEI.2)EXTENT>
</(TEI.2)MONOGR></(TEI.2)BIBL>
<![ %(TEI.2)HTMLonly; [
    <(HTML)HR>
    <(HTML)P>Webmaster:
    <(HTML)A href="mailto:webmaster@our-site.com">
    webmaster@our-site.com</(HTML)a>
    </(HTML)P>
]]>
</(HTML)BODY>
</(TEI.2)TEI.2></(HTML)HTML>
```

The indented material belongs to only one of the structures. The marked section delimiters will ensure that any enclosed text will not be reproduced as part of the structure to which it does not belong.

Marked sections provide a useful method of overcoming one of the major problems with using concurrent structures. *Where data occurs in the document instance, it must be valid in all structures at the point entered.* To understand the types of problems that can occur because of this rule you should note the difference between the example given above and the earlier example which did not use marked sections. In the initial example the TEI <AUTHOR> element is associated with the HTML <TITLE> element, which forms part of the header of the HTML document, rather than part of the main body text. Once marked sections are used, it becomes possible to provide a separate HTML title (which is only used as a window title) and move the author details into the text body.

Note: *If the latter version of the <TITLE> element had been used in the first example, an error would be reported because the <MONOGR> element cannot contain parsed character data. (Its model is purely element content.)*

Not all SGML features can be used within concurrent document structures. In particular, those SGML features that may only be used within the base document type, such as empty start-tags and net-enabling start-tags, cannot be used within concurrent document structures. Similarly, care must also be taken to ensure that notation names associated with data entities or attribute lists are declared in each of the DTDs with which they are associated.

10.4 Linking document structures

SGML uses five types of declarations to link concurrent document structures:

- link type declarations to set up links between different document types;

- attribute definition list declarations to link processing attributes to elements;
- entity type declarations to assign process-specific definitions to general entities or to define parameter entities used in the definition of link processing attributes or link sets;
- link set declarations, which are used, when document instances are parsed, to control how individual elements are to be linked to processes or element structures;
- link set use declarations to switch from one set of links to another.

Link type declarations are similar in structure to document type declarations. They must be entered in the document prolog *after* the DTDs to which they relate. Like other markup declarations, link type declarations begin with the markup declaration open delimiter (`MDO`) delimiter followed, without any intervening spaces, by a reserved name, `LINKTYPE` by default. This is followed by a **link type name** that uniquely identifies the **link process definition**. As well as being different from that of any other link type declaration in the same prolog, this name must also be different from the names used for document type definitions in the same prolog.

Link type declarations may be separated from DTDs, and other link type declarations, by comment declarations, spaces, record start and end codes, valid separator characters or processing instructions, which are collectively referred to within ISO 8879 as **other prolog**.

Except for link set use declarations, which are used in a way similar to short reference maps, link-related declarations must be either embedded within a **link type declaration subset** within the link type declaration or stored in a separate file that is referenced as all or part of the link type declaration subset. The mechanism used is similar to that used for document type definitions (see Chapter 11), with any definitions called from a separate file being read after any local definitions encountered between a matched pair of declaration subset open (`DSO`) and declaration subset close (`DSC`) delimiters.

Three types of link are recognized by SGML:

- simple links to allow processing attributes to be associated with the base document element;
- implicit links to allow processing attributes to be associated with any element in any DTD;
- explicit links, which allow the relationship between two document structures to be controlled explicitly by the DTD developer.

The types of links that can be used within a document are controlled by the `LINK` entries in the `FEATURES` clause of the SGML declaration. In the reference concrete syntax the `LINK` features are disabled by entry of the following line:

```
LINK  SIMPLE NO  IMPLICIT NO  EXPLICIT NO
```

If simple links are required in a document, the first entry in this line must be changed to `SIMPLE YES`, followed by a number indicating the maximum number of simple links to be used in the document. If implicit links are to be used, the second entry changes to `IMPLICIT YES` (without a qualifying number). Where explicit links are required, the maximum number of links to be used within a single chain in the document must be stated after the entry `EXPLICIT YES`, giving a composite entry of the form:

```
LINK   SIMPLE YES 4   IMPLICIT NO   EXPLICIT YES 2
```

If `EXPLICIT YES` is specified, multiple DTDs can be declared in the prolog. The number of explicit links allowed in the `FEATURES` clause must be, at least, one less than the number of document type declarations in the longest chain of linked documents declared in the prolog.

10.4.1 Simple links

A **simple link specification** takes the form:

```
<!LINKTYPE proof #SIMPLE #IMPLIED
 [<!ATTLIST book style CDATA #FIXED "300dpi.prn">]>
```

This declaration tells the system to 'use the style sheet that generates 300 dot per inch proofs of books when this link type declaration is active.'

The link type name (`proof`) that follows the `LINKTYPE` declaration type keyword is followed by two, compulsory, keywords (`#SIMPLE` and `#IMPLIED`) to indicate the type of link being specified and the type of result expected.

The link type declaration subset that follows the specification, between the square brackets, contains a single attribute definition list declaration that defines one or more *fixed* attributes that are to be assigned to the base document type element (the first one defined in the prolog).

Note: *When used in link type declaration subsets, the attribute's declared value cannot be defined by use of the* `ID, IDREF, IDREFS` *or* `NOTATION` *keywords, and* `#CURRENT` *and* `#CONREF` *cannot be used for the default value. (These restrictions apply because link attributes cannot be used within an element's start-tag. In each of the above cases users would need to specify the applicable attribute values or supply the contents to which the attributes are to apply.)*

More than one simple link can be specified in a prolog. For example, the following link types could be associated with the TEI DTD:

```
<!LINKTYPE print #SIMPLE #IMPLIED
 [<!ATTLIST tei.2 style CDATA #FIXED "postscript">]>
<!LINKTYPE load-dbs #SIMPLE #IMPLIED
 [<!ATTLIST tei.2 dbs-name CDATA #FIXED "catalogue">]>
```

to specify the way the TEI.2 document should be processed before being sent for printing or loading into a bibliographic catalogue. Note, however, that a simple link could not be associated with the HTML DTD shown in the examples of the concurrent document given above, because only the base document type can be linked to the implied structure.

As with document type declarations, the declaration subset can be stored in an external file, which can be referenced using system or public identifiers. For example, the two entries shown above could be shortened to:

```
<!LINKTYPE print #SIMPLE #IMPLIED SYSTEM "print.lpd">
<!LINKTYPE load-dbs #SIMPLE #IMPLIED
  PUBLIC "-//our-firm//LPD Database loading link process definition//EN">
```

Note particularly the use of the LPD public class name in the formal public identifier to indicate that the file to be referenced contains a link type declaration subset.

The way a link is activated depends on the application. For conformance testing purposes an SGML parser should be able to use a processing instruction of the following form to activate both of the link type definitions given above:

```
<?rast-active-lpd: print load-dbs>
```

10.4.2 Implicit links

Implicit link specifications can be used to associate processing attributes with any element in any DTD. When the LINK entries in the FEATURES clause of the SGML declaration contain the entry IMPLICIT YES, the link type name can be followed by the name of a document type, the document type declaration for which precedes it in the prolog, and the word #IMPLIED. This tells the system that this link type declaration, when activated as detailed above, will add **link attributes** to elements in the named DTD.

The following example shows how some printing properties could be associated with elements making up a TEI bibliographic entry for a monograph:

```
<!LINKTYPE print tei.2 #IMPLIED
[<!ENTITY % bibl "(author|title|publisher|pubPlace|date|extent)"
>
 <!ATTLIST %bibl; align (start|end|centered|justified) start
                  family   CDATA   "Times Roman"
                  weight   NAME    medium
                  posture  NAME    upright
                  size     NUTOKEN 12pt
                  measure  NMTOKEN 36pi
                  l-indent NUTOKEN 0
                  r-indent NUTOKEN 0
                  attcond  CDATA   #IMPLIED                            >
```

```
<!LINK #INITIAL
        author     [centered weight=bold size=18pt]
        title      [attcond="type=main" centered size=24pt]
        title      [attcond="type=subordinate" centered size=16pt]
        publisher  [weight=bold]
        date       [family="Arial" posture=italic]
        extent     [end family="Arial"]                     >
]>
```

The parameter entity defined at the start of the link set declaration subset identifies all the elements in a monograph's bibliographic entry that have text associated with them. The attribute definition list declaration then associates nine attributes with each of these elements, and assigns default values to eight of the nine attributes.

Each implicit link type declaration must have at least one **link set declaration** whose associated name is a special reserved name, `#INITIAL`. This identifies the start point for the link process. Like other markup declarations the link set declaration begins with a markup declaration open (`MDO`) delimiter followed, without intervening spaces, by the reserved name identifying the type of declaration, `LINK`. The name assigned to the link set must follow this reserved name, separated from it and the subsequent **link rules** by one or more spaces or other separator characters. The link set declaration ends when the next markup declaration close (`MDC`) delimiter is encountered.

For implicit links the link rules take the form of one or more **source element specifications**, each of which consists of the name of an **associated element type**, which must be that of an element defined in the DTD identified by the link type declaration, and a **link attribute specification**. As in other SGML declarations, the associated element type specification can be either a single element name or a bracketed name group. The link attribute specification consists of an attribute specification list, as found within an element's start-tag, bracketed by the current declaration subset open (`DSO`) and declaration subset close (`DSC`) delimiters.

Notice that there are two declarations for the `title` element. Multiple entries are permitted where the selection of an appropriate option can be determined using some application-specific rule. In this example an attribute condition (`attcond`) attribute has been defined to check the current value of the `type` attribute. If the value of the `type` attribute is `main` the title will be set in 24 pt Times Roman centered on the 36 pica (6 inch) default measure. If the value is `subordinate` the title will be set, centered on the measure, in 16 pt Times Roman.

Notice also that there is no entry for the `pubPlace` element. This is because this element should be set using the default settings for the attributes, which specify that the text should be set in 12 pt Times Roman, using a medium weight and upright posture, so that the start of the place of publication's name is aligned with the start of the 36 pica measure, to which no indents are to be applied.

Where style sheets are used to record the details of the parameters to be associated with each element, implicit links provide a natural route for linking elements to style sheets. The following example shows that the name assigned to the style sheet specification (h1) is the only attribute needed to control the link process:

```
<!LINKTYPE format tei.2 #IMPLIED
[<!ENTITY  % bibl  "(author|title|publisher|pubPlace|date|extent)" >
 <!ATTLIST %bibl; style NAME "normal"
                  attcond CDATA #IMPLIED        >

 <!LINK #INITIAL
        author    [style=h1]
        title     [attcond="type=main" style=h2]
        title     [attcond="type=subordinate" style=h3]
        publisher [style=p]
        date      [style=date]
        extent    [style=extent]                                >
 ]>
```

In this case the style sheet name, which is passed to the text-formatting routines, activates a predefined set of formatting instructions which control the appearance of the element's text.

As explained above, the link type declaration subset can be stored in a separate, easily reusable, file that can be associated with many document instances. A typical implementation might add the following prolog to the TEI example document shown above:

```
<!DOCTYPE TEI.2 SYSTEM "tei2.dtd">
<!LINKTYPE format tei.2 #IMPLIED
  PUBLIC "-//our-firm//LPD Styles for TEI Bibliography//EN">
```

10.4.3 ID-specific links

Sometimes you need to associate a specific set of processing rules with a particular occurrence of an element. If an element has been assigned a unique identifier, an **ID link set declaration** can be used to assign link attributes to elements with relevant IDs.

When the reference concrete syntax is being used, ID link set declarations are defined, within the link type declaration subset, in a declaration that begins `<!IDLINK` and ends with `>`. Between these markup delimiters there must be one or more entries consisting of:

- a unique identifier,
- an element name, and
- an optional link attribute specification.

The following example shows how an ID link set declaration could be used to provide overrides for specific instances of a publisher name:

```
<!IDLINK
 isea      publisher [family="Avant Garde"]
 OPOCE     publisher [family="Helvetica"]
 sgml-cen publisher [weight=bold posture=italic] >
```

If the publisher element in the TEI bibliographic entry used above had been:

```
<(TEI.2)PUBLISHER id=isea>isea sa</(TEI.2)PUBLISHER>
```

the `IDLINK` definition would ensure that the company name would be printed using the house style for that company, which requires that the name be set in 12 pt Avant Garde.

Note: *Only one ID link set declaration may be specified in each link type declaration.*

10.4.4 Explicit links

Explicit links are used to link elements in a *source* document structure to elements in a *result* document structure. The **explicit link specification** that follows the `LINKTYPE` keyword and the link type name consists of the names of *two* DTDs defined earlier in the prolog. The subsequent link type declaration subset, between the square brackets, will contain:

- a link set declaration, the name of which is the keyword `#INITIAL`, which will form the start point for the link process;
- optionally, alternative link set declarations that can be called from within other link set declarations, or from within the document instance by a link set use declaration;
- optionally, a set of link rules to be associated with elements assigned a specific ID;
- optionally, parameter and general entity declarations that will extend the set defined in the DTD of the source document;
- optionally, attribute definition list declarations defining processing attributes to be associated with the source document structure.

The following prolog could be used to link a TEI bibliographic entry for a monograph to an HTML document structure:

```
<!DOCTYPE TEI.2 SYSTEM "tei2.dtd">
<!DOCTYPE HTML PUBLIC "-//IETF//DTD HTML 2.0//EN">
<!LINKTYPE CreateCD TEI.2 HTML
 [<!ATTLIST title attcond CDATA #IMPLIED>
  <!LINK #INITIAL author                              title
                  title [attcond="type=main"]         h2
                  title [attcond="type=subordinate"] h3
```

```
                imprint                          address
                pubPlace                         br
                date                             strong
                extent                           p        >
]>
```

For explicit links the link set name (for example, `#INITIAL`) is followed by matched pairs of element names, optionally qualified by attribute specifications, that form an **explicit link rule**. The first element name and attribute specification pair is known as the **source element specification**. This starts with the name(s) of one of the elements defined in the source DTD, the base document element of which is the first DTD named in the link type declaration. The element name can be qualified by one or more attributes forming a **link attribute specification**, as can be seen in the entries for the two variants of the TEI `<TITLE>` element.

The source element specification is followed by a **result element specification**, which also starts with an element name. This second name must be one the element names defined in the result DTD, the base document element of which is the second DTD named in the link type declaration. This element name can, optionally, be followed by a **result attribute specification** showing the attributes to be associated with the selected element in the result document. These attributes must be ones whose attribute definition list declaration has been declared as part of the second of the DTDs named in the link type declaration.

The following document instance could be processed using the prolog shown above:

```
<TEI.2>
<!--TEI header elements omitted here for simplicity-->
<BIBL><MONOGR>
<AUTHOR>Shirley, James</AUTHOR>
<TITLE type=main>
The Gentlemen of Venice
</TITLE>
<TITLE type=subordinate>
A tragi-comedie presented at the private house in Salisbury Court
by Her Majesties servants
</TITLE>
<IMPRINT>
<PUBLISHER>H. Moseley</PUBLISHER>
<PUBPLACE>London</PUBPLACE>
<DATE>1655</DATE>
</IMPRINT><EXTENT>78pp</EXTENT>
</MONOGR></BIBL></TEI.2>
```

The HTML document structure produced as a result of processing the link process definition will be:

```
<TITLE>
Shirley, James
</TITLE><H2>
```

```
The Gentlemen of Venice
</H2><H3>
A tragi-comedie presented at the private house in Salisbury Court
by Her Majesties servants
</H3><ADDRESS>
H. Moseley
<BR>
London
<STRONG>
1655
</STRONG></ADDRESS><P>
78pp
</P>
```

This is not a complete HTML document, but it will be accepted by most HTML-based programs, because the only elements missing from it are ones that are declared omissible in the HTML DTD. When the output of the link process is parsed against this DTD it will generate a file of the form:

```
<HTML VERSION= "-//W3C//DTD HTML 2.0//EN">
<HEAD><TITLE>
Shirley, James
</TITLE></HEAD><BODY><H2>
The Gentlemen of Venice
</H2><H3>
A tragi-comedie presented at the private house in Salisbury Court
by Her Majesties servants
</H3><ADDRESS>
H. Moseley
<BR>
London
<STRONG>
1655
</STRONG></ADDRESS><P>
78pp
</P></BODY></HTML>
```

Note that the parser has determined from the HTML DTD that the <TITLE> element should be placed in the <HEAD> section of the HTML document instance and that all the other elements should be placed in the <BODY> section. It has also added the default values to those attributes that were assigned one in the DTD.

If you compare this document structure with that given as an example of concurrent markup earlier in the chapter, you will find that they are not identical. Using SGML links it is not possible to position the date outside the <ADDRESS> result element generated by the <IMPRINT> source element or to generate more than one start-tag in the result structure when a source element is encountered. (To get the structures to be the same both a <P> and a <STRONG> start-tag would have needed to be generated in response to the <DATE> start-tag.)

If you compare the document structure with the example showing the use of both concurrent markup and marked sections, you will find that the TEI `<AUTHOR>` element, has been linked to the HTML `<TITLE>` element, rather than to the `<H1>` element, because without this, the compulsory title element in the header would not be present and an error would be reported when the HTML file was parsed.

10.4.5 Using alternative link sets

Sometimes problems such as those illustrated by the last example can be overcome by using one of the two mechanims provided by SGML for switching link sets:

- `#USELINK`, which allows an alternative link set to be used within a specified element;
- `#POSTLINK`, which allows an alternative link set to be activated when the end-tag for an element is encountered.

USELINK

The `#USELINK` option is particularly useful for differentiating between the ways in which an element can be processed in different contexts. For example, one of the DTDs used by the Office for Official Publications of the European Communities (OPOCE) contains the following specification for a paragraph:

```
<!ELEMENT (p|elem)    -- (#PCDATA|list)+ >
<!ELEMENT list        -O (elem)+ >
```

Notice that this definition is recursive: lists are made up of elements (`elem`) that can themselves contain lists.

The following, made-up, example shows how a complex paragraph could be marked up using these elements. The marked-up text, which contains four levels of nested lists, has been indented to make it clear which level each component is nested to.

```
<P>The budget for 1996 will be distributed as follows:
   <LIST>
      <ELEM>Payments to Directorates
      <LIST>
         <ELEM>DGI
         <LIST>
            <ELEM>Division: A
            <LIST>
               <ELEM>Brussels:  12 Mecus</ELEM>
               <ELEM>Luxembourg: 8 Mecus</ELEM></LIST>
            <ELEM>Division: B
            <LIST>
               <ELEM>Brussels:  10 Mecus</ELEM>
               <ELEM>Luxembourg: 6 Mecus</ELEM></LIST>
            <ELEM>Division: C
            <LIST>
```

```
            <ELEM>Brussels:    9 Mecus</ELEM>
            <ELEM>Luxembourg:12 Mecus</ELEM></LIST></LIST>
      <ELEM>DGII
      <LIST>
         <ELEM>Division: D
         <LIST>
            <ELEM>Brussels:   21 Mecus</ELEM>
            <ELEM>Luxembourg:18 Mecus</ELEM> </LIST>
         <ELEM>Division: E
         <LIST>
            <ELEM>Brussels:    5 Mecus</ELEM>
            <ELEM>Luxembourg:  2 Mecus</ELEM></LIST>
      <ELEM>Division: F
      <LIST>
            <ELEM>Brussels:   19 Mecus</ELEM>
            <ELEM>Luxembourg:  2 Mecus</ELEM></LIST></LIST></LIST>
   <ELEM>Payments to Member States
   <LIST>
      <ELEM>Greece:  25 Mecus</ELEM>
      <ELEM>Austria: 12 Mecus</ELEM>
      <ELEM>Finland:  8 Mecus</ELEM></LIST>
   <ELEM>Payments to Other Bodies
   <LIST>
   <ELEM>OPOCE: 10 Mecus</ELEM></LIST>
</P>
```

It could be decided that, when distributed over the World Wide Web, the first two levels of list should be numbered, but subsequent levels should be bulleted. The following (simplified) example of an explicit link shows how the #USELINK option can be used to enforce the correct nesting and numbering of lists:

```
<!DOCTYPE blk0 SYSTEM "cat2.dtd">
<!DOCTYPE HTML PUBLIC "-//W3C//DTD HTML 3.2//EN">
<!LINKTYPE to-HTML blk0 HTML [
 <!LINK #INITIAL  p                        p
                  list #USELINK level-1   ol                   >
 <!LINK level-1   elem                     li
                  list #USELINK level-2   ol [type=a]          >
 <!LINK level-2   elem                     li
                  list                     ul [type=disc]       >
]>
```

HTML distinguishes between two types of lists, ordered lists (<OL>), which are preceded by an automatically generated number or letter (depending on the level of nesting), and unordered lists (<UL>), which are preceded by a bullet or dash (depending on both level and the style specifications of the browser you are using).

The rules for processing paragraphs are defined in the initial link set. OPOCE paragraphs are to be mapped to HTML paragraphs. In this case the same markup tag (<P>) is used in both DTDs. (It should be noted, however, that the two elements have different content models.)

When a top-level list (<LIST>) element is identified within the OPOCE paragraph, it will be associated with an HTML ordered list (<OL>) element with the default rules relating to numbering. Within the top-level list the parser will use the link set called `level-1` to link elements. This will link any OPOCE <ELEM> elements to HTML list items (<LI>). If a nested list is encountered this will be mapped to a nested ordered list, within which the setting for the value of the `type` attribute is `a` to ensure arabic numbering of the nested list. Within the nested list the rules defined in the link set called `level-2` will be used.

Within a second level list any <ELEM> elements will be linked to HTML list items and any nested lists will be linked to HTML unordered lists (<UL>). To ensure that the list will be bulleted, a `type=disc` attribute value has been specified. Note that there is no `#USELINK` statement at this level. If there are further levels of nesting, they will continue to use the current link set, `level-2`, which will map all levels of nested list in the same way.

When the link rules are applied to the sample paragraph they will generate an HTML file of the form:

```
<P>The budget for 1996 will be distributed as follows:
   <OL>
      <LI>Payments to Directorates
      <OL type="a">
         <LI>DGI
         <UL type="disc">
            <LI>Division: A
            <UL type="disc">
               <LI>Brussels:     12 Mecus</LI>
               <LI>Luxembourg:    8 Mecus</LI></UL>
            <LI>Division: B
            <UL type="disc">
               <LI>Brussels:     10 Mecus</LI>
               <LI>Luxembourg:    6 Mecus</LI></UL>
            <LI>Division: C
            <UL type="disc">
               <LI>Brussels:      9 Mecus</LI>
               <LI>Luxembourg:   12 Mecus</LI></UL></UL>
         <LI>DGII
         <UL type="disc">
            <LI>Division: D
            <UL type="disc">
               <LI>Brussels:     21 Mecus</LI>
               <LI>Luxembourg:   18 Mecus</LI></UL>
            <LI>Division: E
            <UL typ="disc">
               <LI>Brussels:      5 Mecus</LI>
               <LI>Luxembourg:    2 Mecus</LI></UL>
            <LI>Division: F
            <UL type="disc">
               <LI>Brussels:     19 Mecus</LI>
               <LI>Luxembourg:    2 Mecus</LI></UL></UL></OL>
         <LI>Payments to Member States
```

```
<OL type="a">
   <LI>Greece:    25 Mecus</LI>
   <LI>Austria:   12 Mecus</LI>
   <LI>Finland:    8 Mecus</LI></OL>
<LI>Payments to Other Bodies
<OL type="a">
   <LI>OPOCE:     10 Mecus</LI></OL></OL>
```

This will generate a listing of the following form:

The budget for 1996 will be distributed as follows:

1. Payments to Directorates
    a. DGI
        - Division: A
            - Brussels: 12 Mecus
            - Luxembourg: 8 Mecus
        - Division: B
            - Brussels: 10 Mecus
            - Luxembourg: 6 Mecus
        - Division: C
            - Brussels: 9 Mecus
            - Luxembourg: 12 Mecus
    b. DGII
        - Division: D
            - Brussels: 21 Mecus
            - Luxembourg: 18 Mecus
        - Division: E
            - Brussels: 5 Mecus
            - Luxembourg: 2 Mecus
        - Division: F
            - Brussels: 19 Mecus
            - Luxembourg: 2 Mecus
2. Payments to Member States
    a. Greece: 25 Mecus
    b. Austria: 12 Mecus
    c. Finland: 8 Mecus
3. Payments to Other Bodies
    a. OPOCE: 10 Mecus

Where special instructions are to be associated with specific instances of an element, the source document type definition must include an attribute definition list declaration for that element which contains an attribute declared using the ID keyword as its declared value. In the source document instance each element that is to be treated differently must be given a unique identifier which the system can use to determine where one of the link rules defined in the ID link set declaration defined in the current link type declaration subset is to be applied.

When ID link sets are prepared, it is important to remember that each link set must cater for any subelements that the model allows to be embedded within the element being linked to the result document. Failure to do so may result in embedded elements not being formatted properly; at best, it will result in their being given default formatting parameters. To overcome this problem the `#USELINK` option can be combined with the `IDLINK` option to give a declaration of the form:

```
<!IDLINK special p #USELINK #INITIAL block [style=special-p] >
```

POSTLINK

The `#POSTLINK` option can be used to specify that an alternative link set is to be activated when the end-tag for the specified element is encountered, or is implied by the program.

The classic example of the need to change the link rules immediately after a specific element is provided by books in which the first paragraph of text after a chapter heading is set in a different format from other paragraphs. This could be handled using a link set of the following type:

```
<!LINKTYPE fromHTML HMTL page [
[<!LINK #INITIAL
   h1 #POSTLINK firstpar block [style=chapter-head]
   p                     block [style=para] >
<!LINK firstpar
   p #POSTLINK #INITIAL block [style=initial-para] >
] >
```

In the initial link set the first level of heading, say, the chapter heading, has been declared in such a way that, when the end-tag for the heading (`</H1>`) is encountered, the parser will switch to a special link set (`firstpar`) before processing the following text. The first paragraph differs from other paragraphs: it uses the style sheet known as `initial-para` to format the `block` it forms on the page.

When the end-tag for the first paragraph (`</P>`) is detected by the parser, the `#POSTLINK #INITIAL` entry associated with the paragraph element name (`P`) in the `firstpar` link set will cause the parser to revert to using the link definition for paragraphs given in the initial link. This will ensure that subsequent paragraphs use the normal style sheet for paragraph blocks (`para`).

10.4.6 Short cuts

As will be obvious from the complexity of the above, simplified, examples, preparing link type declarations for a document structure of the complexity of that defined for a book can be a time-consuming task. Fortunately a number of short cuts are available.

As with the other markup declarations, parameter entities can be used to reduce the amount of repetitive keying required. As the following example shows, this can greatly reduce the length of link attribute specifications:

```
<!LINKTYPE print act page [
<!ENTITY % catalog  SYSTEM "catalog.lpd"  >
<!ENTITY % preamble SYSTEM "preamble.lpd" >
<!ENTITY % terms    SYSTEM "terms.lpd"    >
<!LINK #INITIAL    %catalog;
 title [attcond="type='main'"] block [style="big-title"]
 title [attcond="type='subordinate'"] block [style="small-title"]
 %preamble;
 %terms;                                                        >
```

Here the majority of the links to be used are defined in three link process definition files stored on the local systems. These standard link set definitions are called using parameter entities, with any elements not covered by standard definitions being added to the stored definitions.

Entity declarations defined within the document type declaration subset of the document that is identified in the linktype declaration as the source document type for the current link type declaration can also be used within the link type declaration subset if they are appropriate. If entity declarations of the same name occur in both the link type declaration and the document type declaration, however, the one in the link type declaration will have priority while the link is active.

Another short cut is to use a name group for the associated element type part of a source element specification in the link set declaration (or in the link attribute set declarations). For example, if the HTML tags for entering computer coding examples are to have the same format when printed, they could be declared as:

```
<!LINK #INITIAL ...
  (xmp|listing|code|plaintext) block [face=courier]
                  ...                                  >
```

Care must, however, be taken in using this technique. In particular, it is important to check that the linked elements require the same set of attributes for both the source and result elements. If different sets of attributes apply on either side of the link, this technique should not be used.

Where a number of elements share the same output format, the values should be used as the default values in the specification of the attributes in the result DTD. This will allow the attribute specification list to be omitted where the result element only requires these default values.

Another possible short cut is to let the program imply the elements to which a link applies, together with the relevant attribute values. This can be done for individual elements within an explicit link set by replacing the details of the result element specification with the keyword `#IMPLIED` to give a link set declaration of the form:

```
<!LINK linkname element [attributes] #IMPLIED>
```

Here the result of the link process will automatically be implied by the formatting program whenever the specified element is encountered, and the optional link attribute specification associated with the source element specification will define the parameters to be passed to the program.

The parser can also be instructed to link all otherwise unlinked source elements to a default result element by using the `#IMPLIED` keyword in place of the source element specification, for example:

```
<!LINK linkset1 #IMPLIED block [style=normal]>
```

10.4.7 Overriding link declarations

Link type declarations can be controlled from within the text by use of **link set use declarations**. (These have a very similar form to the short reference map use declarations.) The general form of such declarations is:

```
<!USELINK setname linkname>
```

where `USELINK` is the default version of the keyword defined in the reference concrete syntax, `setname` is the name given to one of the link set declarations (`<!LINK ...>`) in the document's prolog and `linkname` is the link type name used to identify the link type declaration (`<!LINKTYPE ...>`) that contains the relevant link set declarations. A typical entry would be:

```
<!USELINK #INITIAL to-HTML >
```

As with the `USEMAP` declaration, the special `#EMPTY` keyword can be used to switch off a link. To disable the `to-HTML` link type once it has been enabled, for example, you could enter the following declaration at any point in the text:

```
<!USELINK #EMPTY to-HTML >
```

If the link set map is switched off within an element by entry of a link set use declaration with the keyword `#EMPTY`, the original link set can be restored by entering a declaration of the form:

```
<!USELINK #RESTORE to-HTML >
```

On seeing this markup declaration, the SGML parser will restore the link set that was associated with the current element prior to the preceding link set use declaration (for example, the one that was current when the element began).

10.4.8 Using publicly declared link type declaration subsets

Where a publicly declared link type declaration subset is already known to the receiving system, it can be invoked, like other publicly declared declaration sets, by use of a formal public identifier. In this case the public identifier qualifies a link type declaration and so the public text class keyword used in the formal public identifier is LPD. A typical declaration might be:

```
<!LINKTYPE create-CD OPOCE HTML PUBLIC
      "-//OPOCE//LPD CD creation link set//EN">
```

If the publicly declared link set is to be extended by local definitions, which may override some of the definitions in the publicly declared set, the formal public identifier can be followed by a link type declaration subset. It should be noted that, as with DTDs, externally stored link declarations are added to the end of the local definitions, the first definition always taking precedence. To ensure the proper handling of entity references, all entities declared within the link process definition are treated as preceding entities declared in the source DTD. This means that any entity declarations within the link will take precedence over entities with the same name declared in the DTD. Similarly, if the link declarations contain attributes that reference general entities not declared in the link type declaration, entities of the same name declared as part of the source or result DTDs will be used, if present; if no name match is found, the default entity for the appropriate DTD will be invoked.

From the above examples, it can be seen that SGML provides both document creators and document designers with a number of techniques for controlling how entered text is to be processed. It should not, however, be thought that link statements and concurrent document types provide all the tools needed to produce paginated text. Fully paginated text requires a powerful text formatter, which will normally need to be set up for specific applications. The degree of interaction possible between the SGML document designer and the text formatter will depend on the skill of the system's designers in linking the formatter to the information stored as an integral part of the SGML document.

A new standard, ISO/IEC 10179, provides the power needed to manage the more complex forms of transformations required for formatting documents. The *Document Style Semantics and Specification Language (DSSSL)* defined in ISO/IEC10179 uses a variant of the LISP-based Scheme programming language to control the way in which SGML document trees are converted for formatting. The language also defines an SGML Document Query Language (SDQL) that can be used to identify specific components of an SGML document tree.

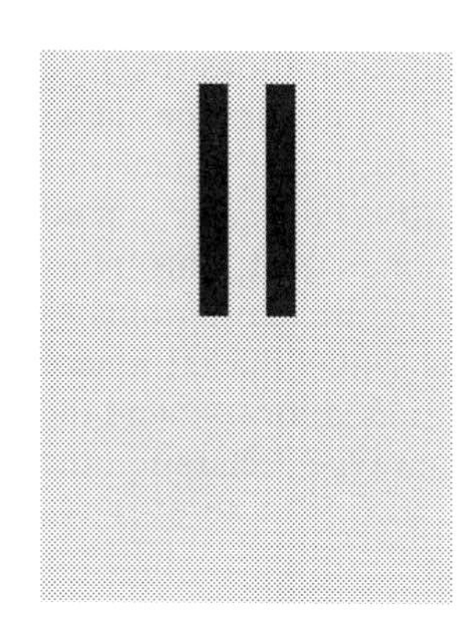

Building a document type definition

The document type declaration • Using publicly declared document type declarations • Element sets • The effect of record boundaries

This chapter reviews how the declarations described in the preceding chapters can be combined to form a document type definition.

11.1 The document type declaration

The rules that are required by an application to control the markup of a document are known as a **document type definition** (DTD). The prolog of each DTD must contain at least one **document type declaration**. The first document type declaration in any prolog is referred to as the **base document type declaration**.

Note: *Short references may only be associated with the base document type declaration.*

A document type declaration is an SGML markup declaration, which starts with the keyword `DOCTYPE` (or its declared replacement). When the reference concrete syntax is being used a document type declaration starts:

```
<!DOCTYPE docname
```

where `docname` is a unique **document type name** used to identify the base document element of one of the logical structures used in the document/subdocument.

Where an externally stored document type definition is being used as part (or all) of the document type declaration, the relevant external identifier can be entered immediately after the document type name to give the document type declaration the form:

```
<!DOCTYPE docname external-identifier ... >
```

The start of any locally defined set of entity and element declarations (referred to as the **document type declaration subset**) is identified by a **declaration subset open** (DSO) delimiter entered immediately after the document's name or external identifier. A matching **declaration subset close** (DSC) delimiter is used to identify the end of the document type declaration subset; this must immediately precede the markup declaration close (MDC) code that terminates the document type declaration. In the reference concrete syntax the left square bracket ([ ) is used for DSO, the right square bracket ( ]) is used for DSC and the MDC code is the greater than sign (>), giving the document type declaration the overall form:

```
<!DOCTYPE docname optional-external-identifier [ local
  declarations ] >
```

Only markup declarations, including comment declarations and marked sections, processing instructions and valid SGML separator characters, as defined in the associated SGML declaration, may be entered within the document type declaration subset.

11.2 Using publicly declared document type declarations

External identifiers can be used to add externally stored declarations to a document type declaration. Two mechanisms are provided for this:

- use of an external identifier immediately after the document type name;
- referencing a parameter entity that identifies the file containing the required declarations within the document type declaration subset.

It is important to understand the difference between these two approaches. Declarations that are called using parameter entity references are activated at the point indicated by the parameter entity reference. Files that are associated with the document type name are not activated until the closing delimiter of the document type declaration subset (for example, the] character) is encountered, even though the SYSTEM or PUBLIC keyword and the file identifier immediately follow the document type name at the start of the document type declaration.

Typically, the files identified through an external identifier in a document's prolog will identify a file containing the markup declarations required for the document type declaration subset. A typical example might be:

```
<!DOCTYPE act PUBLIC "-//OPOCE//DTD Act of the European
  Commission//EN" [ <!-- local declarations -->
  ]>
```

Because SGML only recognizes the first definition of an entity it receives, the fact that the externally stored declarations are added to the end of the subset ensures that any entity declarations entered in the local document type declaration subset will override a definition with the same name in the externally stored declarations. For example, if the document type declaration subset contains the definition:

```
<!ENTITY p CDATA "<p>">
```

while the recalled document type definition contains the entity:

```
<!ENTITY p STARTTAG p>
```

the local definition would be used within the document, causing all `&p;` entity references (or short references calling this entity) to be output as the character string <p> rather than being recognized as a paragraph element tag.

Only one external identifier can be associated with each document type declaration. Where more than one set of externally stored set of declarations needs to be referenced in a document type definition, subsequent files will have to be declared and called within the document type declaration subset. For example, a document type declaration might start:

```
<!DOCTYPE act PUBLIC
  "-//OPOCE//DTD Act of the European Commission//EN"
  [ <!ENTITY % ISOchem PUBLIC
      "ISO 9573-13:1991//ENTITIES Chemistry//EN">
    %ISOchem;
    <!-- other local declarations -->
  ]>
```

Where required, public identifiers can be further qualified by system identifiers showing where the relevant details can be found on the originating system. For example, if the required declarations were stored in a separate file called `a-100296.dtd` a document type declaration might start:

```
<!DOCTYPE act PUBLIC
    "-//OPOCE//DTD Act of the European Commission//EN" "a-010296.dtd"
  [ ... ]>
```

Notice that, for publicly declared entities, the word `SYSTEM` does not precede the system identifier.

11.3 Element sets

Element sets are sets of inter-linked declarations that define the structure of a document, or part of a document. Element sets can contain:

- element declarations;
- attribute definition list declarations;

- notation declarations;
- parameter entity declarations;
- comment declarations;
- processing instructions;
- marked section declarations.

Where element sets are stored in entities that can be identified using formal public identifiers, they should be assigned a public text class of `ELEMENTS`.

11.3.1 The role of comment declarations

Each element set should contain a number of **comment declarations** that uniquely identify its provenance and history. Comment declarations should be used to identify:

- the public name normally used to invoke an element set;
- the owner of the DTD, and any copyright conditions pertaining to it;
- which revision of the DTD is stored in the file;
- what changes have been made in this version of the DTD;
- major groupings of elements within the DTD;
- comments that apply to more than one declaration.

Comment declarations are declarations that contain only comments. The markup declaration open (`MDO`) delimiter must be followed *immediately* by the two hyphens identifying the start of a comment, or by whatever alternative comment (`COM`) delimiter has been defined in the current concrete syntax. The closing comment delimiter is followed by the markup declaration close symbol to give a declaration of the form:

```
<!-- Elements used in a typical textbook -->
```

Note: *Unlike comments embedded within element and entity declarations, comment declarations cannot have spaces on either side of the comment delimiters, because spaces are not permitted between the initial markup declaration open sequence (`<!`) and the opening comment delimiter. The following declaration is, therefore, illegal:*

```
<! -- Elements used in a typical textbook -- >
```

as it should have been entered as:

```
<!-- Elements used in a typical textbook -->
```

Note, however, that a space is permitted after the second of the comment delimiters.

More than one comment can be included in a single comment declaration, if required.

A special short form of comment declaration, consisting of a markup declaration open delimiter immediately followed by a markup declaration close delimiter (<!>) can be used where the comment declaration is simply being inserted to provide a blank space between markup declarations. (This form of dummy line should be used wherever a blank line is required between element declarations in an element set to indicate that the line has deliberately been left blank.)

Note: *The format of comments used within Netscape, whereby the hyphen pairs are omitted, is not valid SGML and should be carefully guarded against.*

11.3.2 Modifying existing element and entity sets

It will be found that most of the declarations required for textual elements embedded within paragraphs are similar to those used in existing element sets. In most cases it will be simpler to copy an existing definition from another set rather than try to redefine the embedded elements from first principles.

Before modifying an existing element set, it is important that the currently declared document structure is fully understood. If the relevant tree diagrams and element descriptions are available, this should not be difficult, but if all you have is an uncommented document type definition it may take some time to work out all the details of the existing structure.

Where the changes required to the existing structure are minor, their incorporation into the document type declaration subset is usually a simple matter. Major changes may, however, require a careful reappraisal of the parameter entities used within the document. This latter point is especially important where two or more existing element sets are being combined, because the two sets may contain parameter entities which have the same name, but different declarations.

11.3.3 Creating new element sets

When creating a completely new element set, you should try to start by identifying a base document element that the element set is to cover. Sometimes this is not possible because the element set is designed to provide facilities for a number of DTDs, but, where this is the case, it will not be possible to test the validity of the element set outside the context in which it is used. Where a single element, or a set of elements, has been identified as a potential base document element for the element set, it will become possible to test the element set before referencing it in other DTDs. This will assist the DTD maintenance process.

It is advisable to use existing element names wherever possible, even when the use of the element slightly changes between applications. Where elements are named consistently, users will find it easier to recognize the elements and will be less likely to enter the wrong tags. As well as reducing the likelihood of keying errors, using commonly recognized names will also reduce the time needed to train document creators in the use of a new document structure.

11.3.4 Structured element sets

Another way of making element sets easier to understand is to structure the declarations so that elements declared at the same level start underneath each other. By applying this technique you can build up structured element sets in simple stages.

The following DTD fragment shows how part of a FORMEX-coded multi-level table, as used within the OPOCE, has been defined:

```
<!ELEMENT BLKROW                -- (#PCDATA, ROW1+)>
  <!ELEMENT ROW1                -- (#PCDATA, ROW2*)>
    <!ELEMENT ROW2              -- (#PCDATA, ROW3*)>
      <!ELEMENT ROW3            -- (#PCDATA, ROW4*)>
        <!ELEMENT ROW4          -- (#PCDATA, ROW5*)>
          <!ELEMENT ROW5        -- (#PCDATA, ROW6*)>
            <!ELEMENT ROW6      -- (#PCDATA, ROW7*)>
              <!ELEMENT ROW7    -- (#PCDATA, ROW8*)>
                <!ELEMENT ROW8 -- (#PCDATA)>
```

While such structured sets can make the relationships of elements easier to understand, structures can be complicated by use of parameter entities. Where a large number of parameter entities are used in model group definitions a structured format may not be advantageous.

11.4 The effect of record boundaries

A record is defined within SGML as any data between a record start (RS) and a record end (RE) code. In the reference concrete syntax the record start code is hexadecimal 0A (the ASCII line feed code) while the record end code is hexadecimal 0D (the ASCII carriage return code).

SGML does not restrict the length of a record and record boundaries do not *need* to be present. Where they are present within parsed text (as opposed to within marked sections or markup declarations), their effect depends on their position.

When parsing the data within mixed content, an SGML program ignores any record start codes, using the record end code as the sole guide to record boundaries. Three rules control the effect of the record end code:

(1) The *first* RE in an element is ignored if it is not preceded by an RS code, some recognized data or a proper subelement (that is, a subelement that is specified in the model group for the element, rather than in an inclusion clause associated with the element or one of its parents).

(2) The *last* RE in an element is ignored if the record is not followed by data or a proper subelement.

(3) RE codes that do not immediately follow an RS code, or another RE code, are ignored unless the program identifies data, or a proper subelement, between the codes.

In the application of these rules, subelement content is ignored because both proper and included subelements are treated as an atom which ends in the record they start in.

Note: *When start-tag omission is in force, omitted markup recognition occurs before the above rules are applied.*

The effect of these three rules on an element containing mixed content can be seen in the following example:

```
Record Contents
--------------------------------------------------------
1     <P>
2     Record end codes immediately after tags are ignored.
3
4     <EM>
5     Emphasized phrases
6     </EM> do not always start on a new line.
7     </P>
```

Each of the records shown above starts with a record start code and ends with a record end code (the record numbers are not part of the file; they are simply shown for reference).

The first element of the text is the paragraph element of which start-tag appears in line 1. As this start-tag is immediately followed by a record end code, without any preceding text, rule 1 will result in the record end code on line 1 being ignored. This means that the program will treat the first two lines of coding as if they had been entered in a single line reading:

```
<P>Record end codes immediately after tags are ignored.
```

The third record appears to consist simply of a record start code followed by a record end code, but it could also contain other, hidden, codes such as Tab codes and Backspaces. If this is the case, rule 3 above may result in the record end code at the end of the line being ignored. If the line is a true blank line, consisting of a record start code followed immediately by a record end code, however, the record end code will be retained when the document is parsed because the following element is a proper subelement.

As with the first record, the record end code at the end of the fourth record will be ignored because no data for the embedded subelement precedes it. At the end of the fifth record, rule 2 will cause the last record end of the embedded subelement to be ignored because, in this case, it is followed by the end-tag of the subelement rather than data or another level of embedded subelement. The program will, therefore, treat the records 4 to 6 as if a single record had been entered as:

```
<EM>Emphasized phrases</EM> do not always start on a new line.
```

As the record end code at the end of the sixth record is the last such code in the paragraph element, this will also be ignored, following rule 2, so the whole example will be treated by the program as if it had been entered as:

```
<P>Record end codes immediately after tags are ignored.

<EM>Highlighted phrases</EM> do not always start on a new line.</P>
```

Note: *The blank line will only be retained if the third record was actually empty.*

Where an element only contains nested subelements (that is, its model group identifies it as having element content), record start and end codes will always be treated as separator characters, which are ignored within markup. Each proper or included subelement is treated as an atom that ends in the same record in which it begins.

Note: *In the days when the SGML standard was being written, record-based mainframes were commonplace. Today, as such systems become less common, the anomalies introduced by adopting this approach are beginning to appear to be a bit dated. It is likely that this area of the SGML standard will be simplified when the standard is next extended.*

12 Interpreting the HTML DTD

DTD history • DTD identification • Deprecated features • Imported Internet specifications • Shared parameters • Character mnemonics • Text markup • Shared content models • Body components • Anchors and links • Images and maps • Applets • Paragraphs and headings • Preformatted text • Lists • Forms • Tables • HTML document headers • HTML document structure

In this chapter the rules of creating SGML DTDs described in the preceding chapters are used to identify the significant features of the version of the HTML DTD that was released in January 1997 to indicate the current direction of HTML development. The way in which the elements defined in this DTD can be used to mark up documents are covered in detail in the following chapters.

Version 3.2 has been selected in preference to Version 2.0, which is formally defined in IETF Request for Comments (RFC) 1866, because it makes more complete use of SGML features. Using this DTD as a starting point makes it easier, therefore, to comment on significant features of preceding chapters. The sections in this chapter reflect the sectioning applied in the DTD.

Note: *To make it easier to explain the DTD, I have reordered some of the sections, but only in situations where reordering does not affect interpretation of the DTD.*

12.1 DTD history

A good indication of the quality of a DTD can often be found at the very start. If the DTD starts with a comprehensive record of its development history, in the form of an SGML comment declaration, you can be sure that the DTD has been developed as the result of extensive evaluation and testing. The Version 3.2 history statement reads:

```
<!--
    W3C Document Type Definition for the HyperText Markup Language
    version 3.2 as ratified by a vote of W3C member companies.
    For more information on W3C look at URL http://www.w3.org/

      Date: Tuesday January 14th 1997

      Author: Dave Raggett <dsr@w3.org>

    HTML 3.2 aims to capture recommended practice as of early '96
    and as such to be used as a replacement for HTML 2.0 (RFC 1866).
    Widely deployed rendering attributes are included where they
    have been shown to be interoperable. SCRIPT and STYLE are
    included to smooth the introduction of client-side scripts
    and style sheets. Browsers must avoid showing the contents
    of these elements. Otherwise support for them is not required.
    ID, CLASS and STYLE attributes are not included in this
    version of HTML.

-->
```

Note particularly the dating of the DTD and a clear indication of how to contact its author.

12.2 DTD identification

DTDs that are intended to be widely used should always be assigned a formal public identifier (FPI). A good DTD will contain a comment showing how the FPI can be used in a <!DOCTYPE declaration to invoke the element set. In the case of the HTML DTD this comment has been added to a parameter entity that can be used to record the HTML version used to check the encoding of a document as an attribute of the <HTML> element:

```
<!ENTITY % HTML.Version
        "-//W3C//DTD HTML 3.2 Final//EN"

        -- Typical usage:

            <!DOCTYPE HTML PUBLIC "-//W3C//DTD HTML 3.2 Final//EN">
            <html>
            ...
            </html>
        -->
```

12.3 Deprecated features

Marked sections provide a useful mechanism for allowing users to select relevant parts of large element sets. In the case of the HTML DTD they are used to identify declarations for elements whose use in new documents is deprecated:

```
<!-============== Deprecated Features Switch =====================-->

<!ENTITY % HTML.Deprecated "INCLUDE">
```

By default such elements are included as part of the DTD to ensure that any existing HTML documents that contain these elements can be read using the latest version of the DTD. Where the DTD is being used to control the authoring of new documents, however, the replacement text for this parameter entity should be changed from `"INCLUDE"` to `"IGNORE"` to ensure that deprecated elements cannot be used.

12.4 Imported Internet specifications

While most DTDs use notation declarations to identify entities containing types of data other than SGML, the nature of the World Wide Web requires a different mechanism for handling references to externally stored data units. For HTML, external references are based on the concepts of Uniform Resource Locators (URLs), the HyperText Transfer Protocol (HTTP) and the Multipurpose Internet Mail Extension (MIME), which have been formally defined in Request For Comment (RFC) documents issued by the Internet Engineering Task Force (IETF).

Note: *A separate RFC is to be created to describe the use of* `<SCRIPT>` *elements within HTML browsers.*

To make it clear where each of these specifications applies to the use of the DTD the following parameter entities have been declared:

```
<!-================== Imported Names ===============================-->

<!ENTITY % Content-Type "CDATA"
        -- meaning a MIME content type, as per RFC1521 -->

<!ENTITY % HTTP-Method "GET | POST"
        -- as per HTTP specification -->

<!ENTITY % URL "CDATA"
        -- The term URL means a CDATA attribute
           whose value is a Uniform Resource Locator,
           See RFC1808 (June 95) and RFC1738 (Dec 94). -->

<!ENTITY % script "CDATA" -- scriptlet -->
```

The replacement text for each of these parameter entities is designed to be used as the declared value in an attribute declaration, as will be seen shortly.

12.5 Shared parameters

A number of SGML model groups are referenced at multiple points in the document. To ensure that these groups are declared before they are referenced, they have been entered in a special part of the DTD, before any elements have been declared:

```
<!-- Parameter Entities -->

<!ENTITY % head.misc "SCRIPT|STYLE|META|LINK" -- repeatable head
elements-->

<!ENTITY % heading "H1|H2|H3|H4|H5|H6">

<!ENTITY % list "UL | OL | DIR | MENU">

<![ %HTML.Deprecated [
   <!ENTITY % preformatted "PRE | XMP | LISTING">
]]>

<!ENTITY % preformatted "PRE">
```

Note: *Remember that parameter entities must always be declared before being referenced. For this reason it is good practice to keep such declarations in a separate section of the DTD, as has been done here.*

12.6 Character mnemonics

HTML uses the standard Added Latin 1 character set declared in the SGML standard as the basis for defining characters outside the range provided by ISO 646:

```
<!--============== Character mnemonic entities =====================-->

<!ENTITY % ISOlat1 PUBLIC
       "ISO 8879-1986//ENTITIES Added Latin 1//EN//HTML">
%ISOlat1;
```

In addition, the HTML DTD provides the following definitions for characters that are commonly required in HTML documents, but which cannot be entered directly. The replacement text for these characters is defined in terms of SGML numeric character references, because such references will not be recognized by the parser as markup.

```
<!--================ Entities for special symbols ====================-->

<!-- &trade and &cbsp are not widely deployed and so are not included here -->

<!ENTITY amp    CDATA "&#38;"  -- ampersand -->
<!ENTITY gt     CDATA "&#62;"  -- greater than -->
<!ENTITY lt     CDATA "&#60;"  -- less than -->
```

In practice, the above list has been extended by including in the HTML 3.2 definition of the Latin-1 entity set some additional entities. These entities are not strictly speaking part of the ISO 8879-1986 ISO Latin-1 entity set identified by the `%ISOlat1;` parameter entity. They are as follows:

```
<!ENTITY nbsp   CDATA " " -- no-break space -->
<!ENTITY iexcl  CDATA "&#161;" -- inverted exclamation mark -->
<!ENTITY cent   CDATA "&#162;" -- cent sign -->
<!ENTITY pound  CDATA "&#163;" -- pound sterling sign -->
<!ENTITY curren CDATA "&#164;" -- general currency sign -->
<!ENTITY yen    CDATA "&#165;" -- yen sign -->
<!ENTITY brvbar CDATA "&#166;" -- broken (vertical) bar -->
<!ENTITY sect   CDATA "&#167;" -- section sign -->
<!ENTITY uml    CDATA "&#168;" -- umlaut (diaresis) -->
<!ENTITY copy   CDATA "&#169;" -- copyright sign -->
<!ENTITY ordf   CDATA "&#170;" -- ordinal indicator, feminine -->
<!ENTITY laquo  CDATA "&#171;" -- angle quotation mark, left -->
<!ENTITY not    CDATA "&#172;" -- not sign -->
<!ENTITY shy    CDATA "&#173;" -- soft hyphen -->
<!ENTITY reg    CDATA "&#174;" -- registered sign -->
<!ENTITY macr   CDATA "&#175;" -- macron -->
<!ENTITY deg    CDATA "&#176;" -- degree sign -->
<!ENTITY plusmn CDATA "&#177;" -- plus-or-minus sign -->
<!ENTITY sup2   CDATA "&#178;" -- superscript two -->
<!ENTITY sup3   CDATA "&#179;" -- superscript three -->
<!ENTITY acute  CDATA "&#180;" -- acute accent -->
<!ENTITY micro  CDATA "&#181;" -- micro sign -->
<!ENTITY para   CDATA "&#182;" -- pilcrow (paragraph sign) -->
<!ENTITY middot CDATA "&#183;" -- middle dot-->
<!ENTITY cedil  CDATA "&#184;" -- cedilla -->
<!ENTITY supl   CDATA "&#185;" -- superscript one -->
<!ENTITY ordm   CDATA "&#186;" -- ordinal indicator, masculine -->
<!ENTITY raquo  CDATA "&#187;" -- angle quotation mark, right -->
<!ENTITY frac14 CDATA "&#188;" -- fraction one-quarter -->
<!ENTITY frac12 CDATA "&#189;" -- fraction one-half -->
<!ENTITY frac34 CDATA "&#190;" -- fraction three-quarters -->
<!ENTITY iquest CDATA "&#191;" -- inverted question mark -->
```

As the Latin-1 code set actually being referenced by HTML is that defined in ISO 10646, the entity declaration used to invoke it should read:

```
<!ENTITY % ISOlat1 PUBLIC
      "ISO 10646-1:1993//ENTITIES Latin 1 Supplement//EN//HTML">
%ISOlat1;
```

12.7 Text markup

The next set of parameter entity declarations is used to simplify subsequent element declarations by providing an easy-to-understand name for groups of elements that share common characteristics:

```
<!--==================== Text Markup ====================================-->

<!ENTITY % font "TT | I | B | U | STRIKE | BIG | SMALL | SUB | SUP">

<!ENTITY % phrase "EM | STRONG | DFN | CODE | SAMP | KBD | VAR | CITE |">

<!ENTITY % special
"A|IMG|APPLET|BASEFONT|FONT|BR|SCRIPT|STYLE|MAP">

<!ENTITY % form "INPUT | SELECT | TEXTAREA">

<!ENTITY % text "#PCDATA | %font | %phrase | %special | %form">
```

The HTML DTD is particularly good in that it defines the most commonly used elements first, with the least commonly used elements afterwards. This technique can reduce considerably the average amount of time spent searching for a definition. The most used elements of the HTML DTD are those that can occur within paragraphs and other blocks of text. These elements identify phrases or text set in specific fonts. They share an infinitely recursive model:

```
<!ELEMENT (%font|%phrase) - - (%text)*>
```

New elements have been added to the DTD to allow a base character size (`BASEFONT`) to be selected from a set of seven predefined text sizes, and to allow text to be set in a specific size and/or color (`FONT`). For some reason text character color is only applicable to text marked for setting in a specific font, or as a parameter shared by all elements permitted in the body of the document. There are two methods for specifying color, by color name, or by specification of an RGB color number:

```
<!ELEMENT BASEFONT - O EMPTY -- base font size (1 to 7) -->>
<!ATTLIST BASEFONT
   size  CDATA #IMPLIED    -- for example, size=3 -->
<!ELEMENT FONT - - (%text)* -- local change to font -->
<!ATTLIST FONT
   size  CDATA #IMPLIED    -- [+]nn for example, size="+1", size=4 --
   color CDATA #IMPLIED    -- #RRGGBB in hex for example, red:
                              color="#FF0000" --

<!-- There are also 16 widely known color names although the
resulting colors are implementation-dependent:

   aqua, black, blue, fuchsia, gray, green, lime, maroon, navy,
   olive, purple, red, silver, teal, white, and yellow

These colors were originally picked as being the standard 16 colors
supported with the Windows VGA palette.
-->
```

The final element in the text markup group has been declared using SGML's EMPTY keyword to indicate that only a start-tag needs to be entered to mark the point at which action, in this case a forced line break, is required:

```
<!ELEMENT BR - O EMPTY -- forced line break -->
<!ATTLIST BR
       clear (left|all|right|none) none -- control of text flow -- >
```

12.8 Shared content models

The following parameter entities are used to group together those elements that share common properties, so that they can be sensibly referenced in the model for the main body of a document:

```
<!--================== HTML content models ===========================-->

<!--
    HTML has three basic content models:

      %text          character level elements and text strings
      %flow          block-like elements for example, paragraphs
                     and lists
      %body.content  as %flow plus headers H1-H6 and ADDRESS
-->

<!ENTITY % block
    "P | %list | %preformatted | DL | DIV | CENTER |
    BLOCKQUOTE | FORM | ISINDEX | HR | TABLE">

<!-- %flow is used for DD and LI -->

<!ENTITY % flow "(%text | %block)*">
```

Note that the %flow parameter entity is used for the model of elements that can contain formatted text intermixed with larger blocks of text, such as paragraphs, lists, tables or freestanding quotes.

12.9 Body components

The following parameter entities are shared by those elements that form the body of the text in an HTML document:

```
<!--=================== Document Body ================================-->

<!ENTITY % body.content "(%heading | %text | %block | ADDRESS)*">

<!ENTITY % color "CDATA" -- a color specification: #HHHHHH or color name -->
```

```
<!ENTITY % body-color-attrs "
        bgcolor %color #IMPLIED
        text %color    #IMPLIED
        link %color    #IMPLIED
        vlink %color   #IMPLIED
        alink %color   #IMPLIED">
```

Note: *As the* `%color` *parameter entity would also be appropriate for the* `color` *attribute on the <FONT> element, it is likely that the parameter entity for this attribute will be moved to join the rest of the color-related information at a later date.*

The elements given below are used to identify the main components of the body of the document. Their use is explained in detail in Chapter 13.

```
<!ELEMENT BODY O O %body.content>
<!ATTLIST BODY
        background %URL #IMPLIED -- texture tile for document
        background --
        %body-color-attrs; -- bgcolor, text, link, vlink, alink -- >

<!ENTITY % address.content "((%text;) | P)*">

<!ELEMENT ADDRESS - - %address.content>

<!ELEMENT DIV - - %body.content>
<!ATTLIST DIV
        align (left|center|right) #IMPLIED

<!-- CENTER is a shorthand for DIV with ALIGN=CENTER -->
<!ELEMENT center - - %body.content>
```

Note particularly the use of the `%URL` parameter entity reference, to indicate that the `CDATA` content of the `background` attribute should be a valid URL.

12.10 Anchors and links

The elements given below are used to identify the links to other parts of the body of the document, or to other files. Their use is explained in detail in Chapter 13. Note the comment within the definition of the `%Types` parameter entity refers to an IETF working draft that defines how the `rel` and `rev` attributes could be used.

```
<!--================== The Anchor Element ============================-->

<!ELEMENT A - - (%text)* -(A)>
<!ATTLIST A
    name   CDATA   #IMPLIED  -- named link end --
    href   %URL    #IMPLIED  -- URL for linked resource --
    rel    CDATA   #IMPLIED  -- forward link types --
    rev    CDATA   #IMPLIED  -- reverse link types --
    title  CDATA   #IMPLIED  -- advisory title string --          >
```

```
<!--================== The LINK Element ==============================-->
<!ENTITY % Types "CDATA"
      -- See Internet Draft: draft-ietf-html-relrev-00.txt
         LINK has been part of HTML since the early days although few
         browsers as yet take advantage of it.

         Relationship values can be used in principle:

            a) for document specific toolbars/menus when used with
               the LINK element in document head:
            b) to link to a separate style sheet
            c) to make a link to a script
            d) by stylesheets to control how collections of html
               nodes are rendered into printed documents
            e) to make a link to a printable version of this document
               e.g. a postscript or pdf version (rel=print) -->

<!ELEMENT LINK - O EMPTY>
<!ATTLIST LINK
      href   %URL    #IMPLIED -- URL for linked resource --
      rel    %Types  #IMPLIED -- forward link types --
      rev    %Types  #IMPLIED -- reverse link types --
      title  CDATA   #IMPLIED -- advisory title string -->
```

12.11 Images and maps

The elements given below are used to identify images and the active hotspots (maps) that can be associated with them. Their use is explained in detail in Chapter 13.

```
<!--================== Images ========================================-->

<!ENTITY % Length "CDATA" -- nn for pixels or nn% for percentage
length -->
<!ENTITY % Pixels "NUMBER" -- integer representing length in pixels -->

<!-- Suggested widths are used for negotiating image size with the
     module responsible for painting the image. align=left or right
     cause image to float to margin and for subsequent text to wrap
     around image -->

<!ENTITY % IAlign "(top|middle|bottom|left|right)">

<!ELEMENT IMG      - O EMPTY -- Embedded image -->
<!ATTLIST IMG
    src    %URL     #REQUIRED -- URL of image to embed --
    alt    CDATA    #IMPLIED  -- for display in place of image --
    align  %IAlign  #IMPLIED  -- vertical or horizontal alignment --
    height %Pixels  #IMPLIED  -- suggested height in pixels --
```

```
    width  %Pixels #IMPLIED  -- suggested width in pixels --
    border %Pixels #IMPLIED  -- suggested link border width --
    hspace %Pixels #IMPLIED  -- suggested horizontal gutter --
    vspace %Pixels #IMPLIED  -- suggested vertical gutter --
    usemap %URL    #IMPLIED  -- use client-side image map --
    ismap  (ismap) #IMPLIED  -- use server image map -- >

<!-- USEMAP points to a MAP element which may be in this document or
an external document, although the latter is not widely supported -->

<!--================== Client-side image maps =======================-->

<!-- These can be placed in the same document or grouped in a separate
     document although this isn't yet widely supported -->

<!ENTITY % SHAPE "(rect|circle|poly)">
<!ENTITY % COORDS "CDATA" -- comma separated list of numbers -->
<!ELEMENT MAP - - (AREA)*>
<!ATTLIST MAP
    name  CDATA  #IMPLIED  >

<!ELEMENT AREA - O EMPTY>
<!ATTLIST AREA
   shape  %SHAPE   rect
   coords %COORDS  #IMPLIED -- defines coordinates for shape --
   href   %URL     #IMPLIED -- this region acts as hypertext link --
   nohref (nohref) #IMPLIED -- this region has no action --
   alt    CDATA    #REQUIRED -- label for non-graphical user-agents --
   tabindex    NUMBER   #IMPLIED -- position in tabbing order --
   notab       (notab)  #IMPLIED -- exclude from tabbing order -- >
```

Note particularly the heavy use of parameter entity references to identify the type of attributes that have been defined using the CDATA and NUMBER declared value keywords. Note also that CDATA is the only type of attribute value that can include a # or other characters that are not part of the currently defined name character set.

12.12 Applets

The <APPLET> element is used to identify Java programs containing small pieces of application code (*applets*) that are to be incorporated into a document. Their use is explained in detail in Chapter 13.

```
<!--=================== Java APPLET tag ============================-->
<!--
This tag is supported by all Java enabled browsers. Applet resources
(including their classes) are normally loaded relative to the
document URL (or <BASE> element if it is defined). The CODEBASE
attribute is used to change this default behavior. If the CODEBASE
```

```
attribute is defined then it specifies a different location to find
applet resources. The value can be an absolute URL or a relative URL.
The absolute URL is used as is without modification and is not
affected by the document's <BASE> element. When the codebase
attribute is relative, then it is relative to the document URL
(or <BASE> tag if defined).
-->

<!ELEMENT APPLET - - (PARAM|%text)>
<!ATTLIST APPLET
  codebase %URL     #IMPLIED  -- codebase --
  code     CDATA    #REQUIRED -- class file --
  name     CDATA    #IMPLIED  -- applet name --
  alt      CDATA    #IMPLIED  -- for display in place of applet --
  align    %IAlign  #IMPLIED  -- vertical or horizontal alignment --
  height   %Pixels  #REQUIRED -- suggested height in pixels --
  width    %Pixels  #REQUIRED -- suggested width in pixels --
  hspace   %Pixels  #IMPLIED  -- suggested horizontal gutter --
  vspace   %Pixels  #IMPLIED  -- suggested vertical gutter -->
<!ELEMENT PARAM - O EMPTY>
<!ATTLIST PARAM
  name     NMTOKEN  #REQUIRED -- the name of the parameter --
  value    CDATA    #IMPLIED  -- the value of the parameter -- >

<!-- Here is an example:
  <applet codebase="applets/NervousText"
    code=NervousText.class
    width=300
    height=50>
  <param name=text value="Java is Cool!">
  <img src=sorry.gif alt="This looks better with Java support">
</applet>
-->
```

Note particularly the use of comment declarations to provide additional information on the use of these complex elements, as well as to provide an example of their use.

12.13 Paragraphs and headings

The elements given below provide the main text containers in the body of an HTML document. Their use is explained in detail in Chapter 13.

```
<!--=================== Paragraphs===================================-->

<!ELEMENT P     - O (%text)*>
<!ATTLIST P
    align (left|center|right)#IMPLIED >
```

```
<!--================== Headings ======================================-->

<!--
  There are six levels of headers from H1 (the most important)
  to H6 (the least important).
-->

<!ELEMENT ( %heading ) - - (%text;)*>
<!ATTLIST ( %heading )
     align (left|center|right) #IMPLIED >
```

The following empty element can be used to insert rules between blocks of text:

```
<!--================== Horizontal Rule ==============================-->

<!ELEMENT HR       - O EMPTY>
<!ATTLIST HR
   align (left|right|center) #IMPLIED
   noshade (noshade) #IMPLIED
   size    %Pixels   #IMPLIED
   width   %Length   #IMPLIED              >
```

Note particularly the use of an attribute, `noshade`, for which only one entry is permitted, which is the same as the attribute name. Because of SGML's default rules for attribute minimization, attributes defined using name tokens can be entered without specifying their name, for example, `<HR center noshade>` rather than `<HR align="center" noshade="noshade">`. By setting the only permitted value of the `noshade` attribute to the same value as the name, users can more easily identify which attribute is being specified.

12.14 Preformatted text

The elements given below are used to identify code or other forms of example inserted into body of the document. Their use is explained in detail in Chapter 13.

```
<!--================== Preformatted Text ============================-->

<!-- excludes images and changes in font size -->

<!ENTITY % pre.exclusion "IMG|BIG|SMALL|SUB|SUP|FONT">

<!ELEMENT PRE - - (%text)* -(%pre.exclusion)>
<!ATTLIST PRE
       width NUMBER #implied -- is this widely supported? --     >

<![ %HTML.Deprecated [
```

```
<!ENTITY % literal "CDATA"
        -- historical, non-conforming parsing mode where the only
        markup signal is the end tag in full--      >

<!ELEMENT (XMP|LISTING) -- %literal>
<!ELEMENT PLAINTEXT - O %literal>

]]>

<!--=================== Block-like Quotes ==============================-->

<!ELEMENT BLOCKQUOTE - - %body.content>
```

Note particularly the use of a marked section, whose action is controlled through the `%HTML.Deprecated` parameter entity, to control whether or not to use deprecated elements, the model of which is based on the `CDATA` content model identified through the `%literal` parameter literal. As elements using this model cannot contain nested tags, or an end-tag open (`ETAGO`) delimiter sequence, their use tends to lead to errors. The newer `<PRE>` element, the model for which has been defined using the `%text` parameter entity and from which images and the newer text elements are excluded through the `-(%pre.exclusion)` exception specification, is less prone to user error.

12.15 Lists

The elements given below are used to identify lists within the body of the document. Their use is explained in detail in Chapter 13.

```
<!--=================== Lists ==========================================-->

<!--
HTML 3.2 allows you to control the sequence number for ordered lists.
You can set the sequence number with the START and VALUE attributes.
The TYPE attribute may be used to specify the rendering of ordered
and unordered lists.
-->

<!-- definition lists - DT for term, DD for its definition -->

<!ELEMENT DL      - - (DT|DD)+>
<!ATTLIST DL
        compact (compact) #IMPLIED -- more compact style --      >

<!ELEMENT DT - O (%text)*>
<!ELEMENT DD - O %flow;>

<!-- Ordered lists OL, and unordered lists UL -->
<!ELEMENT (OL|UL) - - (LI)+>
```

```
<!-- Numbering style
  1  arabic numbers  1, 2, 3, ...
  a  lower alpha     a, b, c, ...
  A  upper alpha     A, B, C, ...
  i  lower roman     i, ii, iii, ...
  I  upper roman     I, II, III, ...

  The style is applied to the sequence number which by default
  is reset to 1 for the first list item in an ordered list.

  This can't be expressed directly in SGML due to case folding.
-->

<!ENTITY % OLStyle "CDATA" -- constrained to: [1|a|A|i|I] -->

<!ATTLIST OL -- ordered lists --
  type     %OLStyle  #IMPLIED -- numbering style --
  start    NUMBER    #IMPLIED -- starting sequence number --
  compact (compact)  #IMPLIED -- reduced interitem spacing -- >

<!-- bullet styles -->

<!ENTITY % ULStyle "disc|square|circle">

<!ATTLIST UL -- unordered lists --
  type     (%ULStyle) #IMPLIED  -- bullet style --
  compact  (compact)  #IMPLIED  -- reduced interitem spacing -- >

<!ELEMENT (DIR|MENU) - - (LI)* -(%block)>
<!ATTLIST DIR
      compact (compact) #IMPLIED        >
<!ATTLIST MENU
      compact (compact) #IMPLIED        >

<!-- <DIR>            Directory list                          -->
<!-- <DIR COMPACT>    Compact list style                      -->
<!-- <MENU>           Menu list                               -->
<!-- <MENU COMPACT>   Compact list style                      -->

<!-- The type attribute can be used to change the bullet style in
     unordered lists and the numbering style in ordered lists -->

<!ENTITY % LIStyle "CDATA" -- constrained to: "(%ULStyle|%OLStyle)" -->

<!ELEMENT LI - O %flow -- list item -->
<!ATTLIST LI
  type    %LIStyle  #IMPLIED   -- list item style --
  value   NUMBER    #IMPLIED   -- reset sequence number -- >
```

Note particularly the last line of the comment declaration on numbering styles for ordered lists and the definition immediately following for the %OLstyle parameter entity. For ordered lists the default value for the type attribute is set to CDATA, which would allow any string of data to be entered as the attribute value. For HTML, however, a comment constrains the contents of this character data string to being one of five single character entries.

The last line of the comment declaration on numbering styles highlights a problem that comes from trying to use different cases to distinguish between options in a list of permitted attribute values. In SGML the name case folding rules for both attribute values and element names are controlled through the NAMECASE GENERAL YES statement in the SGML declaration. If you change this to NAMECASE GENERAL NO to allow an SGML parser to differentiate between attribute values such as a and A, you would also be instructing the parser to differentiate between a <p> and a <P> element start-tag. As this would invalidate many HTML documents, it would not make sense. By using CDATA instead of NAMES it is no longer necessary for HTML browsers to override SGML's rules for name case folding when interpreting the value of the type attribute, because character data is always retained in the case in which it is entered. However, adoption of this approach relies on author discipline to restrain the values to those specified, because the parser is unable to identify the use of arbitrary character strings without special lexical processing of its contents.

12.16 Forms

The elements given below are used to create data capture forms in the body of an HTML document. Their use is explained in detail in Chapter 14.

```
<!--================ Forms ===========================================-->

<!ELEMENT FORM - - %body.content -(FORM)>
<!ATTLIST FORM
  action %URL                #REQUIRED -- server-side form handler --
  method (%HTTP-Method)      GET       -- see HTTP specification --
  enctype %Content-Type;     "application/x-www-form-urlencoded" >

<!ENTITY % InputType
   "(TEXT | PASSWORD | CHECKBOX | RADIO | SUBMIT |
   RESET | FILE | HIDDEN | IMAGE)"
>

<!ELEMENT INPUT - O EMPTY>
<!ATTLIST INPUT
   type  %InputType TEXT -- what kind of widget is needed --
   name  CDATA #IMPLIED  -- required for all but submit and reset --
   value CDATA #IMPLIED  -- required for radio and checkboxes --
```

```
  checked (checked) #IMPLIED -- for radio buttons and check boxes --
  size   CDATA #IMPLIED  -- specific to each type of field --
  maxlength NUMBER #IMPLIED
  src    %URL #IMPLIED   -- for fields with background images --
  align (top|middle|bottom|left|right) top -- image alignment -->

<!ELEMENT SELECT - - (OPTION+)>
<!ATTLIST SELECT
  name      CDATA       #REQUIRED
  size      NUMBER      #IMPLIED
  multiple (multiple)  #IMPLIED >

<!ELEMENT OPTION - O (#PCDATA)*>
<!ATTLIST OPTION
  selected (selected) #IMPLIED
  value CDATA #IMPLIED -- defaults to element content -- >

<!-- Multi-line text input field. -->

<!ELEMENT TEXTAREA - - (#PCDATA)*>
<!ATTLIST TEXTAREA
  name        CDATA    #REQUIRED
  rows        NUMBER   #REQUIRED
  cols        NUMBER   #REQUIRED >
```

The definition of the %InputType parameter entity is a good example of how to simplify the structure of attribute definitions where long lists of permitted values, which are likely to grow with time, are required. An editor can make use of the current value of this parameter entity when creating a pull-down option list for form creation.

12.17 Tables

The elements given below can be used to code tables in the body of an HTML document. Their use is explained in detail in Chapter 13. The formal specification for HTML tables is given in IETF RFC 1942, the URL for which is specified in the second comment declaration of the section. Note that the definition given in this DTD represents a subset of the full table specificiation.

```
<!--======================= Tables ===================================-->

<!-- Widely deployed subset of the full table standard, see RFC 1942
     e.g. at http://www.cs.uci.edu/pub/ietf/html/rfc1942.txt -->

<!-- horizontal placement of table relative to window -->
<!ENTITY % Where "(left|center|right)">

<!-- horizontal alignment attributes for cell contents -->
<!ENTITY % cell.halign
       "align (left|center|right) #IMPLIED >
```

```
<!-- vertical alignment attributes for cell contents -->
<!ENTITY % cell.valign
      "valign (top|middle|bottom) #IMPLIED" >

<!ELEMENT table - - (caption?, tr+)>
<!ELEMENT CAPTION - - (%text;)* -- table or figure caption -->
<!ATTLIST CAPTION
  align (top|bottom)#IMPLIED>
<!ELEMENT tr - O (th|td)+>
<!ELEMENT (th|td) - O %body.content>

<!ATTLIST table            -- table element --
   align       %Where;  #IMPLIED -- table position relative to window --
   width       %Length; #IMPLIED -- table width relative to window --
   border      %Pixels; #IMPLIED -- controls frame width around table --
   cellspacing %Pixels; #IMPLIED -- spacing between cells --
   cellpadding %Pixels; #IMPLIED -- spacing within cells -- >

<!ATTLIST tr               -- table row --
   %cell.halign;           -- horizontal alignment in cells --
   %cell.valign;           -- vertical alignment in cells -- >

<!ATTLIST (th|td)                 -- header or data cell --
   rowspan  NUMBER 1              -- number of rows spanned by cell --
   colspan  NUMBER 1              -- number of cols spanned by cell --
   %cell.halign;                  -- horizontal alignment in cells --
   %cell.valign;                  -- vertical alignment in cells --
   width  %Pixels #IMPLIED -- suggested width for cell --
   height %Pixels #IMPLIED -- suggested height for cell -- >
```

Note that the model for table headers and data elements (<TH> and <TD>) is defined using the `%body.content` parameter entity. As this includes tables and images, it is possible to define subtables within table entries.

Note: *The comment associated with the <CAPTION> element is misleading as captions can only be entered inside <TABLE> elements.*

12.18 HTML document headers

The elements given below can be used within HTML document headers to associate metadata with the text that forms the document body. Data stored within these elements is not displayed in the text area of the screen, but can be displayed in menus by browsers with a suitable user interface. Their use is explained in detail in Chapter 13. Note particularly the use of a comment at the start of the section to remind readers that the parameter entity, `%head.misc`, used to define an inclusion for the header, was defined in an earlier part of the DTD.

```
<!--================ Document Head ===================================-->

<!-- %head.misc defined earlier on as "SCRIPT|STYLE|META|LINK" -->

<!ENTITY % head.content "TITLE & ISINDEX? & BASE?">

<!ELEMENT HEAD O O (%head.content) +(%head.misc)>


<!ELEMENT TITLE - - (#PCDATA)* -(%head.misc)
    -- The TITLE element is not considered part of the flow of text.
       It should be displayed, for example as the page header or
       window title. -->

<!ELEMENT ISINDEX - O EMPTY>
<!ATTLIST ISINDEX
       prompt CDATA #IMPLIED -- prompt message -->

<!--
  The BASE element gives an absolute URL for dereferencing relative
  URLs, e.g.

  <BASE href="http://foo.com/index.html">
  ...
  <IMG SRC="images/bar.gif">

The image is deferenced to

  http://foo.com/images/bar.gif

In the absence of a BASE element the document URL should be used.
Note that this is not necessarily the same as the URL used to request
the document, as the base URL may be overridden by an HTTP header
accompanying the document.
-->

<!ELEMENT BASE - O EMPTY>
<!ATTLIST BASE
  href        %URL     #REQUIRED    >

<!ELEMENT META - O EMPTY -- Generic Metainformation -->
<!ATTLIST META
  http-equiv NAME   #IMPLIED   -- HTTP response header name --
  name       NAME   #IMPLIED   -- metainformation name --
  content    CDATA  #REQUIRED  -- associated information -- >

<!-- SCRIPT/STYLE are place holders for transition to next version
of HTML -->

<!ELEMENT STYLE - - (#PCDATA)*-(%head.misc) -- style info -->

<!ELEMENT SCRIPT - - (#PCDATA)*-(%head.misc)
  -- script statements -->
```

12.19 HTML document structure

The very last element to be defined in the HTML DTD is that for the omissible <HTML> element. Note how the %HTML.Version parameter entity is used to assign a fixed default value to each instance of this element.

```
<!--================ Document Structure ============================-->

<!ENTITY % version.attr "VERSION CDATA #FIXED '%HTML.Version;'">

<![ %HTML.Deprecated [
  <!ENTITY % html.content "HEAD, BODY, PLAINTEXT?">
]]>

<!ENTITY % html.content "HEAD, BODY">

<!ELEMENT HTML O O (%html.content)>
<!ATTLIST HTML
  %version.attr;
  >
```

The Hypertext Markup Language (HTML)

The HTML header • Text blocks in the HTML body • Embedded text • The role of HTML anchors • Images and maps • Tables • Applets

The HTML document type definition (DTD) is the most commonly used example of the use of SGML in electronic publishing on the Internet. This chapter provides a detailed explanation of the roles of the elements provided in Version 3.2 of the HTML DTD that is shown in Chapter 12. The use of forms in an HTML environment is covered in the next chapter.

Figure 13.1 provides a graphical illustration of the main structural elements of the HTML DTD. It should be noted, however, that this simplified tree diagram does not fully illustrate the recursive nature of the HTML DTD.

13.1 The HTML header

Each HTML document starts with a `<HEAD>` element that has embedded within it:

- a compulsory `<TITLE>` element;
- an optional `<BASE>` element;
- an optional `<ISINDEX>` element;
- optionally, one or more `<STYLE>` elements;
- optionally, one or more `<SCRIPT>` elements;
- optionally, one or more `<META>` elements;
- optionally, one or more `<LINK>` elements.

The header *must* contain a title, for which the start-tag (`<TITLE>`) and end-tag (`</TITLE>`) are compulsory. Text placed between these tags will be displayed

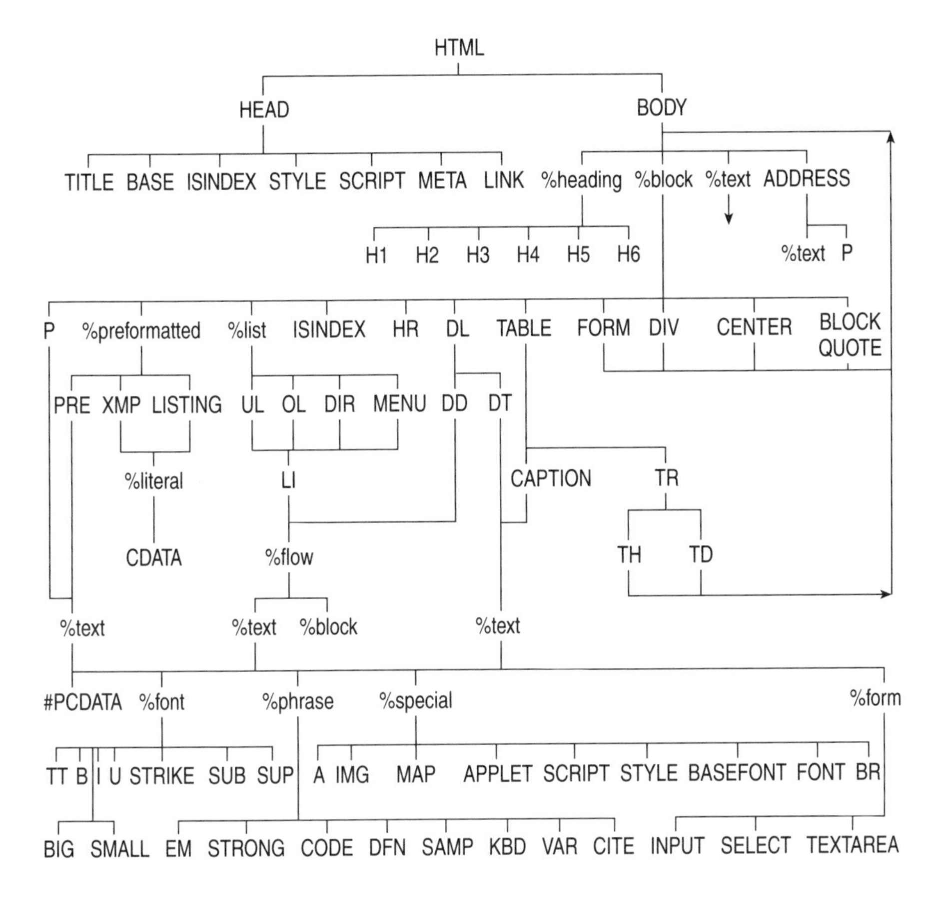

Figure 13.1 Relationships between main structural elements in the HTML 3.2 DTD

by the browser as the window title and will be used as the title of the file in any history or bookmark record.

Note: *The two start-tags that can precede the start-tag for the title, <HTML> and <HEAD>, are both omissible.*

If the anchors in the file are defined using relative URLs that reference files in a directory other than the one containing the current file, the referenced directory should be identified by entry of a start-tag of the form `<BASE href="URI">`, where `URI` (Uniform Resource Identifier) is a fully resolved URL that identifies the directory containing the referenced files. The URI should always begin with a *scheme specification*, for example, `http:`, and be followed by a *network location*, such as `//www.echo.lu`, and a *pathname* identifying a route to a directory at that location, such as `/oii/en`. A typical entry is:

```
<BASE href="http://www.echo.lu/oii/en">
```

Note: *Some browsers also require the addition of a filename component, but this is not part of the HTML specification.*

As the <BASE> element has been declared to be an EMPTY SGML element, it can have no textual contents and, therefore, will have no end-tag.

Where users are expected to generate input as a result of reading a file that needs to be sent to a search engine, or another program, the <BASE> element can be followed by an <ISINDEX prompt="Message"> start-tag. This tells the system that it should display a text input field, preceded by the contents of the prompt attribute, into which users can enter a search string. When the return key is pressed the browser should append the contents of the input field, using a GET-data search request, to the URI specified by the <BASE> element.

As the <ISINDEX> element has been declared to be an EMPTY element, it can have no textual contents and will have no end-tag.

The <STYLE> element will normally contain information coded using the World Wide Web Consortium's (W3C) Cascading Style Sheet (CSS) specification for the formatting rules to be applied to the document.

The <SCRIPT> element allows JavaScript, Visual Basic and related *scripts* to be used to control the way in which embedded HTML objects are presented to users. Both elements use the CDATA keyword as their content model. This is intended to prevent users from embedding markup tags, or character sequences that could be mistaken for HTML markup tags, within the script or style sheet data.

A simple example of JavaScript is:

```
<SCRIPT LANGUAGE="JavaScript">
// CursorOver() and OnClick() are functions used to display text
// in the status bar when the mouse is near a given link
function CursorOver ()
{     window.status="Click for more information" }
function OnClick ()
{     window.status="Please wait while we retrieve the relevant file" }
</SCRIPT>
```

Note: *Details of the coding of styles and scripts is beyond the scope of this book. References to the formal specifications of JavaScript and the W3C Cascading Style Sheets specifications are provided in the references section at the end of the book.*

The <META> element can be used to assign metadata to a file. Each <META> element sets up a name/value pair, defined using attributes called name and content, which contain information that can be used to identify or manage the file when it is stored within a filestore. Where the information defined is of a type normally transmitted in an HTTP message header, the name of the equivalent HTTP field can be specified as the value of an http-equiv attribute in place of assigning a name to the property. Examples of the use of metadata include:

```
<META name="Author" content="Martin Bryan">
<META name="Copyright" content="The SGML Centre">
<META http-equiv="Expires" content="Fri, 08 Mar 1996 23:59:59 GMT">
<META http-equiv="Keywords" content="SGML HTML">
```

On some browsers the <META> element can also be used to set up what are known as *client pull* scenarios, whereby calling a file automatically invokes the display of a second page after a specific period of time. For example, if the header contains the following <META> element:

```
<META http-equiv="refresh" content="120;URL=timeout.gif">
```

the browser will automatically switch to a timeout image 120 seconds after first displaying the page.

The <LINK> element allows pointers to other files to be stored as part of the header of a file. The <LINK> element is typically used to identify related indexes and glossaries, older and younger versions of the files, available translations and associated resources such as style sheets. As the <LINK> element has been declared to be an EMPTY element, it has a start-tag, but, unlike the <A> element used to identify anchors in the body of the text, can have no textual contents or end-tag. The following attributes can be associated with the <LINK> start-tag:

- an href attribute, used to specify the URL of the file to which this file is to be linked;
- an optional rel attribute, used to identify the relationship(s) described by the link; the value is a list of relationship names separated by white space;
- an optional rev attribute, used to identify the relationship between the file being pointed to and the file containing the link; this relationship is the reverse of that specified by the rel attribute;
- an optional title attribute, used to suggest a title for the linked data; this title may be used for display prior to accessing the data, for example, as a margin note or window message;

  Note: *Titles must be specified in the local code set and should not, therefore, include SGML entity references to accented characters. To ensure that titles work in all environments, they should be restricted to ASCII alphanumeric and basic punctuation characters.*

Typical examples of the use of <BASE> and <LINK> elements include:

```
<BASE "http://www.myco.org/pub/subject/en/">
<LINK href="bibliography.html" title="Bibliography" rel=author rev=wrote>
<LINK href="../sp/file234.html" title="Espanol" rel=translation>
<LINK href="../fr/file234.html" title="Francais" rel=translation>
<LINK href="../de/file234.html" title="Deutsch" rel=translation>
<LINK href="index.html" rel=index
```

13.2 Text blocks in the HTML body

The header of each HTML file must be followed by one or more of the elements defined as valid `body.content` elements, which can, optionally, be enclosed within a `<BODY>` element. The following attributes can be associated with the `<BODY>` element:

- an optional `background` attribute, used to identify an image to be used as a background to any text or images in the body of the text;
- a set of overrides to the reader's stated display preferences, as defined through the `body-color-attrs` parameter entity:
  - an optional `bgcolor` attribute that changes the colour used as the background to any text displayed on the screen;
  - an optional `text` attribute that changes the colour used for displayed text;
  - an optional `link` attribute that changes the colour used to display text within anchors;
  - an optional `alink` attribute that changes the colour used to display anchors whose links are being activated;
  - an optional `vlink` attribute that changes the colour used to display anchors that have already been visited.

The colors that can be defined for each of the `%body-color-attrs` options must be entered either in a standardized RGB format as three pairs of hexadecimal numbers (for example, `#C0FFC0`) or as one of 16 widely understood color names: `aqua`, `black`, `blue`, `fuchsia`, `gray`, `green`, `lime`, `maroon`, `navy`, `olive`, `purple`, `red`, `silver`, `teal`, `white` and `yellow`. (These represent the standard 16 colors in the Windows VGA palette.)

To force the user to read the text of a document as red letters on a white background, with links defined using colors chosen by the author, the `<BODY>` element could be assigned the following additional attributes:

```
<BODY bgcolor=white text=red link=green alink=teal vlink=blue>
```

Warning: *Changing the user's stated preferences can be very dangerous. Remember that 14% of the population is color blind to some extent. Selecting colors such as red and green as your overrides may make it impossible for some readers to see the file. Forcing a white on black screen, which is increasingly being done on many web sites, can cause unnecessary eye strain. Web page creators should be aware that they risk prosecution in some jurisdictions if they try to enforce color choices that damage the health of the reader.*

A better use of the attributes associated with the <BODY> element would be:

```
<BODY background="watermark.gif">
```

When the &body.content parameter entity is expanded, the model for the <BODY> element becomes:

```
<!ELEMENT BODY O O ( %heading | %text | %block | ADDRESS )>
```

Six levels of heading are defined by the %heading parameter entity, numbered from H1 to H6. The HTML DTD places no restrictions on the order in which these headings are used, but does require that the user enter both a start-tag and an end-tag, for example </H1>, for each heading.

Note: *Users expect authors to apply some logic to their selection of appropriate heading levels, but the DTD does not enforce the use of such logic.*

Headings may contain the elements defined in the %text parameter entity. These elements may also be included at any point within the body of the document. %text is defined as:

```
<!ENTITY % text "#PCDATA | %font | %phrase | %special | %form">
```

The first keyword, #PCDATA, indicates that parsed character data (text) can be entered as the contents of elements that use this parameter entity as their content model. Details of the use of elements that can be embedded within headings and other forms of text, as defined in the nested parameter entities, are provided in later sections of this chapter and, in the case of %form, in the next chapter.

The start-tags for headings can be qualified by align. For example, to set a centered heading, you would enter the heading as:

```
<H1 align=center>Using Centered Headings</H1>
```

13.2.1 Space-delimited text blocks

The definition of the %block parameter entity is:

```
<!ENTITY % block "P | %list | %preformatted | DL | DIV | CENTER |
BLOCKQUOTE | FORM | ISINDEX | HR | TABLE" >
```

These elements create blocks of text that are normally separated from surrounding blocks by white space.

Note: *The coding of tables will be covered in a later section. The role of the <FORM> and <ISINDEX> elements will be explained in the next chapter.*

The paragraph element, <P>, is the main container for text within the body of an HTML-encoded file. Paragraphs may contain any of the elements identified by the `%text` parameter entity.

A typical minimally coded HTML file has a heading containing just a title, followed by a body part consisting of a set of headings and associated paragraphs:

```
<HTML><HEAD><TITLE>HTML Example 1</TITLE>
<BODY>
<H1>Using HTML</H1>
<P>This page gives readers some useful clues in the use of HTML.</P>
<H2>Creating Links To Other Files</H2>
<P>One of the most potent features of HTML is its ability to
interconnect files.</P>
```

13.2.2 Lists

Four forms of list are identified through the `%list` parameter entity. Ordered (numbered) list, <OL>, and unordered (bulletted) list, <UL>, elements can be used to identify lists made up of one or more paragraphs of text. Specialist kinds of list can be identified using the directory, <DIR>, and <MENU> elements, although these elements are now considered to be obsolete. All of the elements indentified through `%list;` contain a sequence of one or more list items, <LI>, which can contain any of the elements identified by the `%text` parameter entity and, when not occurring within a menu or directory element, with the elements defined in the `%block` parameter entity.

Note: *This allows ordered and unordered lists to be nested to any level required, but means that nested menus or directories cannot be represented in HTML. It should be noted that W3C have suggested that <DIR> and <MENU> are to be deprecated in future versions of DTDs produced by members of the consortium. There is, therefore, some doubt as to whether they will be retained.*

Users can request that a list should be displayed in a compact format, without spacing between list items, by adding a `compact` attribute value to the start-tag of any list. For both ordered and unordered lists a `type` attribute can be used to identify the type of bullet or number to be associated with each entry in the list. The definition for this attribute changes for each element. For unordered lists the `%ULStyle` parameter entity defines the following options:

- `disc` for a filled circular bullet;
- `square` for a square bullet;
- `circle` for an open circular bullet.

For ordered lists the keyword CDATA has been defined as the replacement text for the %OLstyle parameter entity, but this has been qualified by a comment that restricts the character data which can be used to one of the following single character entries.

- 1 (the number 1) for arabic numbering of entries;
- a for lowercase alphabetic numbering of entries;
- A for uppercase alphabetic numbering of entries;
- i for lowercase roman numbering of entries;
- I for uppercase roman numbering of entries.

For ordered lists an additional start attribute can be used to enter the number of the first entry in the list. (For alphabetic codes the number identifies the position of the first letter to be used within the 26-character Latin alphabet.)

Note that, within HTML, lists cannot be embedded within paragraphs, but must always be treated as siblings of preceding and (non-nested) following paragraphs. This leads to a degree of illogicality in HTML documents, as the following example illustrates:

```
<HTML>
<HEAD><TITLE>HTML Example 2</TITLE>
<BODY>
<P>In this paragraph there is a list containing the following
items:
<OL type=1>
<LI>A numbered list containing four items
<LI>An embedded alphabetically numbered list containing three
subitems:
    <OL type=a>
    <LI>Subitem 1
    <LI>Subitem 2
    <LI>Subitem 3</OL>
<LI>An embedded unordered list that has square bullets:
    <UL type=square>
    <LI>bulleted item 1
    <LI>bulleted item 2
    <LI>bulleted item 3</UL>
<LI>A bulleted list with items that contain multiple paragraphs:
    <UL type=disc>
    <LI>This is a multiple paragraph list item.
        <P>This is the second paragraph of the first item
    <LI>This is the second item in the list, which does not have a
         second paragraph.</UL></OL>
<P>This is the second, and last, paragraph of the example.</BODY></HTML>
```

It should be noted that the indenting of the markup is purely to help users understand the nesting levels. It will be ignored by an HTML browser. It should also be noted that the last two end-tags are not compulsory, but have been entered to clearly indicate the end of the example.

When this list is displayed in a browser it will appear as follows:

In this paragraph there is a list containing the following items:

1. A numbered list containing four items
2. An embedded alphabetically numbered list containing three subitems:
    a. Subitem 1
    b. Subitem 2
    c. Subitem 3
3. An embedded unordered list that has square bullets:
    - bulleted item 1
    - bulleted item 2
    - bulleted item 3
4. A bulleted list with items that contain multiple paragraphs:
    - This is a multiple paragraph list item.

      This is the second paragraph of the first item

    - This is the second item in the list, which does not have a second paragraph.

This is the second, and last, paragraph of the example.

Warning: *Netscape browsers do not always properly support the* `type` *options in the way documented in the HTML specifications.*

As can be seen from the above example, the list that logically belongs with the first paragraph is formatted as a separate block, as is the embedded paragraph. This lack of context sensitivity often gives lists, and especially paragraphs within lists, a disconnected appearance.

The treatment of menus and directories differs from browser to browser. Sometimes a different typeface can be used for their display, but some browsers will display them as if they were unordered list. The following shows a simple example of a menu and a directory:

```
<HTML>
<HEAD><TITLE>HTML Example 3</TITLE>
<BODY>
<P>Lists fall into four categories:</p>
<OL><LI>Ordered (numbered) lists, such as this one, into which can
be embedded
<UL><LI>lower levels of ordered (numbered or lettered) lists
<LI>unordered (bulleted) lists such as this one</ul>
<LI>directory lists such as:
<DIR><LI>File-1
<LI>File-2
<LI>File-3</dir>
```

```
<LT>menus such as:
<MENU><LI>Option 1
<LI>Option 2
<LI>Option 3</menu></ol></body></html>
```

This example would be displayed as:

Lists fall into four categories:

1. Ordered (numbered) lists, such as this one, into which can be embedded
   - lower levels of ordered (numbered or lettered) lists
   - unordered (bulleted) lists such as this one
   - directory lists such as:
     File-1
     File-2
     File-3
   - menus such as:
     Option 1
     Option 2
     Option 3

A special kind of list, known as a definition list (<DL>), is provided for lists that consist of term/definition pairs. A definition list consists of a set of defined terms, <DT>, and their definitions, <DD>. The order in which these are entered is not controlled by the HTML DTD. Whilst defined terms can only be specified using the elements identified by the `%text` parameter entity, their definitions can include any of the elements defined in the `%block` parameter entity as well.

A typical example of a definition list might contain the following entries:

```
<DL><DT>SGML</DT><DD>Standard Generalized Markup Language</DD>
<DT>HTML</DT><DD>HyperText Markup Language</DD></DL>
```

These would be presented by the browser as:

SGML
  Standard Generalized Markup Language
HTML
  HyperText Markup Language

13.2.3 Preformatted and quoted text

The `%preformatted` parameter entity within the definition of `%block` identifies elements in which line breaks are to be retained as entered. Only one type of preformatted element, <PRE>, is allowed if the `%HTML.Deprecated` parameter entity is set to `IGNORE`. If the default value of `INCLUDE` is retained, however, two now deprecated forms of preformatted element, <XMP> and <LISTING>, can also be used.

The <PRE> element used to capture preformatted text can contain most forms of text, but some of the newer textual elements, such as those for creating smaller or larger characters, subscript or superscript characters and characters in special fonts, are specifically excluded from the default model. This restriction is necessary because preformatted text is normally displayed using a fixed width font that resembles the output of a typewriter or a computer printout. The alignment of the displayed characters would, therefore, be affected if the size of the type changed. For this reason, all elements that would alter the alignment of characters in a preformatted block have been excluded from the content model for the <PRE> element. In addition, images cannot be embedded within this element. Because <PRE> elements can have parsed character data (#PCDATA) they are permitted to contain entity references to accented characters and to characters that would otherwise be treated as markup characters.

The definitions for the <XMP> and <LISTING> elements, like that for the deprecated <PLAINTEXT> element, use the %literal parameter entity for the content model. This restricts the content of these elements to CDATA, which has led in the past to problems with their use, particularly in non-English texts. As the model for <PRE> is much less prone to user error, use of these older forms of defining preformatted text elements is now deprecated.

The <BLOCKQUOTE> element allows blocks of quoted text to be indented on the left and right and separated from surrounding text blocks by white space. As the <BLOCKQUOTE> element can contain any element that can occur within the body of an HTML document, it is very useful for showing examples of the presentation of HTML elements, as the previous examples have shown.

13.2.4 The <DIV>ision element

One problem with earlier HTML DTDs was that they provided no mechanism for identifying the relationship between headings and associated text. Because headings can be used in any order, and there is no constraint that any text be associated with a heading, there was scope for confusion, as the following example shows:

```
<HTML><HEAD><TITLE>HTML Example 4</TITLE>
<BODY>
<H1>Creating Chaos out of Order</H1>
<P>This example shows how easy it is to get paragraphs out of step
with headings.</P>
<H2>Order, Order</H2>
<P>This paragraph is obviously associated with the preceding
heading.</P>
<H3>An Example</H3>
```

```
<PRE>This is an example of HTML data</PRE>
<P>Is this paragraph part of the example, or does it belong with the
"Order, Order" heading?</P></BODY>
```

The <DIV> element, for which both the start-tag and end-tag must be present, can be used to clarify such situations, as the following example shows:

```
<HTML><HEAD><TITLE>HTML Example 5</TITLE>
<BODY><DIV>
<H1>Creating Chaos out of Order</H1>
<P>This example shows how easy it is to get paragraphs out of step
with headings.</P>
<DIV>
<H2>Order, Order</H2>
<P>This paragraph is obviously associated with the preceding
heading.</P>
<DIV><H3>An Example</H3>
<PRE>This is an example of HTML data</PRE></DIV>
<P>Is this paragraph part of the example, or does it belong with the
"Order, Order" heading?</P></DIV></DIV></BODY>
```

The first of the </DIV> end-tags makes it clear that the example ends at the end of the preformatted block. The second </DIV> indicates that the division that began with the <H2> heading also includes the final paragraph. The last </DIV> closes down the division that shows the text associated with the main title of the document.

The <DIV> element is particularly useful for maintaining relationships within SGML-coded files that have been converted to HTML for transmission over the WWW. It can also be used to control the formatting of sets of text blocks through the addition of an `align` attribute, and the other generic attributes asociated with it, as the following example shows:

```
<HTML><HEAD><TITLE>HTML Example 6</TITLE>
<BODY><DIV align=left>
<H1>Creating Chaos out of Order</H1>
<P>This example shows how easy it is to get paragraphs out of step
with headings.</P>
<DIV>
<H2>Order, Order</H2>
<P>This paragraph is obviously associated with the preceding
heading.</P>
<DIV align=center><H3>An Example</H3>
<PRE>This is an example of HTML data</PRE></DIV>
<P>Is this paragraph part of the example, or does it belong with the
"Order, Order" heading?</P></DIV></DIV></BODY>
```

In this case, the heading for the example, and the example itself, will be centered, the rest of the text having the default left alignment.

This example would be displayed as:

Creating Chaos out of Order

This example shows how easy it is to get paragraphs out of step with headings.

Order, Order

This paragraph is obviously associated with the preceding heading.

An Example

`This is an example of HTML data`

Is this paragraph part of the example, or does it belong with the "Order, Order" heading?

Users of Netscape may be familiar with their shorthand form of the `<DIV align=center>` sequence, `<CENTER>`. This tag is also available in the HTML DTD, but is likely to be deprecated in future versions of the DTD. The following example shows how this tag could be used to center the example in the previous example, if the other attributes previously associated with the `<DIV>` start-tag were assumed to be unnecessary:

```
<HTML><HEAD><TITLE>HTML Example 7</TITLE>
<BODY><DIV align=justify>
<H1>Creating Chaos out of Order</H1>
<P>This example shows how easy it is to get paragraphs out of step
with headings.</P>
<DIV>
<H2>Order, Order</H2>
<P>This paragraph is obviously associated with the preceding
heading.</P>
<CENTER><H3>An Example</H3>
<PRE>This is an example of HTML data</PRE></CENTER>
<P>Is this paragraph part of the example, or does it belong with the
"Order, Order" heading?</P></DIV></DIV></BODY>
```

13.2.5 Other elements defined as blocks

Horizontal rules, `<HR>`, can only be inserted between text blocks, not within them. This means that they cannot, for example, be placed between the items in a list. The following attributes can be used to control the format of a rule:

- an optional `align` attribute that can be used to align the rule with the `left` or `right` margin, or to `center` it;
- an optional `noshade` attibute that is used to inhibit any shadowing effect;
- an optional `size` attribute that can be used to define the depth of the rule as an integer number of pixels;

- an optional `width` attribute that is used to define the length of the rule in terms of either an integer number of pixels (`nn`) or a percentage of the line length (`nn%`).

For example, to create a 4 pixel deep unshadowed rule half the width of the column, centered on the width, you would enter `<HR align=center noshade size=4 width="50%">`.

The last element in the model of the `<BODY>` element is `<ADDRESS>`. Addresses may consist of either the elements identified by the `%text` parameter entity or paragraphs. Addresses are typically displayed in italic with a left indent. An address would typically be encoded as:

```
<ADDRESS>Martin Bryan<BR>
The SGML Centre<BR>
29 Oldbury Orchard<BR>
Churchdown<BR>
Glos. GL3 2PU<BR>
U.K.</ADDRESS>
```

and displayed as:

Martin Bryan
The SGML Centre
29 Oldbury Orchard
Churchdown
Glos. GL3 2PU
U.K.

13.3 Embedded text

The elements covered in this section may be embedded within text contained within paragraphs and other text-containing elements, the model of which includes the `%text` parameter entity. When the parameter entities referenced in the model provided in the `%text` parameter entity are expanded, you end up with a content model of the form:

```
( #PCDATA | TT | I | B | U | STRIKE | BIG | SMALL | SUB | SUP |
EM | STRONG | DFN | CODE | SAMP | KBD | VAR | CITE |
A | IMG | APPLET | BASEFONT | FONT | BR | SCRIPT |
MAP | INPUT | SELECT | TEXTAREA )
```

Except where otherwise stated, the model for the contents of these elements is defined using the `%text` parameter entity, so each of the elements can be used recursively. For this reason it is essential that both start-tags and end-tags are entered for all embedded elements other than the empty tags for base font specifications, `<BASEFONT>`, line breaks, `<BR>`, and images, `<IMG>`.

Note: *Some earlier versions of HTML required <IMG> to have end-tags.*

The #PCDATA at the start of the model group indicates that parsed character data can occur at any point in an element assigned this model. If a line break is required at a particular point in a line, a <BR> start-tag can be entered. This element has been defined as an empty element, so must contain no content and have no end-tag. The <BR> element has an optional clear attribute which defaults to none, but can be changed to left, all and right if a break is to be forced to a point at which the left or right margin(s) are clear of any images or other data placed on the specified side(s) of the window.

The emphasis, <EM>, element, or its font-based equivalent for the use of an italic typeface, <I>, can be used to highlight phrases within a paragraph. Where a stronger degree of emphasis is required the <STRONG> element, or its font-based equivalent for the use of a bold typeface, <B>, can be used. By embedding these elements inside one another you can produce strongly emphasized text, which will normally be displayed using bold italic characters.

References to book titles that are to be printed in italics should be marked up using the citation element, <CITATION>. The latest versions of HTML have reintroduced a tag for defining instances of terms using the <DFN> element.

To indicate that in-line text is to be presented using fixed-width characters, it can be marked up as computer code, <CODE>, sample text, <SAMP>, or keyboard characters, <KBD>. Alternatively, the font-based equivalent for the use of a fixed width typewriter typeface, <TT>, can be used. Computer coding can also have components that are identified as a variable, <VAR>. This element is normally presented in italic.

Version 3.2 of the HTML DTD introduced two elements that are particularly important for those creating scientific texts:

- The <SUB> element can be used to code subscripts (inferior characters), such as H₂O.
- The <SUP> element can be used to code superscripts (superior characters) and other forms of indices, such as x².

In addition, Version 3.2 of the HTML DTD has introduced two new elements, <U> and <STRIKE>, that can be used to indicate that text embedded within them is to be underlined or struck through.

Unfortunately the latest versions of the HTML DTD have also introduced the following formatting-related elements, rather than having text formatting controlled through application of the rules defined as part of a <STYLE> element:

- <BIG> to set enclosed text in a larger point size;
- <SMALL> to set enclosed text in a smaller point size;
- <FONT> for controlling typeface size, color and shape more precisely using the following attributes:
  - size to specify the relative size of the font in terms of position in a list of seven available type sizes, either relative to the current type size (for

example, +2 or -1) or absolutely (for example, 5 for the fifth entry in the size table);

Note: *The negative option for specifying smaller sizes is not, according to the comment in the DTD, part of the official definition, but it is supported by popular browsers.*

– color to indicate the RGB code or name of the color to be used to display embedded characters.

The default size of font to be used for subsequent text can be selected from the list of seven font sizes known to each HTML browser by entering a <BASEFONT size="n"> tag, where n is the number (1–7) of the size to be used for the presentation of normal sized text.

The example below illustrates the use of the main textual elements in the HTML DTD. To emphasize that the end-tags for many text block elements are optional, they have been omitted where appropriate.

```
<HTML><HEAD><TITLE>Using HTML Text Elements</TITLE>
<BASE href="http://www.echo.lu/icons">
<LINK href="mailto:mtbryan@sgml.u-net.com" rel=author>
<META http-equiv="Keywords" content="HTML elements examples">
<META name="Copyright" content="The SGML Centre">
<BODY>
<H4>Using HTML Text Elements</H4>
<P>Paragraphs can have <EM>emphasized</EM> and <I>italic</I> text,
<STRONG>strongly emphasized</STRONG> and <B>bold</B> text, and
<EM><STRONG>both</STRONG></EM> options
to produce <B><I>bold italic</I></B> text.</P>
<P>In <CITATION>SGML and HTML Explained</CITATION> by Martin
Bryan, you will find a paragraph with <CODE>computer coding</CODE>,
<SAMP> sample text</SAMP>, <KBD>keyboard codes</KBD> and
<VAR>variables </VAR> displayed, together with text presented
using the <TT> typewriter</TT> typeface.</P>
<P>For scientific text it is important to be able to enter
<DFN>chemical formulae</DFN> such as <FONT size="+1"
color=aqua>H<SUB>2</SUB>O</FONT> and <DFN>mathematical
formulae</DFN> such as <FONT size="+2" color="#00FFFF">
x<SUP>2</SUP></FONT>.</P>
<P>Note: Some browsers<STRIKE>, such as Netscape,</STRIKE> do not
differentiate <U>underlined text</U>.</P>
<HR>
<PRE>This is preformatted text.
The line breaks in it are those entered by the user.
It is often displayed using fixed width characters.</PRE>
<BLOCKQUOTE>
<BIG>This is an example of a block quote containing big and small
sentences.</BIG>
<P>
<SMALL>It contains two paragraphs of text.</SMALL>
</BLOCKQUOTE>
</HTML>
```

This file would be displayed as:

> **Using HTML Text Elements**
>
> Paragraphs can have *emphasized* and *italic* text, **strongly emphasized** and **bold** text, and ***both*** options to produce ***bold italic*** text.
>
> In *SGML and HTML Explained* by Martin Bryan, you will find a paragraph with `computer coding`, `sample text`, `keyboard codes` and *variables* displayed, together with text presented using the `typewriter` typeface.
>
> For scientific text it is important to be able to enter *chemical formulae* such as H_2O and mathematical formulae such as x^2.
>
> Note: Some browsers~~, such as Netscape,~~ do not differentiate underlined text.

```
This is preformatted text.
The line breaks in it are those entered by the user.
It is often displayed using fixed width characters.
```

> This is an example of a block quote containing big and small sentences.
>
> It contains two paragraphs of text.

Warning: *Do not be surprised if your browser does not display underlined or struck through text correctly, because only the latest versions of WWW browsers will be able to process the new elements introduced by the DTD.*

13.4 The role of HTML anchors

The most important of the embedded elements in the HTML DTD is the anchor element, <A>. Anchors are used to name points within a file that other documents can point to and to identify hotspots within the text that users can click on to move to another part of the same file, or to open another file.

The definition of the anchor element in Version 3.2 of the HTML DTD is:

```
<!ELEMENT A - - (%text)* -(A)>
<!ATTLIST A
     name      CDATA  #IMPLIED -- named link end --
     href      %URL   #IMPLIED -- URL for linked resource --
     rel       CDATA  #IMPLIED -- forward link types --
     rev       CDATA  #IMPLIED -- reverse link types --
     title     CDATA  #IMPLIED -- advisory title string --     >
```

The content model for the anchor element shows that it can contain any of the elements defined in the `%text` parameter entity, including parsed character data. An anchor cannot, however, contain headings, paragraphs or other blocks of text, *or nested anchors*, as the exclusion definition at the end of the declaration makes clear.

Note: *Many HTML browsers do not enforce this exclusion, or the rules about not nesting text blocks, because many existing HTML files ignore these rules.*

No mechanism is provided for identifying arbitrary sets of text blocks within HTML. For part of a text block to be named so that it can be pointed to from elsewhere in a document, the text should be placed within an anchor element assigned a `name` attribute. As the `name` attribute is defined using the `CDATA` keyword, SGML places no restrictions on the lengths of anchor names and permits them to contain spaces. The rules for URLs, however, do not permit spaces, requiring that any spaces in the string be replaced by `%20` to indicate the hexadecimal value of the space code.

A named anchor would typically have the form:

```
<P>The role of <A name="anchors">HTML anchors</A>...
```

To reference a named anchor from elsewhere in the same file requires the use of an anchor with a URL *fragment identifier* as the value of its `href` attribute, for example:

```
... in the section on <A href="#anchors">The Role of the A Element</A>.
```

Note that the name must, in this case, be preceded by a # symbol to identify it as an IETF fragment identifier. As this character is not part of the standard set of SGML name characters, the `href` attribute has also been declared as containing character data (`CDATA`), rather than a name, in the definition for the `%URL` parameter entity.

Note: *The HTML anchor element does not use the SGML ID/IDREF mechanism to identify and reference elements. There is, therefore, no way of confirming that a reference to an HTML fragment identifier within the same document is a valid one.*

To reference data in another file stored in the same directory as the file containing the reference, the relevant *file name* can be entered as the value of the `href` attribute, for example:

```
... shown in <A href="annex-a.html">Annex A</A>.
```

Where the referenced file is an HTML file that contains named anchors, the relevant anchor name can be entered as a fragment identifier after the file name, for example:

```
... shown in <A href="chapter5.html#clause5-2">Clause 5.2</A>.
```

Where the referenced file is stored in a directory that is a subdirectory of the parent directory of the directory containing the referenced file, the relevant directory can be specified using a *relative path* of the form:

```
... provide the text in <A href="../sp/file134.html">Spanish</A>.
```

Warning: *It is important that PC users note that URLs require that the divider between the directory name and the file name is a Unix-conformant forward slash, rather than a PC-conformant backward slash. Macintosh users should take care not to use colons in file or directory names. When referencing files on VMS systems, care must be taken to avoid the use of square brackets or periods within file and path names.*

Where the text is held in another directory of the same file server, the full *path name* of the relevant directory can be specified, for example:

```
... in <A href="/pub/1995/statement-13-04">our earlier statement</
A>.
```

Where the document is stored on another system, the URL should start with *scheme* and *network location* identifiers, for example:

```
... as described by Bryan in
<A href="http://www.sgml.u-net.com/sgml.htm#LINK">
<CITATION>Using Multiple SGML Document Structures</CITE></A>.
```

If the file is not an HTML document that is retrievable using the HTTP protocol, it can be recalled using other schemes, such as anonymous FTP or Gopher. In such cases, there should not be a fragment identifier at the end of the URL as these can only be identified within HTML documents. Typical examples of this type of anchor include:

```
... in <A href="ftp://ftp.cwi.nl/pub/audio/
  AudioFormats.part1">Part 1</A> and
<A href="gopher://kupe.itu.ch:70/11/.1/itudoc/public/
  gophermenus/.1/.itu-t/.rec/.x/.x200-499/.22320">ITU X.400</A>.
```

Anchors share the following optional attributes with the `<LINK>` element:

- an optional `rel` attribute, used to identify the relationship(s) described by the hyperlink; the value is a white-space-separated list of relationship names;
- an optional `rev` attribute, used identify the relationship between the file being pointed to and the file containing the link; this relationship is the reverse of that specified by the `rel` attribute;

- an optional `title` attribute, used to suggest a title for the destination resource, which could be displayed prior to accessing it, for example, as a margin note or in a separate menu;

Note: *Titles must be specified in the local code set and should not, therefore, include SGML entity references to accented characters. To ensure that titles work in all environments, they should be restricted to unaccented alphanumeric and basic punctuation characters.*

13.4.1 Link relationships

An Internet Draft specification, *Hypertext Links in HTML*, which expired in August 1996, suggested the following possible values for the `rel` and `rev` attributes associated with anchors and links:

- `CONTENTS`, or `TOC`, to identify tables of contents
- `INDEX`
- `NAVIGATOR`
- `CHILD`
- `PARENT`
- `SIBLING`
- `TOP`, or `ORIGIN`, to identify the root of the document tree
- `BEGIN`, or `FIRST`, to identify the first document in a set
- `END`, or `LAST`, to identify the last document in a set
- `NEXT`
- `PREVIOUS`, or `PREV`
- `BIBLIOGRAPHY`
- `CITATION`
- `BIBLIOENTRY`
- `FOOTNOTE`
- `GLOSSARY`
- `AUTHOR`
- `EDITOR`
- `PUBLISHER`
- `COPYRIGHT`
- `DISCLAIMER`
- `TRADEMARK`
- `META` to identify links to files containing meta data relating to the current file.

13.4.2 Link management in an HTML environment

Whilst the <A> element is the most important element in the HTML DTD, it is also the one that leads to the most problems as systems are normally unable to validate, or otherwise manage, entered URLs. It is, therefore, important to develop strategies for testing the currency of links created between documents within a managed set, and between locally controlled documents and external data sources.

If you can afford the time, and have suitably trained staff, the safest method of checking links from anchors is by traversing them and checking that the results are as expected. This latter can be a problem if the staff concerned do not fully understand the role of the link, because it is possible that the anchor or file pointed to does exist, but no longer points to the data originally being linked to because someone has changed the contents of the referenced file. (HTML anchors provide no mechanism for recording the creation date/time of the version of the file being used when the link was created.)

It is generally a fairly simple matter to write a program that can check the validity of anchors whose addresses reference local data sources. Normally, this will involve splitting the anchor at the # symbol, if it is present, and checking that the data to the left of the symbol is a valid filename on the local system and that the data to the right of the symbol identifies an anchor that has been named within the referenced document.

Checking the validity of data stored on other systems is a much more complicated affair and yet is the area in which errors are most likely to occur. In general, those creating links to files have no control over their contents, or where, or for how long, they will be stored at the identified location. To check that a referenced file is still available over the network, the checking program must issue a request for the file. If the file is not immediately available, one of the following HTTP status messages is likely to be returned by the HTTP server:

- 204; No Content
- 301; Moved Permanently
- 302; Moved Temporarily
- 400; Bad Request
- 401; Unauthorized
- 402; Payment Required
- 403; Forbidden
- 404; Not Found
- 405; Method Not Allowed
- 407; Proxy Authentication Required
- 408; Request Timeout

- 409; Conflict
- 410; Gone
- 502; Bad Gateway
- 503; Service Unavailable
- 504; Gateway Timeout

Whilst the first eight of these messages suggest that the file being referenced no longer exists at the specified location, or is now only available to a known set of subscribers, the other error messages simply indicate that it has not been possible to access the file for the time being. With the exception of message 502, most of these errors could be removed by requesting the file at a later time, perhaps using a different configuration.

Checking the validity of fragment identifiers within externally stored files is much more difficult than checking those within locally held files, because the fragment identifiers can only be checked by requesting the file, storing it locally and then processing the fragment identifiers using the programs created for checking fragment identifiers in local files. This process is, of course, entirely dependent on being able to obtain access to the requested files. Correction of any errors, however, can only be done at the end of the calling anchor, since it is not possible to correct retrieved files and then update their source.

13.5 Images and maps

If an image is to be embedded within text, or entered as a component of the body of the text between paragraphs, it must be specified just as a start-tag because the `<IMG>` element is declared as being an `EMPTY` element. The attributes that can be associated with images in Version 3.2 of the DTD are:

- a compulsory source, `src`, attribute that contains the URL of the file in which the image has been stored;
- an optional alternative text, `alt`, attribute, used to enter a text string that is to be displayed if the image is not available, or if the user has requested that images not be retrieved by default;
- an optional `align` attribute, used to say whether the image should be aligned with the `top`, `middle`, `bottom`, `left` or `right` of any text on the same line;
- an optional `height` attribute, used to indicate the preferred height of the image in terms of number of pixels;
- an optional `width` attribute, used to indicate the preferred width of the image in terms of number of pixels;
- an optional `border` attribute, used to indicate the width, as a number of pixels, of a line to be drawn as a border around the image;

- an optional `vspace` attribute, used to indicate the number of pixels of blank space to be left at top and bottom of the image;
- an optional `hspace` attribute, used to indicate the number of pixels of blank space to be left on either side of the image;
- an optional `usemap` attribute, used to associate a client-side image map with the image;
- an optional `ismap` attribute, used to tell browsers that the image is to be treated as a mappable area using a server-based image map.

The following example shows how the alignment attribute affects the position of an image embedded within a line:

```
<P>An embedded image looks like this
<IMG src="web.gif" alt="Sample Image"> by default, <BR>
like this
<IMG src="web.gif" alt="Sample Image" align=top>
when aligned at the top,<BR>
or like this
<IMG src="web.gif" alt="Sample Image" align=middle>
when aligned in the middle,<BR>
and like this
<IMG src="web.gif" alt="Sample Image" align=bottom>
when aligned at the bottom.</P>
<P align=center>
<IMG src="de.gif" alt="German Flag" align=right hspace=4><BR>
<IMG src="fr.gif" alt="French Flag" align=left hspace=4>
Images can also be positioned to left and right of a line.
```

This example would be presented on your browser as:

An embedded image looks like this by default,

like this when aligned at the top,

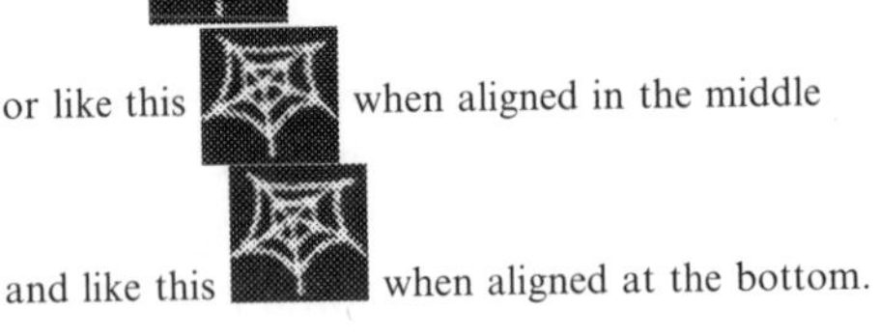
or like this
when aligned in the middle
and like this
when aligned at the bottom.

Images can also be positioned to left and right of a line.

If the `ISMAP` attribute is present, the image must be embedded within an `<A>` element, the `href` attribute of which identifies a server-based program that can process a Common Gateway Interface (CGI) search query for image maps. This construct represents a set of hyperlinks. When the user clicks on a pixel of an image that has been identified as a server-based image map by addition of the `ismap` attribute value, the browser computes the URL of the file identified by the containing anchor, appends a `?` to this, and then adds the *x* and *y* coordinates of the pixel. This query is then sent to the server's search program, which will normally return the contents of another file for presentation to the user.

Where support for client-side image maps is provided by the browser being used, a `<MAP>` element can be used to identify a set of active areas (hotspots) within each image. Each `<MAP>` element can optionally be assigned a `name` that can be used to reference the map from an anchor.

Note: *Full details of the use of client-side maps can be found in the Internet draft proposal on A Proposed Extension to HTML: Client-Side Image Maps* *(`http://ds.internic.net/internet-drafts/draft-seidman-clientsideimagemap-02.txt`).*

The `<MAP>` element contains a number of `<AREA>` elements, each of which identifies part of the image. The `<AREA>` element is an `EMPTY` element, so it has no contents or end-tag. It must, however, have one or more of the following attributes:

- a compulsory `alt` attribute that contains alternative text, which is to be displayed if the map is sent to a browser that does not support client-side image maps;
- an optional `shape` attribute, used to define the shape of the hotspot if it is not the default rectangular, `rect`, shape; the default can be changed to `circle` or `poly` (polygon);
- an optional `coords` attribute, used to describe the area to be identified as the hotspot; if this attribute is omitted, the whole image is taken as a hotspot;
- the `href` attribute that specifies the URL that is to be accessed when the hotspot is clicked on, unless the alternative `nohref` attribute is present to say that this area of the image is not to be active.

Where the `shape` attribute has the value of `circle` the `coords` attribute should contain three comma-separated numbers. The first two numbers indicate the *x* and *y* coordinates of the circle's center point with respect to the top left-hand corner of the image, expressed as a number of pixels. The third number indicates the radius of the circle, expressed in pixels.

Where the `shape` attribute has the default value, `rect`, the `coords` attribute must have four comma-separated numbers, which identify the *x* and *y* coordinates of the top left and bottom right corners of the rectangle required.

When the value of the `shape` attribute is `poly` the `coords` attribute will contain *n* pairs of comma-separated *x* and *y* coordinate values, where *n* indicates the number of sides to the polygon.

To see the effect of these rules consider the following example:

```
<IMG src="oii-logo.gif" alt="OII Logo" usemap="#OII-map">
<MAP name="OII-map">
<AREA shape=circle coords="16,16,13" href="http://europa.eu.int"
      alt="About the European Union">
<AREA shape=rect coords="28,2,52,29"
      href="http://www.echo.lu/oii/en/oii-info.html"
      alt="About the Open Information Interchange initiative">
</MAP>
```

This example would appear on the screen as:

If you click on the circle of stars in the electronic version of the file, you will be taken to the European Union's home page. If you click on either of the letter I components of the image, you will be taken to the home page of the European Commission's Open Information Interchange initiative.

13.6 Tables

The formal specification for the elements that can occur within an HTML table can be found in Internet RFC 1942. Version 3.2 of the HTML DTD identifies a subset of this specification that is supported by most Internet browsers.

The following elements and attributes are used for encoding tables:

- `<TABLE>`, which identifies the boundaries of the tables and allows the following attributes to be applied to the table:
  - `align` to position the table to the `left`, `right` or `center` of the window in which it is displayed;

    Note: *Many browsers ignore this attribute.*
  - `width` to specify the width to be made available for displaying the table;
  - `border` to define the width of any border to be placed around the table;
  - `cellspacing` to specify spacing between cells;
  - `cellpadding` to specify spacing between cell contents and cell boundaries;

- an optional <CAPTION> element, which can have the following attributes associated with it:
  - `align` to specify whether the caption is to be placed at the `top` or `bottom` of the table;

    Note: *This attribute is, unfortunately, ignored by many browsers.*
- one or more table rows, <TR>, which can have the following attributes associated with them:
  - `align` to indicate whether the contents of all the cells in the row are to be aligned to the `left`, `right` or `center` of the cell if no other instructions are given regarding the alignment of cell contents;
  - `valign` to identify whether cell contents are to be aligned with the `top`, `middle` or `bottom` of all the cells in the rows for which a specific `valign` attribute has not been given.
- within table rows, individual cells can be defined either as table headers, <TH>, or as table data, <TD>. These elements share the following attributes:
  - `nowrap` to indicate that wrapping of contents is not permitted;
  - `rowspan` to indicate the number of adjacent columns the cell is to span;
  - `colspan` to indicate the number of adjacent columns the cell is to span;
  - `align` to indicate whether the contents of the cell are to be aligned to the `left`, `right` or `center` of the cell;
  - `valign` to identify whether cell contents are to be aligned with the `top`, `middle` or `bottom` of adjacent cells;
  - `width` to specify the number of pixels of the screen display to be used as the width of the cell;
  - `height` to specify the number of pixels of the screen display to be used as the height of the cell.

The following file shows an example of an HTML table:

```
<TABLE border="10" cellspacing="2" cellpadding=6>
<CAPTION>Relationship between HTML and other table models</CAPTION>
<TR valign=bottom align=center><TH></TH>
<TH>HTML Tables</TH>
<TH>US CALS Tables</TH>
<TH>Swedish CALS Tables</TH>
<TH>ISO 12083 Tables</TH></TR>
<TR align=center valign=middle>
<TH align=left>Outermost element</TH>
<TD colspan="2">&lt;TABLE&gt;</TD>
<TD>&lt;TABELL&gt;</TD> <TD>&lt;TBL&gt;</TD></TR>
<TR align=center valign=middle>
<TH align=left>Table header element</TH>
<TD colspan="2">&lt;THEAD&gt;</TD>
```

```
<TD>&lt;KOLHUVUD&gt;</TD>
<TD>&lt;TH&gt;</TD></TR>
<TR align=center valign=middle>
<TH align=left>Table body identifier</TH>
<TD colspan="2">&lt;TBODY&gt;</TD>
<TD>&lt;TABELL.BLOCK&gt;</TD>
<TD>&lt;TBY&gt;</TD></TR>
<TR align=center valign=middle>
<TH align=left>Table row identifier</TH>
<TD>&lt;TR&gt;</TD> <TD>&lt;ROW&gt;</TD>
<TD>&lt;RAD&gt;</TD> <TD>&lt;ROW&gt;</TD></TR>
<TR align=center valign=middle>
<TH align=left>Table cell identifier</TH>
<TD>&lt;TH&gt; or &lt;TD&gt;</TD>
<TD>&lt;ENTRY&gt;</TD>
<TD>&lt;CELL&gt;</TD>
<TD>&lt;C&gt;</TD></TR></TABLE>
```

This table could be presented by an HTML browser as:

Relationship between HTML and other table models

	HTML Tables	US CALS Tables	Swedish CALS Tables	ISO 12083 Tables
Outermost element	<TABLE>		<TABELL>	<TBL>
Table header element	<THEAD>		<KOLHUVUD>	<TH>
Table body identifier	<TBODY>		<TABELL.BLOCK>	<TBY>
Table row identifier	<TR>	<ROW>	<RAD>	<ROW>
Table cell identifier	<TH> or <TD>	<ENTRY>	<CELL>	<C>

13.7 Applets

The <APPLET> element was introduced to allow Java-encoded mini-applications (applets) to be called from within an HTML browser.

The <APPLET> element, used for HTML calls to Java programs, has a content model that consists of a set of parameter definitions, defined using the <PARAM> element, and textual elements that contain text or images to be displayed, in place of the Java applet, by browsers that do not support Java. The attributes that can be associated with the <APPLET> element are:

- `codebase`, which can contain a URL that identifies the source of the applet program, if this is not held in the directory identified by the <BASE> element or is not stored in the directory containing the file making the call;
- `code`, which is used to identify the Java class file that invokes the application program;
- `name`, which can be used to assign a name to the applet;

- `alt`, which can be used to provide alternative text to be displayed by browsers not able to run the applet;
- `align`, which can be used to position the object with respect to the window;
- `height`, which can be used to control the height of the display area assigned to the applet;
- `width`, which can be used to control the width of the display area assigned to the applet;
- `hspace`, to indicate the amount of space to be maintained to the left and right of the applet;
- `vspace`, to indicate the amount of space to be maintained above or below the applet;

The `<PARAM>` element is used to pass name/value pairs to the program identified by `<APPLET>` and `<OBJECT>` elements. This empty element can have the following attributes associated with its start-tag:

- `name`, which names the relevant parameter;
- `value`, which supplies the named parameter with a value.

The following example shows how the `<APPLET>` and `<PARAM>` elements interact:

```
<APPLET codebase="java" code="TumbleItem.class" name="Flags"
  alt="Java applets not supported on this system" width="60"
  height="40">
<PARAM name="nimgs" value="15">
<PARAM name="img" value="flags">
<PARAM name="speed" value="1">
<PARAM name="pause" value="50">
<IMG src="flags/eu.gif" alt="EU Flag" align="bottom"><BR>
A Java-enabled browser will display national flags followed by the
EU flag.
</APPLET>
```

The precompiled Java-encoded program stored in the `java` subdirectory of the current directory is stored in a file called `TumbleItem.class`.

Note: *The source code for the `TumbleItem` class can be obtained from Sun Microsytems at `http://java.sun.com/applets/applets/TumblingDuke/TumbleItem.java`.*

The `TumbleItem` application requires four input parameters:

- `nimgs`, which identifies the number of images to make up the revolving image;

  Note: *For some reason, with the version of the applet being used in the electronic version of this book, this needs to be one greater than the actual number of images displayed.*

Figure 13.3 The EU national flags which will be displayed by a Java-enabled browser

- `img`, which identifies either the source directory of the images displayed relative to that of the calling file or the directory specified by the file's `<BASE>` element;
- `speed`, which indicates the relative speed of display (`1` being the lowest possible speed between images);
- `pause`, to indicate the number of PC-clock pulses to be left between each sequence of images.

When viewed on a browser this applet will display a set of national flags (Figure 13.3). If Java support is not available, the EU flag will be displayed instead, together with a message explaining that this replaces a changing Java image.

Creating HTML forms

Basic principles • The <FORM> element • The <INPUT> element • The <SELECT> element • The <TEXTAREA> element • The <ISINDEX> element • Form submission • Form processing

One area where HTML is particularly useful is in the area of on-line data capture. Many companies have found the HTML <FORM> element so useful that they have converted their main data capture processes to HTML. This chapter explains how this can be achieved using a combination of SGML elements and special processing programs.

14.1 Basic principles

An HTML form consists of a set of input fields, selection menus, and explanatory text. When users have selected relevant options from menus and completed all the input fields as instructed within the text associated with the form, the contents of the input fields and details of selected options are packaged up into a compressed format that conforms to the Internet Common Gateway Interface (CGI) specification. The compressed data package is *submitted* to a program on a WWW server using the HyperText Transfer Protocol (HTTP). This program uses the CGI specification to control the decoding of the input into the format it requires for processing the data.

HTTP provides two mechanisms for delivering data, GET and POST. While most modern HTTP servers can handle most forms processing using the GET option, some older servers restrict the data strings associated with this option to 255 characters. Where large amounts of data are required to be transmitted when a form's contents are submitted to a server (for example, where files for storage at the server need to be attached to forms) or where the requested information will require an update to the forms generation database, the POST method should be used instead.

When the GET method of form generation is used, the server will normally return an HTML message acknowledging receipt of the form contents. When the POST method is used users will normally need to select manually the next page to work on.

14.2 The <FORM> element

The <FORM> element is defined as follows in Version 3.2 of the HTML DTD released in January 1997:

```
<!ELEMENT FORM -- %body.content -(FORM)>
<!ATTLIST FORM
  action   %URL            #REQUIRED -- server-side form handler --
  method   (%HTTP-Method) GET -- see HTTP specification --
  enctype  %Content-Type; "application/x-www-form-urlencoded">
```

Note particularly the use of the -(FORM) exclusion declaration, to preclude the nesting of forms within forms, and the use of parameter entities to identify the type of data that is expected to be found in attributes that have been declared using the CDATA attribute declared value keyword.

While a <FORM> can contain any element which has been defined by the %body.content parameter entity, it will normally consist principally of elements defined as part of the %form parameter entity. This is defined as:

```
<!ENTITY % form "INPUT | SELECT | TEXTAREA" >
```

These three elements allow form creators to define:

- the type of input required, and the size of single line input fields (<INPUT>);
- the properties of larger text input areas (<TEXTAREA>);
- the properties and contents of menus from which users can select options (<SELECT> and its embedded <OPTION> elements).

The attributes associated with the <FORM> element are:

- an action attribute that contains the URL for the program to be used to process the contents of the form (or a URL starting with mailto: to post data to an electronic mailbox);
- a method attribute that identifies the HTTP method (GET or POST) to be used; unless changed, this defaults to GET;
- an encoding type attribute, enctype, that indicates the type of HTTP encoding used for the transmitted data: this defaults to application/x-www-form-urlencoded.

If files are attached to the form using the type=file option of the <INPUT> element, the default entries will need to be changed to give a start-tag for the form such as:

```
<FORM action="http://www.myco.com/cgi/process1" method=POST
     enctype="multipart/form-data" >
```

14.3 The <INPUT> element

The definition assigned to the <INPUT> element in Version 3.2 of the HTML DTD was:

```
<!ELEMENT INPUT - O EMPTY>
<!ATTLIST INPUT
   type     %InputType TEXT -- what kind of widget is needed --
   name     CDATA  #IMPLIED -- required for all but submit and reset --
   value    CDATA  #IMPLIED -- required for radio and checkboxes --
   checked  (checked) #IMPLIED -- for radio buttons and check boxes --
   size     CDATA  #IMPLIED -- specific to each type of field --
   maxlength NUMBER #IMPLIED
   src      %URL   #IMPLIED -- for fields with background images --
   align (top|middle|bottom|left|right) top -- image alignment -->
```

The most important entry in this definition is the %InputType parameter entity used to define the permitted values for the type attribute. This has been defined as:

```
<!ENTITY % InputType
      "(TEXT | PASSWORD | CHECKBOX | RADIO | SUBMIT | RESET |
      FILE | HIDDEN | IMAGE)"    >
```

The types of input field that can be defined using the <INPUT> element are:

- fields for the entry of single lines of data (TEXT);
- a field for the entry of a password, which will be displayed as a sequence of asterisks (PASSWORD);
- boxes which the user can click on to select an option (CHECKBOX);
- sets of related boxes, from which the user can select only one option (RADIO);
- a button that can be pressed to send the contents of the form to the server (SUBMIT);
- a button that can be pressed to reload the original form (RESET);
- fields which have predefined contents that must always be submitted with the form (HIDDEN); these contents must not be altered by users;
- fields that can be used to select a file that is to accompany the form (FILE);
- a field that can be used to select an x/y coordinate from a displayed image (IMAGE).

How the attributes associated with the <INPUT> element are used is dependent on the value of the type attribute.

14.3.1 Text input

Where the contents of a field can be entered in a single line, an <INPUT> element, the `type` attribute of which has been defined as `text`, can be used. In this case the following additional attributes can be specified:

- a compulsory `name` attribute that identifies the name of the field as known to the receiving program;
- an optional `value` attribute that specifies any default contents for the field;
- an optional `size` attribute that identifies the number of characters to be allowed for the display of the field;
- an optional `maxlength` attribute that indicates the maximum length of the field's contents.

If `maxlength` is greater than `size`, the contents of the text field will be scrolled whenever the cursor is positioned outside the displayable area.

A typical example of a text input field specification is:

```
<P>Name: <INPUT type=text name=claimant size=20 maxlength=40></P>
```

This field would be displayed as:

Name:

14.3.2 Password input

Password input is similar to text input except that each character input is replaced by an asterisk if the value of the `type` attribute is `password`. Typically a fixed size, without a maximum length, will be specified for a password field. A typical example would be:

```
<P>Password: <INPUT type=password name=password size=6></P>
```

This field would be displayed as:

Password:

14.3.3 Checkboxes

Checkboxes are buttons that are either on or off. The following attributes can be associated with an <INPUT> element when its `type` attribute has been set to `checkbox`:

- a compulsory `name` attribute that identifies the name of the field as known to the receiving program;

Note: *More than one checkbox can have the same name. Checkboxes with the same name represent* n-*of-many sets.*

- a compulsory `value` attribute that is used to specify the value to be sent to the server when the box has been selected;
- an optional `checked` attribute to show that the checkbox should be marked as checked when initially displayed.

A typical use of checkboxes would be:

```
<P>Send further information? <INPUT type=checkbox name=SendInfo
value=Y checked>
```

This would be displayed as:

Send further information? ☑

14.3.4 Radio buttons

Radio buttons form sets of linked buttons, only one of which can be selected for each submission of the form. The following attributes can be associated with an `<INPUT>` element when its `type` attribute has been set to `radio`:

- a compulsory `name` attribute that identifies the name of the field as known to the receiving program;

  Note: *Only one button with a given name can be selected because radio buttons only cater for 1-of-many selections.*

- a compulsory `value` attribute that is used to specify the value to be sent to the server when the button has been selected;
- an optional `checked` attribute to show which of the radio buttons sharing the same name should be marked as checked when initially displayed.

A typical use of radio buttons might be:

```
<P>Orange Juice <INPUT type=radio name=juice value=orange
checked> Grapefruit Juice <INPUT type=radio name=juice value=
grapefruit> Tomato Juice <INPUT type=radio name=juice value=
tomato></P>
```

This would be displayed as:

Orange Juice ⊙ Grapefruit Juice ⊙ Tomato Juice ⊙

Selecting any one of the three options automatically deselects the other two.

14.3.5 Submit button

The contents of a form are sent to the program identified by its action attribute when a button, for which value for the type attribute is submit, is pressed. The value attribute can be used to label the button. If this value is to be submitted as part of the form contents, a name attribute can be added to identify which field the value is to be stored in.

A typical use of this option is:

```
<P>When you have completed the form:
<INPUT type=submit value="Press here to submit form"></P>
```

This would be displayed as:

When you have completed the form: [Press here to submit form]

14.3.6 Reset button

When a form contains an <INPUT> element with an attribute of type= reset, a reset button will be displayed. When this button is pressed, the browser will remove any existing entries without submitting them and returning the form to the state in which it was first displayed (including any default values for fields). As with the submit button, the value attribute can be used to name the button.

A typical use of this option is:

```
<P><INPUT type=reset value="Press here to clear current entries"></P>
```

This would be displayed as:

[Press here to clear current entries]

14.3.7 Hidden input

Many forms require information about themselves to be submitted as part of the information set sent to the form processor. The form may also need to contain information about the state of the client, or server, from which the form was transmittted. Where users do not need to be made aware of transmitted information, hidden fields can be created in an HTML form by creating an <INPUT> element with a type=hidden attribute. Only two attributes, name and value are used with this element. They identify the name of the field being sent to the server and the value being assigned to the field.

A typical entry would be:

```
<INPUT type=hidden name=form-id value=Form-12>
```

As such fields are not displayed, no example can be given here, but a hidden field is included in the sample form shown in Figure 14.2.

14.3.8 File selection

Where users need to identify a file that should be attached to a form, a special type of `<INPUT>` field, with an attribute value of `type=file`, can be used to associate a Browse button with an input field. The attributes that can be associated with this type of field are:

- a compulsory `name` attribute that identifies the name of the field to contain the file name;
- an optional `size` attribute that identifies the number of characters to be allowed for the display of the field;
- an optional `maxlength` attribute that indicates the maximum length of the field.

A typical entry would be:

```
<INPUT type=file name=file-id size=20 maxlength=40>
```

This would typically be displayed as:

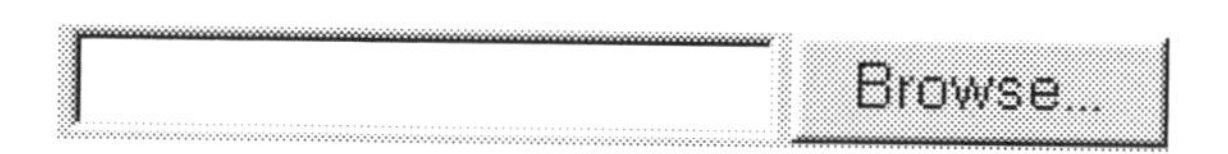

Pressing the Browse button will display the browser's file selection menu. Selecting a file from this menu will result in the full pathname of the file being placed into the field. When the form is transmitted, the file name will be submitted as the value of the field identified by the `name` attribute.

14.3.9 Image spot selection

The `type=image` option for the `<INPUT>` element can by used to allow users to select a spot on an image. When this option is selected the following attributes apply:

- a compulsory `name` attribute that identifies the name of the field, as known to the receiving program;
- an compulsory `src` attribute to specify the URL of a file containing the image to be displayed;
- an optional `align` attribute to determine whether the image is to be aligned with the `top`, `middle`, `bottom`, `left` or `right` of related text.

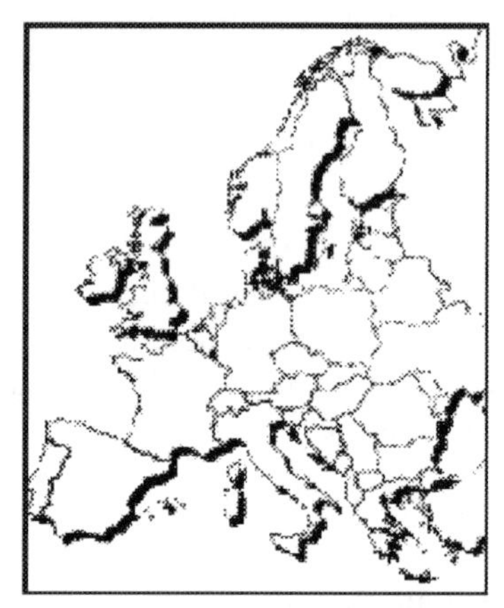

Figure 14.1 A map of Europe in which countries can be selected by clicking on them. The coordinates of the point selected are automatically transmitted

A typical use would be:

```
<INPUT type=image src=europe.gif name=find-co>
```

This would typically be displayed as shown in Figure 14.1. Clicking on a point in this map will automatically send the *x* and *y* coordinates of the selected pixel to the program identified by the form's `action` attribute as the value of the `find-co` field.

Warning: *Clicking on an image in a form has the effect of submitting the current contents of the form.*

14.4 The <SELECT> element

Where users need to be asked to pick one or more options from a menu, the `<SELECT>` element can be used in place of a set of `<INPUT>` buttons. This element is defined in Version 3.2 of the HTML DTD as:

```
<!ELEMENT SELECT -- (OPTION+)>
<!ATTLIST SELECT
    name       CDATA         #REQUIRED
    size       NUMBER        #IMPLIED
    multiple   (multiple)    #IMPLIED >
```

Each `<SELECT>` element forms a container for a list of options that will be selected to form the contents of a particular field in the submitted message. The attributes associated with the `<SELECT>` element are:

- a compulsory `name` attribute that identifies the field to which the selection(s) are to be submitted;

- an optional size attribute that can be used to control the number of entries in the displayed portion of the menu;
- an optional multiple attribute to indicate when more than one entry can be selected from the list.

The model for the <OPTION> element used within the <SELECT> element is:

```
<!ELEMENT OPTION - O (#PCDATA)*>
<!ATTLIST OPTION
     selected (selected) #IMPLIED
     value CDATA #IMPLIED -- defaults to element content -- >
```

Each option element should contain a text string that forms the entry to be displayed in a single line of the menu. Each <OPTION> element can have the following optional attributes associated with it:

- selected to indicate that the entry is to be selected when the menu is first displayed;
- value, which defines the value to be submitted as the value for the field identified by the name attribute of the containing <SELECT> element.

The following coding can be used to set up a menu from which users can select the appropriate option:

```
<SELECT name=juice size=3 title=Juices>
<OPTION value=Orange selected>Fresh Orange Juice</OPTION>
<OPTION value=Grapefruit>Grapefruit Juice</OPTION>
<OPTION value=Pineapple>Pineapple Juice</OPTION>
<OPTION value=Tomato>Tomato Juice</OPTION></SELECT>
```

This menu would be displayed as:

14.5 The <TEXTAREA> element

Where more than one line needs to be allowed for input, the <TEXTAREA> element must be used. The attributes associated with this element are:

- a compulsory name attribute that identifies the field to which the entered text is to be submitted;
- a compulsory rows attribute that identifies the number of text rows to be displayed in the text area;

- a compulsory `cols` attribute that indicates the text area width in terms of number of columns of fixed-width characters.

  A typical text area definition might be:

```
<P>Address<BR>
<TEXTAREA name=address rows=5 cols=25></P>
```

This would appear on the screen as:

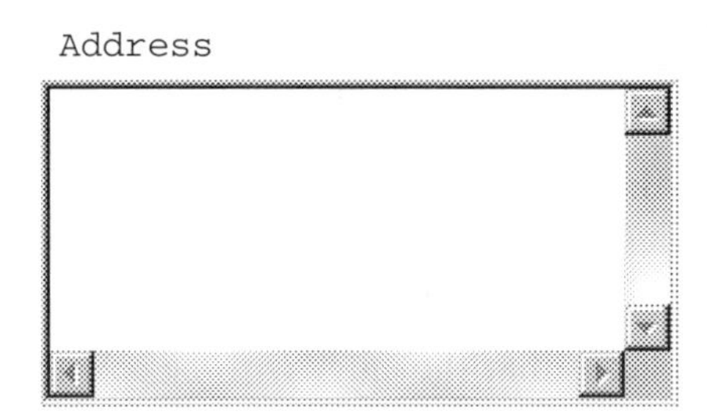

14.6 The <ISINDEX> element

Where only one field is required for input, the empty `<ISINDEX>` element can be used to capture the data to be submitted to the server program identified by the `<BASE>` element in the header. The `<ISINDEX>` element can be assigned a `prompt` attribute to define text that is to precede the box provided for entry of the query string. For example, a tag such as `<ISINDEX prompt="Search for: ">` would be displayed as:

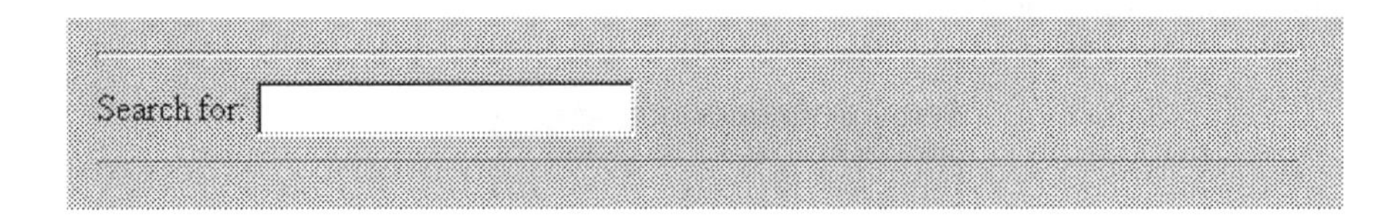

14.7 Form submission

Figure 14.2 shows a typical form ready for submission to the server. When this form is submitted to the server it will generate the following data string:

```
form-id=Form-123&Surname=Bryan&Forenames=Martin&UserID=
sgml66&Type=Malfunction&Problem=The+program+failed+to+copy
+the+selected+area+when+the+%0D%0ACopy+button+was+pressed
+and+then+Paste+was+used.%0D%0A%28I%27ve+been+successful+in
+copying+smaller+pieces+of+text%2C%0D%0Ait+was+trying+to
+copy+the+whole+of+section+5.3+that+failed.%29&Cause=Memory
& file=docs%2Fmtb%2Ffile1.doc
```

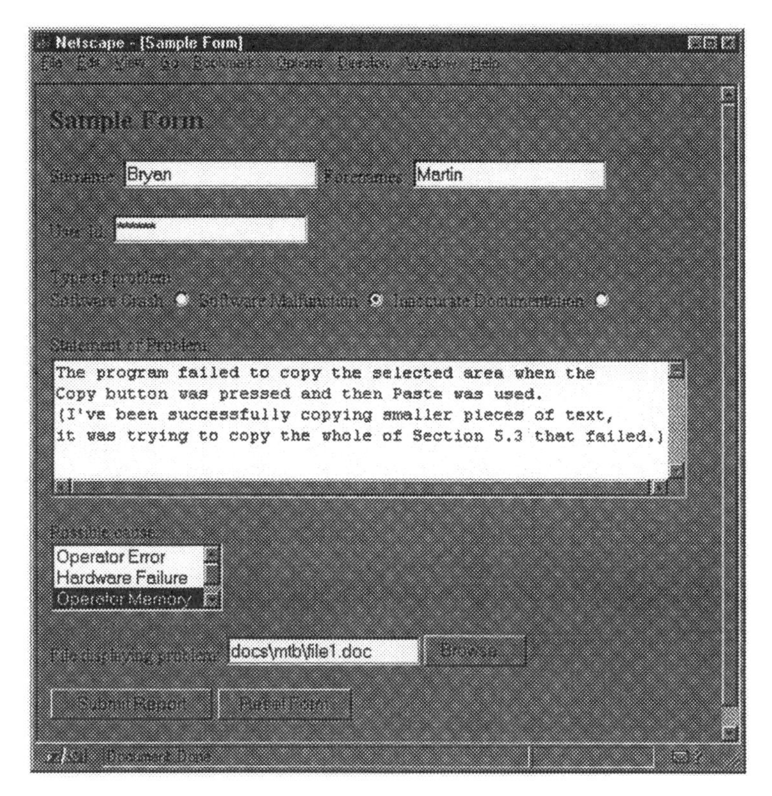

Figure 14.2 Completed form

Note that this string has no spaces, and forms one continuous sequence of characters with no line breaks (although it has been necessary to insert arbitrary line breaks to print the string). The boundary of each field of information is identified by the presence of an `&` character. Each space in the form input has been replaced by a + sign. Each non-alphanumeric character, other than hyphens and periods, has been replaced by a `%` sign followed by a two-digit hexadecimal value of the character. Each carriage return/line feed sequence in the text area has, therefore, been replaced by `%0D%0A`.

Each field definition consists of two parts, separated by the = sign. To the left of the = is the name of the field; to the right is the value to be assigned to the field.

Note that the first field definition, `form-id=Form-123` does not appear on the displayed form. This entry represents the contents of the `name` and `value` attributes of a hidden input field. Note also that the contents of the User ID field are transmitted in clear text form, though the contents of this password field are not displayed on the screen.

For the `Type` and `Cause` fields the field values have been take from the contents of the `value` attributes of the selected radio button or option, rather than from the displayed text.

14.8 Form processing

The submitted contents of a form are normally sent to a program conforming to the Common Gateway Interface specification. WWW servers often contain software, such as UNCGI, that is specifically designed to accept the continuous strings produced as a result of form processing and to break them into a set of discrete fields, reconverting the + signs to spaces and the hexadecimal entries to the equivalent characters.

Normally a CGI program will be associated with facilities for validating specific entries and for passing the validated entries to appropriate programs. If an invalid field is found the program may be able to generate an HTML form that requests that the user provide a corrected entry. Such a form could contain supplementary information on completing the faulty field that was not displayed on the original form.

When a form has been successfully processed, the CGI program will typically respond with a new page of information for the user. Where the `POST` method has been used, however, the only notification that the form has been successfully submitted may be the presence of a `Document Done` message in the window's message area.

The future for SGML and HTML

What DSSSL brought to SGML • The HyTime SGML General Facilities annex • Possible extensions to SGML • Possible extensions to HTML

This chapter looks briefly at extensions to SGML and HTML that are likely to be defined in 1997.

15.1 What DSSSL brought to SGML

April 1996 saw the long-awaited publication of ISO/IEC standard 10179 which defined the *Document Style Semantics and Specification Language* (*DSSSL*) used to describe formally the formatting rules to be associated with an SGML document type definition. The new standard introduced two concepts that are central to the future development of SGML:

- SGML groves;
- the SGML Document Query Language (SDQL).

15.1.1 SGML groves

To make it possible to describe the sort of transformations that are needed to describe formally the relationships between the logical structure of an SGML document and the physical structure of a formatted document, DSSSL introduced a generalized model for the description of SGML document structures that went far beyond that defined in the Element Structure Information Set (ESIS) previously used for SGML conformance testing. To allow for the creation of books from more than one SGML document instance, and for the creation of more than one formatted document from an SGML document instance, the new concept is based on defining one or more **trees** of **SGML properties**. The generic name for this set of trees is an **SGML grove**.

SGML groves are defined in terms of a **grove plan**, which identifies the elements, attributes and related properties that are to form part of the trees in the grove. DSSSL has extended the set of SGML properties defined in ISO/IEC standard 10744, the *Hypermedia/Time-based Structuring Language (HyTime)*, but continues to use HyTime's formal mechanism for describing property sets, so as to allow application developers to define any additional properties they may need to assign to groves over and above the standard set of properties defined in HyTime and DSSSL.

Once a grove plan has been established, it becomes possible to identify **nodes** in an SGML tree. A node is an addressable object in an SGML tree. It should be noted that the nodes in the tree of a document instance differ somewhat from the trees of the DTDs shown in Chapter 2 and elsewhere in this book. For document instances, each occurrence of an element forms a node of the tree, rather than having one node for each type of element. Each element can have a set of **relationships** with other elements. For example, embedded elements have a **parent element**, which will normally be linked to earlier **ancestors** of the element. If the element forms part of a model group, it is likely to have **younger siblings** that precede it in the document instance and **older siblings** that follow it in the document instance. Unless the element is an empty element, it will have **children**, either in the form of parsed data characters or in the form of embedded trees of **descendant elements**. Each attribute of an element will also form a tree attached to the element node. Attributes have properties such as name, value, tokens and characters, that form their own hierarchy of addressable nodes.

15.1.2 The SGML Document Query Language

The SGML Document Query Language (SDQL) is specifically designed to identify nodes within an SGML tree, using the properties identified in the grove plan defined for parsing a document instance. Expressed as extensions to IEEE's LISP-based Scheme programming language, SDQL expressions are designed to provide a transportable form of query that can be interpreted at run-time, without having to be predefined or preprocessed.

SDQL queries use keywords to identify nodes that have specific relationships to previously identified nodes, or to nodes that have identifiable properties, such as a unique identifier. Like all LISP list processing expressions, SDQL expressions can be infinitely nested. For example, to select the children of an element with a particular unique identifier you would enter an expression of the form:

```
(children (select-match (attributes (current-node)) '(name: id
value: object-x)))
```

SDQL expressions can reference a wide range of standard SGML properties and can also map to user-defined properties of trees or documents. For example, they can be set up to look for elements that contain strings that require special processing, or to identify elements containing part-numbers or other data that needs to be processed by querying a relational database using SQL.

15.2 The HyTime SGML General Facilities annex

1997 will see the publication of a new SGML General Facilities annex as part of the *Hypermedia/Time-based Structuring Language* (*HyTime*) published as ISO/IEC standard 10744. The new annex will define a set of facilities that will be applicable to all SGML systems, not just those conforming to HyTime. The new annex will cover three main areas:

- An Architectural Form Definition Requirements (AFDR) section will show how rules for creating the architectural forms used to describe the HyTime application of SGML can be used to define architectural forms for any SGML application.
- A Formal System Identifiers (FSI) section will show how system identifiers can be specified in a manner that makes them more transportable and more flexible.
- A Property Set Definitions Requirements (PSDR) section will show how the properties needed for the definition of an SGML grove can be defined.

15.2.1 Architectural form definition requirements

HyTime introduced the concept of **architectural forms** to SGML to allow a DTD to be defined in terms of known classes of elements. The Architectural Form Definition Requirements (AFDR) section of the SGML General Facilities annex will take those features of HyTime that are applicable to any architectural form and define them in a way that makes them easily referenceable by all SGML applications. It will define a set of attributes, and formal processing instructions, that can be used to identify which architectural forms are associated with a particular document prolog and instance.

The AFDR specifications allow architectural forms to be derived from other architectural forms. This will allow superclasses, such as HyTime, to form the basis of other architectural forms, such as those being defined for topic navigation maps as part of the development of a new ISO 13250 standard.

15.2.2 Formal system identifiers

The SGML General Facilities annex will also contain the definition for the **formal system identifiers** mentioned in Section 6.4.1. Formal system identifiers have been introduced to make SGML system identifiers more transportable, and to add security control features to entity managers. As well as identifying the path and file names of the relevant files in a system independent way, a formal system identifier can also identify features such as its methods of compression, checksum sealing and encryption, any bit combination transformation process (bctp) carried out on data before transmission and the type of record boundaries used within the file.

The HyTime Standardized BENTO (SBENTO) facility for creating a container that will allow a number of related files to be referenced using a single file identifier has also been moved to this part of the SGML General Facilities annex. As well as ensuring that related files can be referenced as a single unit, SBENTO containers also allow streams of data to be multiplexed in such a way that suitable amounts of data are transmitted in an appropriate sequence. This is particularly important when sending multimedia presentations over slow networks such as the Internet, where you need to ensure that both sound and visual components are delivered, in a synchronizable way, at rates that are suitable for presentation on the screen before all of the file has been received.

15.2.3 Property set definition requirements

The SGML General Facilities annex will also contain those parts of the HyTime standard that are used for the definition of the **property sets** that identify the component parts of an SGML grove. This will include a set of definitions that can be used to identify virtually all aspects of SGML. In addition the annex will define mechanisms for defining **classes of properties**.

As well as formally defining SGML groves, this annex will also provide facilities for controlling what SGML parsers will generate when parsing particular document instances. It will also contain the definitions for the HyTime <LEXTYPE> element, which can be used to create user-defined **lexical types**. This will mean that the concepts introduced in HyTime to provide a customizable method for checking the values of attributes or the contents of element will now be usable in non-HyTime applications. To see the effect of this, consider the following attribute list definition, which allows more than one attribute to have a value of YES or NO:

```
<!ATTLIST switch1 CDATA --lextype: ("YES"|"NO")-- NO
          switch2 CDATA --lextype: ("YES"|"NO")-- NO >
```

15.3 Possible extensions to SGML

In November 1996 ISO approved a technical corrigendum that will allow SGML declarations to be extended to allow a full range of ISO 10646 characters to be used as valid SGML name characters. To make this possible, the corrigendum allows character ranges to be defined as part of the name character definition (for example, UCNMCHAR "-." 160-254) and provides new facilities for defining name characters that are not case dependent (NAMESTRT and NAMECHAR). Use of the new facilities will be identified by extending the minimal literal at the start of the SGML declaration to read

"ISO 8879:1986 (ENR)", where ENR is an abbreviation of 'Extended Naming Rules'.

As part of ISO's standard five-year review cycle, SGML is now undergoing its ten-year review. As part of this process during 1996 and 1997, ISO/IEC JTCI SC18/WG8 will be carrying out a clause-by-clause examination of ISO 8879:1986. A number of areas of improvement have already been identified, including:

- deprecating the use of features, such as RANK, which have been shown to lead to confusion among users, and providing extra switches in the FEATURES clause of the SGML declaration to allow options that are currently grouped under one heading, such as the various short tag options, to be switched on and off independently;
- allowing cross-referencing to unique identifiers in other documents by allowing IDREF attributes to be extended to include the identity of the entity containing the ID (for example, refid="#ENTITY entity2 id5");
- to extend the default values for quantities such as NAMELEN and LITLEN to allow for the larger names that are typically used on less memory-constrained systems now generally available to SGML users;
- making the handling of record starts and record ends less prone to introduce unexpected error, especially on systems that do not use the two-code approach used on MS-DOS systems.

Many more extensions to SGML are planned, but the guiding principle behind all extensions will be that any currently valid SGML document will remain valid under any future revision to the standard.

In September 1996 discussions started on the specification of a subset of SGML that could provide an efficient method for transmitting SGML documents over the Internet. The proposed subset is being referred to as the eXtensible Markup Language (XML). At the time of writing (December 1996) it is still too early to be certain what advantages, or disadvantages, may come from restricting which markup constructs and grove properties should be used when transmitting documents over the Internet. However, adoption of a smaller set of markup features and a common set of grove properties should make it easier to construct SGML document browsers that are fully integrated with the Internet.

September 1996 also saw the first release of alpha-test versions of a public domain tool capable of parsing an SGML document to create an SGML grove and, at the same time, applying a DSSSL formatting specification to it. James Clark's JADE processor uses a DSSSL specification to convert SGML documents, including those coded in HTML, into RTF for import into standard processors. During 1997 other tools capable of making use of DSSSL's advanced grove transformation facilities are expected to become available.

15.4 Possible extensions to HTML

Whilst the January 1997 version of the HTML DTD introduced a number of useful new concepts, it still only provides a limited set of elements, which do not include all the elements currently supported by the manufacturers of HTML document browsers.

One area in which extension of the existing HTML DTD will probably be needed concerns the use of multiple-point anchors. At present HTML only allows an anchor to point to one destination. There are, however, many times when you need to reference more than one file from a particular point. Some facility similar to the concept of aggregate locations for multi-headed links provided by HyTime needs to be added to HTML if it is to have a more general application than is currently possible.

The latest version of the HTML DTD presumes that the full ISO/IEC 10646 character set will be supported on future releases of WWW browsers. Mechanisms for identifying language preferences of users at the HTTP level will help in the selection of suitable versions of documents, but, until a better mechanism is provided for switching from one language to another while maintaining the current point in the file, it will not be possible to develop truly multilingual HTML applications. As the existing mechanism provided through the `<LINK>` element is poorly understood, and rarely implemented suitably, it is likely to be some time before facilities for supporting the sort of multicultural applications now being postulated for the WWW are available.

As this book has shown, SGML provides a very flexible method for marking up documents for interchange between computer systems. New facilities are constantly being added to both SGML and HTML as more complex applications are coded using these markup languages. Today's new ideas will be taken for granted in a few years time. By the beginning of the 21st century, the concepts of structurally based generic markup, introduced by the ISO as far back as 1986, will have become a standard part of virtually every word-processing system, and of many millions of computerized data servers. The last 10 years have been very interesting for those of us involved in the development of SGML. The next 10 years are likely to be even more exciting.

References

ISO = International Organization for Standardization
IEC = International Electrotechnical Commission

Bryan M. T. (1988). *SGML: An Author's Guide to the Standard Generalized Markup Language*. Wokingham: Addison-Wesley

CALS (1993). *Exchange of Formatting Information using the Output Specification, Department of Defense Application of MIL-M-28001 Using Standard Generalized Markup Language (SGML)*. MIL-HDBK-SGM. Washington: US Department of Defense

CGI Specification, The (`http://hoohoo.ncsa.uiuc.edu/cgi/interface.html`)

Erwin M., Gaither M., Hassinger S. and Tittel E. (1995). *Foundations of World Wide Web Programming with HTML & CGI*. Foster City: IDG Books Worldwide

Goldfarb C. F. (1990). *The SGML Handbook*. Oxford: Clarendon Press

Goldfarb C. F., Mosher E. J. and Peterson T. I. (1970). An online system for integrated text processing. *Proc. American Society for Information Science*, **7**, 147–150

ISO 639:1988. *Codes for the representation of languages*. Geneva: ISO

ISO/IEC 646:1991. *Information Processing – 7-bit coded character set for information interchange*. Geneva: ISO

ISO/IEC 2022:1994. *Information technology – Character set structure and extension techniques*. Geneva: ISO

ISO/IEC 6937:1994. *Information technology – Coded graphic character set for text communication – Latin alphabet*. Geneva: ISO

ISO 8859:1987. *Information processing – 8-bit single-byte coded graphic character sets. Parts 1–10*. Geneva: ISO

ISO 8879:1986. *Information Processing – Text and Office Systems – Standard Generalized Markup Language (SGML)*. Geneva: ISO

ISO/IEC 9070:1991. *Information Processing – SGML support facilities – Registration procedures for Public Text Object Identifiers*. Geneva: ISO

ISO/IEC TR9573:1991–4. *Information processing – SGML support facilities – Techniques for using SGML – Parts 12–16*. Geneva: ISO/IEC

ISO/IEC 10179:1996. *Information technology – Text and office systems – Document Style Semantics and Specification Language (DSSSL)*. Geneva: ISO/IEC

ISO/IEC 10646:1993. *Information technology – Universal Multiple-Octet Coded Character Set (UCS)*. Geneva: ISO/IEC

ISO/IEC 10744:1992. *Information technology – Hypermedia/Time-based Structuring Language (HyTime)*. Geneva: ISO/IEC

Internet Draft Proposal, *Cascading Style Sheets* (`http://www.w3.org/pub/WWW/TR/WD-css1.html`)

Internet Draft Proposal, *Hypertext Links in HTML* (`http://ds.internic.net/internet-drafts/draft-ietf-html-relrev-00.txt`)

Internet Draft Proposal, *Inserting objects in HTML* (`http://www.w3.org/pub/WWW/TR/WD-object.html`)

Internet Draft Proposal, *Internationalization of the HyperText Markup Language* (`http://ds.internic.net/internet-drafts/draft-ietf-html-i18n-05.txt`)

Internet Draft Proposal, *Proposed Extension to HTML: Client-Side Image Maps* (`http://ds.internic.net/internet-drafts/draft-seidman-clientsideimagemap-02.txt`)

Internet RFC 1521, *MIME (Multipurpose Internet Mail Extensions) Part One: Mechanisms for Specifying and Describing the Format of Internet Message Bodies* (`http://ds.internic.net/rfc/rfc1521.txt`)

Internet RFC 1522, *MIME (Multipurpose Internet Mail Extensions) Part Two: Message Header Extensions for Non-ASCII Text* (`http://ds.internic.net/rfc/rfc1522.txt`)

Internet RFC 1523, *The text/enriched MIME Content-type* (`http://ds.internic.net/rfc/rfc1523.txt`)

Internet RFC 1738, *Uniform Resource Locators (URL)* (`http://ds.internic.net/rfc/rfc1738.txt`)

Internet RFC 1766, *Tags for the Identification of Languages* (`http://ds.internic.net/rfc/rfc1766.txt`)

Internet RFC 1808, *Relative Uniform Resource Locators* (`http://ds.internic.net/rfc/rfc1808.txt`)

Internet RFC 1866, *HyperText Markup Language – Version 2.0* (`http://ds.internic.net/rfc/rfc1866.txt`)

Internet RFC 1942, *HTML Tables* (`http://ds.internic.net/rfc/rfc1942.txt`)

Internet RFC 1945, *Hypertext Transfer Protocol – HTTP/1.0* (`http://ds.internic.net/rfc/rfc1945.txt`)

Java Language Specification, The (`http://java.sun.com/doc/language_specification/`)

JavaScript Authoring Guide (`http://home.netscape.com/eng/mozilla/Gold/handbook/javascript/index.html`)

Microsoft (1989). *Word for Windows Technical Reference*. Redmond, WA: Microsoft Press

Office for Official Publications of the European Communities (1985). *FORMEX – Formalized Exchange of Electronic Publications* (ISBN 92-825-5399-X). Luxembourg: OPOCE

Pepper S. (1996). *The Whirlwind Guide to SGML Tools and Vendors*. Oslo, Norway: Falch Infotek A/S. (`http://www.falch.no/people/pepper/sgmltool/`)

TEI P3. *Guidelines for Electronic Text Encoding and Interchange*. Chicago/Oxford: The Association for Computers and the Humanities (ACH), The Association of Computational Linguistics (ACL) and The Association for Literary and Linguistic Computing (ALLC)

World Wide Web Consortium (1996). *Cascading Style Sheets, level 1*. W3C Working Draft (5 May 96) (`http://www.w3.org/pub/WWW/TR/WD-css1.html`)

Index

<A> 168, 196–199
abstract syntax 38
<ADDRESS> 193
AFDR, *see* Architectural Form Definition Requirements
ambiguous content models 66
American Standard Code for Information Interchange (ASCII) 9
ancestors 222
anchors 168, 196–199
AND connector 47, 62
ANY 64
APPINFO 53
<APPLET> 170, 206–208
applets 170, 206–208
application-specific information 53
architectural forms 223
Architectural Form Definition Requirements (AFDR) 223
<AREA> 203
ASCII, *see* American Standard Code for Information Interchange
associated element type 140
ATTLIST, *see* attribute definition list declarations
attribute definition list declarations (ATTLIST) 71
attribute name 70, 72
attributes 16, 70–81
  calling entities using 77
  numeric 75
  omitting names of 125
  simple 74
attribute specification 70
attribute values 70, 72
  reserved names for 73
attribute value literals 70

<B> 194
<BASE> 181
base character set 41, 49
base document element 14, 59
base document type 134
base document type declaration 153
<BASEFONT> 195
BASESET 41, 49
<BIG> 194
<BLOCKQUOTE> 190
<BODY> 184

 194
browsers, *see* document browsers

CALS Formatting Output Specification Instance (FOSI) 25, 35
capacity set 52
<CAPTION> 205
catalog, *see* SGML catalog
CDATA, *see* character data *or* character data entity *or* marked sections
CGI, *see* Common Gateway Interface
character data (CDATA) 64, 73, 111
character data entity 83, 87, 90
character references 8, 100
character reference open (CRO) 47, 101
character set description 50
CHARSET 40
checkboxes (in HTML) 212
children 222
<CITATION> 194
classes of properties 224
<CODE> 194
color, control of in HTML 166, 184, 195
comment declarations 156
comments 39, 66, 86
Common Gateway Interface (CGI) 209, 220
concrete syntax 38, 40, 53
CONCUR 52, 134
concurrent document types 133–136
connector 61–62
content model 60
  analysis of 66–69

content reference (#CONREF) 74, 80
CRO, *see* character reference open
current attribute value (#CURRENT) 74, 80

data attributes 92
data attribute specifications 93
database, *see* data repository
data conversion tools 28, 31
data repository 28, 33–34
DATATAG 52, 126
data tag group close (DTGC) 126
data tag group open (DTGO) 126
data tag padding template 127
data tag pattern 126
data tags 126
data tag template 126
data tag template group 126
declaration subset open (DSC) 47, 93, 111, 137, 154
declaration subset open (DSO) 47, 93, 111, 137, 154
declared value 72
default entity 87
default value 72
DELIM 41, 46
delimiters 3, 11, 41, 46–49
descendant elements 222
described character set 41
DESCSET 41
<DFN> 194
<DIV> 190–192
document analysis 11
document analysis tools 28, 31
document browsers 36
document instance 37, 82
document prolog 37, 82
document structure 12
Document Style Semantics and Specification Language (DSSSL) 25, 35, 221
document type declaration 153
document type declaration history 161
document type declaration subset 154
document type definition (DTD) 7, 11, 82, 153
document type name 153
document type specification 133
DSC, *see* declaration subset close
DSC, *see* declaration subset open
DSSSL, *see* Document Style Semantics and Specifications Language
DTD, *see* document type definition

element content 64
element declarations 60–69
element names, *see* generic identifier
elements 7, 11, 59–70
element sets 155, 157
Element Structure Information Set (ESIS) 221
element tokens 61
<EM> 194
embedded elements 59
empty element (EMPTY) 64
empty end-tag 122
empty start-tags 122
end-tag omission 120
end-tag open (ETAGO) 47, 69
end-tags 7, 69
ENR, *see* Extended Naming Rules
entities 8, 12, 82–103
  referencing through attributes 77
  storing markup declaration in 89
  storing marked sections in 89, 115
  types of 82, 89
ENTITY/ENTITIES 73, 77–78
entity declaration 85–101
entity end 72, 92
entity manager, *see* SGML entity manager
entity name 84, 85
entity reference 83
entity reference open (ERO) 84
entity set 101, 157
entity types 89, 90
ERO, *see* entity reference open
ESIS, *see* Element Structure Information Set
ETAGO, *see* end-tag open
exceptions 65
exclusions 65
EXPLICIT 52, 138
explicit link rule 143
explicit link specification 142–149
Extended Naming Rules (ENR) 224
eXtensible Markup Language (XML) 225
external entities 89–100
external entity reference 12
external entity specification 89

FEATURES 52
file selection (in HTML forms) 215
File Transfer Protocol (FTP) 2
fixed attribute values (#FIXED) 74, 80
<FONT> 194
<FORM> 210
FORMAL 52
formal public identifier 95, 162
formal system identifier (FSI) 90, 223
formatting 24
forms 175, 209–220
FOSI, *see* CALS Formatting Output Specification Instance
FSI, *see* formal system identifier
FTP, *see* File Transfer Protocol
FUNCHAR 46
FUNCTION 41, 45
function characters 41, 45
function class 45
function name 45

general entities 82
general entity reference 8, 84
generic identifier 11, 60, 126

GI, *see* generic identifier
group close (GRPC) 47, 60
group open (GRPO) 47, 60
grove plan 221–222
GRLPC, *see* group close
GRPLVL 50, 63
GRPO, *see* group open

hidden input (in HTML forms) 214
HR 192
HTML, *see* HyperText Markup Language
HTTP, *see* HyperText Transfer Protocol
hyperdocument 12
Hypermedia/Time-based Structuring Language (HyTime) 223
HyperText Markup Language (HTML) 161–220
  body of text 184–193
  deprecated features in 163
  document headers 177, 180
  header 180–183
  history 2
  possible extensions to 226
  role 9
  SGML declaration for 54–57
  start-tag 179
  structure of DTD 181
  use of other Internet specifications 163
HyperText Transfer Protocol (HTTP) 2, 163
  error messages in 200
  GET method 209
  POST method 209
HyTime, *see* Hypermedia/Time-based Structuring Language

<I> 194
ID/IDREF, *see* unique identifier
ID link set declaration 141
id value 79
ignored marked sections (IGNORE) 111, 113
image maps 169, 201–204
<IMG> 201
IMPLICIT 52, 138
implicit link specifications 139–141
implied attribute values (#IMPLIED) 74, 78
included marked sections (INCLUDE) 112, 113
inclusions 65
information management 26
information modeling 11
<INPUT> 211–216
Internet 1
<ISINDEX> 182, 218
ISO 646 9, 41–45
ISO/IEC 6937 99
ISO 8859-1 50
ISO/IEC TR 9573 102
ISO/IEC 10646 41, 50
ISO Latin-1: use in HTML 164
ISO owner identifiers 94, 96

<KBD> 194

LCNMCHAR 46
LCNMSTRT 46
lexical types 224
<li>, *see* list item
<LINK> 183
LINK 52, 137
link attributes 139
link attribute specification 140, 143
linking document structures 136–152
link management (in HTML) 200
link process definition 137
link relationships (in HTML) 199
link rules 140
link set declaration 140
link set use declarations (USELINK) 145, 151
link type declarations 137, 152
link type declaration subset 137
link type name 137
<LISTING> 190
list items 119, 173, 186
lists 19, 173, 186–189
LIT/LITA, *see* literal delimiters
literal delimiters 47, 70

<MAP> 203
map name 105
marked section close (MSC) 111
marked section declarations 111
marked section end 111
marked sections 110–117, 136
marked section start 111
markup 3
  declarations 7
  delimiters 11
  generic 7
  generalized 6
  specific 4
  tags 4
markup declaration close (MDC) 39, 47, 60
markup declaration open (MDO) 39, 47, 60
markup scan control characters 46
MDC, *see* markup declaration close
MDO, *see* markup declaration open
<META> 182
minimal SGML document 54
minimized elements 60
minimum data characters 95
mixed data 64
model group 61
MSC, *see* marked section close
MSICHAR 46
MSOCHAR 46
MSSCHAR 46
multicode basic concrete syntax 54
multicode core concrete syntax 54
multiple document structures 130–152

NAME 73

NAMECASE 46, 79
name characters 46
name group 60
NAMES 41, 73
name start characters 46
names in SGML markup 46
name tokens 73, 75
NAMING 41, 46
naming rules 41, 46
NDATA, *see* non-SGML data entities
NET, *see* null end-tag
net-enabling start-tag 124
NMTOKEN/NMTOKENS, *see* name tokens
nodes 222
non-SGML data entities (NDATA) 91
null end-tag (NET) 47, 69, 124–125
NUMBER/NUMBERS 73, 77
number tokens 73, 75
NUTOKEN/NUTOKENS, *see* number tokens
NOTATION 73, 91
notation declarations 91
notation identifier 92
notation name 92

occurrence indicator 62
<OL>, *see* lists
older siblings 222
OMITTAG 52, 61, 118
omitted tag minimization 61, 118, 120
OPT 47, 62
<OPTION> 217
or connector 47, 62
other prolog 137

<P> 186
paragraphs (in HTML) 171, 186
<PARAM> 207
parameter entities 24, 82
  declaring 86
  referencing 84
parameter separator 72
parent element 222
parsed character data (#PCDATA) 64
parser, *see* SGML parser
password entry (in HTML) 212
PCDATA, *see* parsed character data
PI, *see* processing instructions
PIC, *see* processing instruction close
PIO, *see* processing instruction open
<PLAINTEXT> 190
PLUS 47, 62
<PRE>, *see* preformatted text
preformatted text 172, 189
primitive content token 63
printing SGML documents 34
processing instruction close (PIC) 47, 117
processing instruction open (PIO) 47, 117
processing instructions 25, 116
prolog, *see* document prolog
property sets 224
public concrete syntax 54
public identifier 54, 94, 152, 154, 162
publicly declared document type definitions 154, 162
publicly declared entity sets 102
publicly declared external entities 93–100
publicly declared link type declarations 152
public text class 97
public text description 98
public text designating sequence 99
public text display version 100
public text language 98

QUANTITY 41, 48
quantity set 41

radio buttons (in HTML forms) 213
RANK 52, 60, 126
ranked elements 126
rank stem 126
rank suffix 126
RCDATA, *see* replaceable character data or marked sections
RE, *see* Record End
record boundaries 158–160
Record End (RE) 45, 158–160
  use as reference end 84
Record Start (RS) 45, 158–160
REFC, *see* reference close
reference capacity set 52
reference close (REFC) 84
reference concrete syntax 39–49
reference end 84
registered owner identifier 96
relationships 222
REP 47, 62
replaceable character data (RCDATA) 64, 111
repository, *see* data repository
required attributes (#REQUIRED) 74, 78
reserved name indicator (RNI) 47, 63, 73
reserved names 41, 72
  for attribute declared values 73
reset button (in HTML forms) 214
result attribute specification 143
result element specification 143
Rich Text Format (RTF) 4
RNI, *see* reserved name indicator
RS, *see* Record Start
RTF, *see* Rich Text Format

<SAMP> 194
SCOPE 52
<SCRIPT> 182
SDATA, *see* specific character data entity
SDQL, *see* SGML Document Query Language
<SELECT> 216
separator 45
separator characters 45, 72
SEPCHAR 46

SEQ, *see* sequence connector
sequence connector (SEQ) 47, 62
SGML, *see* Standard Generalized Markup Language
SGML catalog 37, 100
SGML database, *see* data repository
SGML declaration 37, 39, 82
SGML document 11, 36–37
SGML document editors 28–31
SGML document entity 82
SGML Document Query Language (SDQL) 222
SGML entity manager 33, 223
SGML General Facilities annex (in HyTime) 223
SGML groves 221
SGML parser 28, 32–33
SGML properties 221
SGML subdocument entity 91
SGML text entity 85
SHORTREF 48, 104, 105
short reference delimiters 48–49, 104
short reference mapping declarations 105
short references 104–109
short reference use declarations 106
SHORTTAG 52, 71, 118, 121
SHUNCHAR 41, 45
shunned characters 41, 45
SIMPLE 52, 138
simple link specifications 138–139
<SMALL> 194
source element specification 140, 143
SPACE 45
specific character data entity (SDATA) 83, 88
STAGO, *see* start-tag open
Standard Generalized Markup Language (SGML)
  role of 7
start-tag omission 119
start-tag open (STAGO) 47, 69
start-tags 7, 69
status keyword specification 111
<STRIKE> 194
<STRONG> 194
<STYLE> 182
styles 25
<SUB> 194
SUBDOC 52, 132
subdocuments 8, 91, 131–133
submit button (in HTML forms) 214
<SUP> 194
syntax 38
SYNTAX clause 40–49
system identifier (SYSTEM) 90
system-specific external entities 90

<TABLE> 204
tables 176, 204–206
TAGC, *see* tag close
tag close (TAGC) 47, 69
tag omission 118
tags 7
<TD> 205
temporary marked sections (TEMP) 112, 114
<TEXTAREA> 217
<TH> 205
<TITLE> 180
tokens 74
<TR> 205
trees 221
<TT> 194

<U> 194
UCNMCHAR 46
UCNMSTRT 46
<UL>, *see* lists
unavailable text indicator 98
unclosed end-tag 124
unclosed start-tag 123
unclosed tags 123
Uniform Resource Locator (URL) 90, 163
unique identifier 19, 73, 78–79
  reference to 73, 79–80
unregistered owner identifier 96
URL, *see* Uniform Resource Locator
USELINK, *see* link set use declaration
USEMAP, *see* short reference use declarations

value indicator (VI) 47, 70
<VAR> 194
variant concrete syntax 54
VI, *see* value indicator

XML, *see* eXtensible Markup Language
<XMP> 190

younger siblings 222

#CONREF, *see* content reference
#CURRENT, *see* current attribute value
#FIXED, *see* fixed attribute values
#IMPLIED, *see* implied attribute values
#NOTATION, *see* data attributes
#POSTLINK 149
#REQUIRED, *see* required attributes
#USELINK, *see* link set use declarations